# VANISHING FISHES OF NORTH AMERICA

Distributed by

Stackpole Books
Cameron & Kelker Sts.
Harrisburg, PA 17105

# VANISHING FISHES OF NORTH AMERICA

Dr. R. Dana Ono
Dr. James D. Williams
Anne Wagner

paintings by Aleta Pahl

Stone Wall Press, Inc.
1241 30th Street NW
Washington, DC 20007

dust jacket designed by Hasten Graphic Design
painting by Aleta Pahl
color photograph by James D. Williams

ISBN 0-913276-43-X

Printed in the United States of America.

Library of Congress Cataloging in Publication Data
Catalog Card No. 82-062896
Ono, R. Dana, James D. Williams, and Anne Wagner
    Vanishing Fishes of North America
Washington, D.C.: Stone Wall Press, Inc.

*The naturalist looks upon every species of animal and plant now living as the individual letters which go to make up one of the volumes of our earth's history; and, as a few lost letters may make a sentence unintelligible, so the extinction of the numerous forms of life which the progress of cultivation invariably entails will necessarily render obscure this invaluable record of the past. It is therefore an important object to preserve them. If this is not done, future ages will certainly look back upon us as a people so immersed in the pursuit of wealth as to be blind to higher considerations. They will charge us with having culpably allowed the destruction of some of those records of creation which we had it in our power to preserve, and while professing to regard all living things as the direct handiwork and best evidence of a Creator, yet, with a strange inconsistency, seeing many of them perish irrecoverably from the earth, uncared for and unknown.*

A. R. Wallace, 1863.
Journal of the
Royal Geographic Society

To our families.

# Acknowledgments

The production of a book involves more people than just authors and publishers. Taking on a life of its own and resembling a species of plant or animal living in its habitat, a book finds itself affecting the lives of a web of individuals. These are the people who deserve special thanks and appreciation.

We thank all of our family and friends who put up with what must have appeared to be an endless stream of refusals to dinner invitations and other social festivities, instead telling them, "Thanks for the invitation, but we must work on the book!" To all of you, we express a hearty "thank you" for your support and understanding.

We wish to thank all of the individuals who provided information, reviewed, commented, and advised us on the various chapters. These individuals are: Herbert T. Boschung, Noel M. Burkhead, Glenn H. Clemmer, John E. Cooper, David A. Etnier, William M. Howell, Robert E. Jenkins, James E. Johnson, Gail C. Kobetich, Don E. McAllister, Robert R. Miller, Phil Pister, Henry W. Robison, Don Sada, John R. Shute, Peggy W. Shute, Wayne C. Starnes, Thomas N. Todd, and Jack E. Williams. Their assistance was gratefully appreciated. Any remaining errors, or unclear ideas are solely our fault.

Our expressed appreciation to the following individuals who generously loaned color and/or black and white photographs for the illustrations: Bruce H. Bauer, Michael A. Bell, Noel M. Burkhead, Glenn H. Clemmer, James E. Deacon, Ron J. Gilbert, Terry Hickman, James E. Johnson, Henry W. Robison, Don Sada, Wayne C. Starnes, Thomas N. Todd, and Jack E. Williams. Thanks must also go to the Department of the Interior, U.S. Fish and Wildlife Service for the use of their photographs.

We would also like to thank the Smithsonian Institution for the use of their color plate of the Lahontan cutthroat trout.

Finally, thanks to Henry Wheelwright, publisher, who gave us the chance to share our message with you. And to Rachel Parker, assistant publisher, who did an excellent job of coordinating our deadlines, renewing our energies, and acting as a sounding-board during the low points we faced in assembling this book.

# TABLE OF CONTENTS

Introduction by Dr. Sylvia Earle      1

I. The Vanishing Fishes      3

II. Atlantic and Gulf Coast Freshwater      9
Fishes
    Copper Redhorse - *Moxostoma hubbsi*
    Maryland Darter - *Etheostoma sellare*
    Roanoke Fishes
      Orangefin Madtom - *Noturus gilberti*
      Roanoke Logperch - *Percina rex*
    Lake Waccamaw Fishes
      Waccamaw Killifish - *Fundulus waccamensis*
      Waccamaw Silverside - *Menidia extensa*
      Waccamaw Darter - *Etheostoma perlongum*
    Okaloosa Darter - *Etheostoma okaloosae*

III. Great Lakes Fishes      27
    Lake Sturgeon - *Acipenser fulvescens*
    Shortnose Cisco - *Coregonus reighardi*
    Shortjaw Cisco - *Coregonus zenithicus*

IV. Pacific Coast Freshwater Fishes      37
    Borax Lake Chub - *Gila boraxobius*
    Warner Sucker - *Catostomus warnerensis*
    Modoc Sucker - *Catostomus microps*
    Unarmored Threespine Stickleback -
    *Gasterosteus aculeatus williamsoni*

V. Pyramid Lake Fishes      53
    Lahontan Cutthroat Trout - *Salmo clarki*
      *henshawi*
    Cui-ui - *Chasmistes cujus*

VI. Desert Spring and Pool Fishes    67
    Desert Dace - *Eremichthys acros*
    Ash Meadows Fishes
      Devils Hole Pupfish - *Cyprinodon diabolis*
      Ash Meadows Speckled Dace - *Rhinichthys osculus nevadensis*
      Ash Meadows Amargosa Pupfish - *Cyprinodon nevadensis mionectes*
      Pahrump Killifish - *Empetrichthys latos latos*

VII. Colorado River System Fishes    87
    Humpback Chub - *Gila cypha*
    Bonytail Chub - *Gila elegans*
    Colorado Squawfish - *Ptychocheilus lucius*
    Razorback Sucker - *Xyrauchen texanus*
    Woundfin - *Plagopterus argentissimus*
    Moapa Dace - *Moapa coriacea*

VIII. Western Trouts    109
    Apache Trout - *Salmo apache*
    Greenback Cutthroat Trout - *Salmo clarki stomias*
    Gila Trout - *Salmo gilae*

IX. Texas Spring Fishes    121
    Comanche Springs Pupfish - *Cyprinodon elegans*
    Clear Creek Gambusia - *Gambusia heterochir*
    San Marcos River Fishes
      San Marcos Gambusia - *Gambusia georgei*
      Fountain Darter - *Etheostoma fonticola*

X. Texas Blindcats and Cavefishes    133
    Widemouth Blindcat - *Satan eurystomus*
    Toothless Blindcat - *Trogloglanis pattersoni*
    Ozark Cavefish - *Amblyopsis rosae*
    Northern Cavefish - *Amblyopsis spelaea*
    Alabama Cavefish - *Speoplatyrhinus poulsoni*

XI. Cuatro Ciénegas Fishes    143
    Sardinilla Cuatro Ciénegas - *Lucania interioris*
    Cuatro Ciénegas Platyfish - *Xiphophorus gordoni*
    Cuatro Ciénegas Shiner - *Notropis xanthicara*

XII. Interior Highlands Fishes 167
Niangua Darter - *Etheostoma nianguae*
Peppered Shiner - *Notropis perpallidus*
Leopard Darter - *Percina pantherina*

XIII. Tennessee and Cumberland Fishes 175
Slackwater Darter - *Etheostoma boschungi*
Snail Darter - *Percina tanasi*
Blackside Dace - *Phoxinus cumberlandensis*

XIV. Southeastern Spring Fishes 189
Barrens Topminnow - *Fundulus julisia*
Spring Pygmy Sunfish - *Elassoma* species
Watercress Darter - *Etheostoma nuchale*

XV. Marine and Estuarine Fishes 199
Shortnose Sturgeon - *Acipenser brevirostrum*
Acadian Whitefish - *Coregonus canadensis*
Totoaba - *Cynoscion macdonaldi*

XVI. Extinction and Extinct Fishes 209
Harelip Sucker - *Lagochila lacera*
Tecopa Pupfish - *Cyprinodon nevadensis calidae*
Whiteline Topminnow - *Fundulus albolineatus*
Blue Pike - *Stizostedion vitreum glaucum*

XVII. Biogeography of Endangered and Threatened Fishes 217

XVIII. Acid Rain 221

XIX. Outlook 225

XX. Appendices 229
List of Endangered, Threatened and Extinct Fishes of North America
Map of Endangered and Threatened Fishes of North America
Parts of a Fish
Glossary
References

# COLOR ILLUSTRATIONS

1. Maryland darter - *Etheostoma sellare*
2. Orangefin madtom and Roanoke logperch - *Noturus gilberti* and *Percina rex*
3. Shortjaw cisco - *Coregonus zenithicus*
4. Unarmored threespine stickleback - *Gasterosteus aculeatus williamsoni*
5. Lahontan cutthroat trout - *Salmo clarki henshawi*
6. Devils Hole pupfish - *Cyprinodon diabolis*
7. Humpback chub and Colorado squawfish - *Gila cypha* and *Ptychocheilus lucius*
8. Bonytail chub and Razorback sucker - *Gila elegans* and *Xyrauchen texanus*
9. Greenback cutthroat trout - *Salmo clarki stomias*
10. Northern cavefish - *Amblyopsis spelaea*
11. Slackwater darter - *Etheostoma boschungi*
12. Snail darter - *Percina tanasi*
13. Blackside dace - *Phoxinus cumberlandensis*
14. Barrens topminnow - *Fundulus julisia*
15. Shortnose sturgeon - *Acipenser brevirostrum*
16. Totoaba - *Cynoscion macdonaldi*

# Introduction

If fishes were as easy to watch and to get to know on a day-to-day basis as birds and mammals, they surely would be understood and valued as creatures with curiosity and personality and would be widely admired for their beauty, diversity, and intriguing behavior. Also, it might be easier for people to understand the ways that the lives of fishes are inextricably tied to the lives of all other living things, including humans.

As it is, fishes have attracted only modest attention in the growing awareness and concern about the rapid environmental changes that have characterized recent decades.

The concept of protecting fishes is unimaginable to many, except possibly to ensure a good supply of a few that are valued for sport or commerce. For many people, even the word "fish" inspires only thoughts of a silver-orange creature swimming in a bowl—or a nicely browned fillet swimming in lemon butter sauce. The authors and artist for this volume present a different perspective, one that takes into consideration the interlocking destiny of humanity and fish-kind.

Half a century ago, zoologist William Beebe, renowned for his discoveries concerning deep-sea fishes, expressed alarm at the rapid loss of plant and animal species and habitats. He observed: "The beauty and genius of a work of art may be reconstructed although its first material expression be destroyed; a vanished harmony may yet inspire the composer; but when the last individual of a race of living things breathes no more, another heaven and another earth must pass before such a one may be again."

*Vanishing Fishes of North America* eloquently illustrates that while habitats and fish populations in North America have decreased or disappeared, a relatively small number of researchers have dramatically expanded our knowledge about fishes and their nature. The significance of fishes and their relevance to human civilization has been demonstrated as the number of fishes decline.

With knowing comes caring. Through this volume, people may come to know and understand fishes in ways they have not thought about before, and thus to sense the importance of the survival of seemingly insignificant creatures—for our sake, as well as theirs.

Dr. Sylvia Earle
Marine Biologist

# I.

# The Vanishing Fishes

Almost anywhere a body of water exists, no matter how large or small, the chances are good that this is home for some species of fish. As the largest group of vertebrates on earth, fishes have a total number of species that almost exceeds the number of species from all the other vertebrate classes combined. Fishes have evolved an impressive array of adaptations that have allowed them to live in a wide variety of habitats. Certain fishes can live in high altitude alpine lakes 15,000 feet above sea level, while others survive in the deepest ocean trenches more than 30,000 feet below sea level. Some species of desert fishes have evolved elaborate physiological mechanisms to cope with waters that exceed 110°F. On the other hand, a species of Antarctic fish has a form of "anti-freeze" which allows it to live in bone-chilling waters.

All life depends on water. And like the thousands of species of fishes that depend on water for their very survival, so too does Man. However, unlike fishes, Man has the ability to alter lakes, streams, rivers, and oceans to improve his "quality of life." More and more often, this quality of life unfortunately has not been found to be mutually beneficial to those animals and plants that share the water resources with humans. Some biologists predict that without major efforts to protect their habitats, as many as one million species of plants and animals worldwide may become endangered or disappear by the year 2000 as a result of the ever expanding human populations and the increased consumption of natural resources.

Extinction knows no socioeconomic class, political boundaries, or species specific grouping. It can occur anyplace and at anytime depending on the particular environmental conditions. The process of extinction is a natural biological phenomenon that all species of living things must continually face

3

1-1
Dams, large and small, drastically alter riverine habitat. Aquatic organisms adapted to flowing waters rarely survive in reservoirs. Photo by J. D. Williams.

while on earth. Through Man's ability to exploit natural resources and alter the habitats of other species, the rate of extinction for animals and plants has accelerated dramatically. Some scientists estimate that the rate of extinction for species has accelerated 40 to 400 times over the natural rate without human interference.

In the case of fishes, a variety of ecosystem-altering practices plague the aquatic habitats of these cold-blooded vertebrates. The pumping of ground-waters and diversion of streams for agricultural purposes have played a major role in either decreasing or totally eliminating certain fish species from their spring pools, streams, and lakes. Pesticides and other toxic pollutants from agricultural and industrial runoffs find their way into the aquatic systems causing a variety of problems such as nutrient enrichment of the waters which leads to a proliferation of aquatic vegetation and a lack of dissolved oxygen in the waters. Channelization of streams and damming of rivers to create impoundments destroys or drastically degrades the habitats of fishes living in them. Competition and predation from exotic, introduced species are more subtle threats to native fishes.

The Endangered Species Act of 1973 marked a forceful commitment on the part of the United States government to preserve endangered and threatened animals and plants. Unlike the two preceding acts, the Endangered Species Preservation Act of 1966 and the Endangered Species Conservation Act of 1969, the Endangered Species Act established two conservation status categories: endangered and threatened. An endangered species is defined as any species or subspecies of fish, wildlife, or plant, and any distinct population segment of any species of fish or wildlife or plant, which interbreeds when mature, that is in danger of becoming extinct in all or a significant portion of its range within the foreseeable future. Similarly, a threatened species is any species or subspecies of fish or wildlife or plant, and any distinct population segment of any species of fish or wildlife or plant which interbreeds when mature, that is likely to become an endangered species throughout all or a significant portion of its range within the foreseeable future.

This piece of legislation also provided protection for the ecosystems of the endangered or threatened species from adverse activities. This portion of the environment, legally termed "critical habitat," is that area considered to be essential for the continued existence of the endangered or threatened species. Depending on the living requirements of the particular species, critical habitat may include land areas, lakes, rivers, marshes, or other environments. Because habitat alteration is the primary reason that more and more animal and plant species are heading down the road to extinction, the concept of critical habitat may help save a substantial portion of those species already in trouble.

In 1978 the U.S. Fish and Wildlife Service sponsored a three-year study that showed that about one third of the people interviewed had any knowledge of the Endangered Species Act of 1973! But we should not despair over the results of this study. As incidents involving environmental pollution from acid rain to radioactive waste are more frequently in the news media, the public's awareness of environmental issues grows daily. No longer can threats to the environment and our vulnerability to altered environments be swept under the rug of "progress."

Still, many people continue to ask, "Why should we bother to save endangered and threatened species?" and "What good are these species anyhow?" In these particularly rough economic times, interest in the preservation of endangered and threatened animals and plants may seem to be a low priority for many people. Is it more important that ranchers in the southwestern desert be able to raise their crops and feed their livestock than allow the desert pupfish to survive? Or how do we judge the worth of a seldom-seen, endemic species of fish whose habitat just happens to be considered the ideal site for a multimillion dollar geothermal energy project? The answers to such questions may not be as simple as those who ask them apparently think.

1–2
Channelization destroys stream and riparian habitat and increases flooding in downstream unchannelized areas. Photo by J. D. Williams.

Conservationists often have the tough task of defending an endangered or threatened species with what appears to be ill-conceived reasoning or flawed logic simply because they have no better rationale at their disposal. Such a vulnerable position can be capitalized upon by those who wish to exploit our natural resources using slick business plans complete with concrete dollar values.

There is no crystal ball for us to see into the future and find out which species of animals and plants may hold valuable secrets that could directly benefit Mankind. But lessons from the past tell us that many of the discoveries from nature such as anti-malarial drugs, cardiac and respiratory stimulants, morphine, tumor inhibitors, and a host of other medical products as well as industrial chemical products, food products, and products for space technological purposes, have been somewhat serendipitous. Every species of animal and plant that disappears before its properties are fully known represents the loss of potential discoveries that might improve human welfare. As an example, certain species of desert pupfishes can tolerate spring waters that are several times saltier than seawater. Understanding how the kidneys of the pupfish are able to cope with such extreme salinity could help us redesign kidney dialysis units. By preventing the extinction of living species, we keep intact our treasure chest of practical discoveries that future research will reveal.

No species exists independently of other living species in its environment. All parts within an ecosystem are interrelated. If a particular endangered species becomes extinct, then the health and stability of the entire ecosystem could be jeopardized. In order to preserve a species, one must preserve its habitat. Endangered and threatened species play a crucial role for Mankind by serving as indicators of potentially large-scale environmental problems. By serving as this pulse of an environmental problem, these endangered and threatened species allow us to take steps toward rectifying problems which ultimately could affect our own survival. Those individuals who cannot see the value in preserving species from extinction also fail to recognize their own dependence within the environment.

Perhaps the most compelling reason for preserving living species is to demonstrate the importance of restraint. The significance of any single species is far too complex to be measured simply by how useful it can be to humans, especially in economic terms. We should refrain from thinking about other species solely from the point of view of net worth to our quality of life. There are many non-economic reasons for protecting the endangered and threatened species of wildlife. It might just be the right thing to do; a moral obligation of humans to allow the other plant and animal species to continue to live without interference. Surely we are intelligent enough to solve our pressing space and resource requirements without large-scale habitat destruction that has been synonymous with our past efforts to improve the quality of life.

As public awareness and concern for endangered fish, wildlife, and plants grow, we have observed that the degree of support for protecting individual endangered and threatened species depends to a large extent on how attractive the species is to humans. Also its biological relationship to humans, the reasons why it is endangered, its economic value, and the relative importance of the species to American history and folklore are factors that may generate interest in conservation of a particular species. Consequently, when one thinks about endangered species, it is only natural to pay the most attention to endangered and threatened mammals such as whales, sea otters, wolves, and other furry, soft-eyed animals. Because of their visibility and beauty, people easily identify with birds as well. Logically, these endangered species get most of the conservation dollar and media coverage.

Fishes, on the other hand, live in a world that is quite alien to ours. The general attitude toward preserving fish species that are either endangered or threatened has been one of "out of sight, out of mind." Most people find it difficult to identify with these cold-blooded, scaly vertebrates. But like the other species of wildlife that are losing their habitat through human exploitation, endangered and threatened fishes must be given a fair shot at survival . . . and equal attention.

Our purpose in writing this book about the endangered and threatened fishes of North America is to draw attention to a most remarkable group of vertebrates that most people may only slightly understand. Though we had never worked together in the past, our common interest in wildlife conservation and fish biology created a bond which generated this book after two years of research, writing, and development. We hope that our treatment of this subject will, at the very least, illustrate some of the difficulties facing dozens of species of fishes in North America and motivate many readers to actively assist in the conservation of these aquatic animals.

Toxic chemical pollutants, which are often invisible, are still deadly to aquatic organisms. Photo by J. D. Williams.

# II.

# Atlantic and Gulf Coast Freshwater Fishes

Extending more than 3000 miles from Cape Cod south along the Atlantic seaboard and Gulf Coast to Mexico lies a portion of elevated former sea bottom called the Coastal Plain. The altitude of this plain rarely exceeds five hundred feet and more than 50 percent of its surface is less than one hundred feet above sea level. Deposits of sand and gravel underlie most of the area. Varying from one hundred to two hundred miles in width, it makes up almost 10 percent of the U.S. land area. An area like the Coastal Plain might seem to lack diversity of topography, but significant differences in geology and topography do exist along its length, breaking the Coastal Plain into several distinct regions.

Inland from the Coastal Plain along the Atlantic Coast the elevations gradually increase through the Piedmont Plateau and ultimately reach the highest elevations of the eastern U.S. in the Appalachian Mountains. The Piedmont Plateau extends from New York to eastern Alabama and ranges from 15 to 120 miles in width. It is best described as an area of broadly rolling hills with occasional knobs and ridges. While some elevations reach heights of more than 1500 feet, most are 500 to 1000 feet. Beyond the Piedmont, the Appalachian Mountains are characterized by elevations of 1000 to 5000 feet with the highest peaks towering upward to more than 6000 feet. Streams traversing these regions are varied and offer an incredible variety of habitats for fishes. These same streams have also attracted many people who have left their mark on every major river and many of the large creeks.

The eight species of fishes discussed in this section inhabit several of the many different regions on the Atlantic and eastern Gulf Coasts. The aquatic habitats of the highlighted fishes range from fast-flowing Gulf Coast streams in the panhandle of northwestern Florida where a small darter finds its home, to the middle Atlantic Coastal Plain where a shallow circular lake, one of many Carolina Bays, harbors three endemic threatened fishes. We will also relate the stories of an endangered fish that inhabits the rocky riffles of a small creek just outside of Baltimore, Maryland and a rather large threatened fish that occasionally can be found swimming in the St. Lawrence River and lakes near Montreal. Finally, a large river that meanders over four hundred miles between the Appalachians and the Atlantic Ocean and contains the greatest diversity of fishes found anywhere along the Atlantic Coast has two species of fishes that are currently being considered for the federal list of endangered and threatened species.

All of the fishes portrayed in this section have felt the negative impact of Man's encroachment on their aquatic habitats. Acid rain, a phenomenon that has contributed to the demise of at least one of the fishes in this section, could easily plague the other Atlantic and Gulf Coast fishes in the future. Though these eight species of fishes are separated by hundreds of miles in some cases, all face similar threats to their very survival.

## Copper Redhorse
### *Moxostoma hubbsi*

The copper redhorse is a peculiar name for a species of freshwater fish. "Copper" refers to its bright reddish-copper body sheen and fin color, especially during the spawning season; the appelation, "redhorse," comes from their stout robust body. This label is applied to several species of the genus *Moxostoma* of the sucker family (Catostomidae) and so called because of their reddish fins and/or body and their massive size. Interestingly enough, the buffalo fish is a relative of the copper redhorse, with similar physical attributes.

The copper redhorse is a rather large, deep-bodied member of the sucker family which generally attains a weight between 6 and 7 pounds and reaches lengths of slightly over 22 inches. There is somewhere in the written records an entry for one unusually large copper redhorse that reached almost fourteen pounds. The copper redhorse is fairly long-lived, with a life-span of twelve to fifteen years. It is the second largest of the eighteen species of *Moxostoma*.

Found only in the large rivers and their lake-like expansions around Quebec, the copper redhorse can, if one is lucky, be spotted in the St. Lawrence River, Lac St. Louis, Lac Saint Pierre, Lac des Deux-Montagnes of the Ottawa River near Montreal, the Richelieu River and a widened section called the Chambly Basin, and the Yamaska River system including the Rivière Noire. Nowhere in these waters, however, is the copper redhorse very common. Eighty percent of the sightings and captures of this large fish have occurred in the Yamaska River system. In terms of actual numbers of copper redhorses found, only 164 individuals were collected between 1942 and 1973.

Considered a threatened species in Canadian waters, the copper redhorse, like most other species of fishes in the northeastern United States and eastern Canada, faces the deadly problem of acid rain. The influence of acid rain will depend to a large extent on the intrinsic buffering capacity of the particular body of water. But within the same body of water some animals will succumb more readily than others to the environmental changes associated with this dreaded phenomenon. In the case of the copper redhorse, the snails and aquatic insects that it vacuums up with its small protrusible, ventral sucking mouth (*Moxostoma,* in fact, means "sucking mouth") are quite susceptible to the lethal effects of acid rain. The redhorse has highly specialized molar-like teeth behind the gills to crush these food items. As the snails and aquatic insects die, the copper redhorse's food supply will be directly affected.

Perhaps a more immediate threat to the survival of the copper redhorse is the heavy industrial and domestic pollution from the city of Montreal present along much of its total known range. The Canadian government is not currently taking any steps to safeguard this rare species of sucker from extinction. Spawning, nursery, and adult foraging sites should be set up in a nature preserve as free from pollution as possible.

Very little is known concerning the life history of this rare fish except that it normally prefers quiet waters or slow to sluggish currents. While no one has ever seen actual breeding taking place, the copper redhorse apparently spawns in mid-June in the swift sections of rivers. Timing of the spawning period is based on the development of what are called nuptial or breeding tubercles. These tubercles are small pointed bumps on the fish's skin that develop in males of certain fishes during the spawning season. They are used to physically stimulate the female during the courtship ritual, and in combat with competing males. These tubercles can be found on the snout, body, and fins of the male copper redhorse.

Other than this scant bit about its morphology, no other information concerning the biology of the copper redhorse exists. This species is exceedingly rare. Unless positive steps are taken to clean up and protect the habitat, the threatened status could change to endangered or even extinct. Then we will never be able to learn about this large long-lived redhorse.

# Maryland Darter
## *Etheostoma sellare*

(Color plate 1.)

A small three page scientific paper written by two ichthyologists in 1913 entitled, "Description of a new darter from Maryland," identified a new species of small fish called the Maryland darter, *Etheostoma sellare.* The two scientists, L. Radcliffe and W.W. Welsh, based the results of their study on two specimens that they had collected at "Swan Creek near Havre de Grace, Maryland," the year prior to the paper's publication. For almost a half of a century after their discovery, not a single Maryland darter was collected despite several intensive attempts to find it by experienced field biologists. The failures in finding the darter were due in part to the vagueness of the locality that the two scientists had initially described. Radcliffe and Welsh said that their two Maryland darters came from a long, stony riffle in Swan Creek. The lower reaches of Swan Creek in 1912 probably had less silt buildup than it does now, which may explain the difficulty in finding additional specimens at this location.

2–1
This riffle on Deer Creek in Harford County, Maryland is prime habitat for the Maryland darter. Photo by J. D. Williams.

While sampling fishes in Gasheys Run near Aberdeen, Maryland in 1962, a group of Cornell University students captured a juvenile Maryland darter among their netting of numerous juvenile tessellated darters, *Etheostoma olmstedi,* a rather common darter in these waters. The members of the Cornell group were excited by the find which prompted a flurry of renewed collecting activity. Ichthyologists again took to the lower Susquehanna River drainage with nets and waders in search of this rare darter.

In the spring of 1965 another Maryland darter was taken by Dr. Leslie Knapp and his party. This specimen happened to be an adult female. Soon after this finding, Dr. Edward C. Raney of Cornell University and colleague, Dr. Frank J. Schwartz, located a population of Maryland darters in Deer Creek.

To date, only eighty Maryland darters are known to be preserved in scientific collections across the United States. No specimens have been preserved since 1971. About fifteen additional Maryland darters have been captured and then released since 1974. Author Jim Williams is one of the few biologists to have ever seen living Maryland darters in Deer Creek, where all post-1974 sightings have been made.

This small fish appears to dart around riffles near the bottom of the stream, searching for aquatic insects and snails. Reddish-orange in color with four distinct black saddle-like markings across its long back, the Maryland darter sports a small black spot behind the eye. When looking at juvenile Maryland darters, their body pattern is similar to the more widespread tessellated darter,

*Etheostoma olmstedi,* which is common in the Maryland darters' habitat. Other darter relatives like the banded darter and shield darter share this habitat with the tessellated and Maryland darters.

Because only fifteen Maryland darters have been seen alive since 1974, little is known about the biology of this species. By studying the gonads of some of the eighty preserved specimens in fish collections, ichthyologists have found that spawning probably takes place in late April or early May. Like most other darters, the Maryland darter is rather diminutive, the largest specimen only about 3½ inches in length. Although no one has ever seen a Maryland darter feeding in its habitat, the stomach contents of preserved specimens indicate that they dine on snails, *Elmia virginica,* and a host of aquatic insects such as caddisfly larvae, *Hydropsyche* sp.; stonefly nymphs, Perlidae; and mayflies, Heptageniidae.

This fish, literally in the backyard of the Office of Endangered Species in Washington, D.C., was placed on the endangered species list on March 11, 1967. There are no real solid estimates of how many Maryland darters exist in Harford County, Maryland, but an educated guess is less than 1000 individuals. Currently, the only known population of the Maryland darter is in Deer Creek. Therefore, the greatest problem in preserving this species will be to protect Deer Creek from the detrimental effects of unrestricted water and land uses within the watershed. Prolonged periods of high turbidity, silt, impoundments, pesticide and herbicide run-offs, reduction of stream flow for consumptive uses, construction projects, and waste from sewage treatment plants all pose problems for the Maryland darter population.

"Can we dump chlorinated wastes into Ebaugh's Creek without harming the Maryland darter?" asked the little municipality of Stewartstown, Pennsylvania, in 1974—the owners of a new sewage treatment plant. Ebaugh's Creek just happened to be a headwater tributary of Deer Creek, the habitat of the Maryland darter. There was strong opposition at the public hearing held by the Environmental Protection Agency (EPA), but a permit was granted—chlorinated waters could be channeled into Ebaugh's Creek which could, in turn, threaten the endangered fish. Ammonium nitrogen in the waste combines with the chlorine during the waste treatment process and forms "chloramines." Not only are these compounds toxic to fishes, but they also might be potential carcinogens when found in municipal drinking water supplies.

There is a good chance that the Deer Creek population of Maryland darters is the only remaining permanent population of this species. Although we have no idea as to the former range of this darter, perhaps, like a few other darters, it is restricted to the swift riffles of the Coastal Plain. If so, then the formation of the Chesapeake Bay, resulting from the submergence of coastal areas, may have reduced the Maryland darter's former range in the lower Susquehanna River. More recently, the Maryland darter's range may also have shrunk because of the completion of the Conowingo Dam in 1928 as well as other impoundments in the drainage system. These impoundments have flooded the shallow rocky riffles and decreased the swift flow of clean, clear water required by this darter.

Because the number of Maryland darters that have been seen alive is so few, and we know so little about this species' biology, it is difficult to assess the chances for its survival. In any case, it is fair to say that the total population size is extremely small and its distribution limited. As long as the threat of Man's activities looms so near to the Maryland darter's only habitat in Deer Creek, the Maryland darter will remain one of our most endangered species.

# Roanoke Fishes

## Orangefin Madtom and Roanoke Logperch
### *Noturus gilberti* and *Percina rex*

(Color plate 2.)

What river drainage system can boast of having the most unique and diverse species of fishes inhabiting its waters anywhere on the Atlantic Coast from Maine to Florida? If you guess the Hudson River or Susquehanna River, you would be dead wrong. The Roanoke River in Virginia makes this claim. This river system extends over four hundred miles, rising in south-western Virginia and flowing in a generally southeasterly direction to Albemarle Sound on the North Carolina coast.

Most of the more than two hundred species of fishes that are found in the state of Virginia are in some way connected to the Roanoke River system. Among this diverse assemblage of fishes live a half-dozen species that are found no where else in the world. Two of these endemic species, which are rarely seen, have their largest populations in the Upper Roanoke River basin. The Roanoke logperch and the orangefin madtom are the two small species currently being considered for threatened status. The native range of both species lies solely in the somewhat oblong-shaped mountain-bordered basin known as the Upper Roanoke River system that drains approximately 2800 square miles of land surrounding the Roanoke River. A small, presumably introduced population of orangefin madtoms has been reported from the Craig Creek drainage system in the James River, Virginia. For all practical purposes, these two species overlap in their habitat preferences.

As the North and South Forks of the Roanoke River merge they flow towards the urbanized and industrialized cities of Roanoke and Salem which loom on the horizon. Industrialized centers usually spell trouble to such waterways. As the population expands, the residents of the Roanoke-Salem metropolitan area face the pressing problem of water supply. The increasing population will economically bolster the land developers as they convert more and more of the Upper Roanoke River basin into urban and suburban lots. Additional electric power will be needed and hydroelectric projects have been considered for the upper reaches of the river. The water around the city of Roanoke has had a history of poor condition because of siltation, eutrophication, and chemical waste products that have been dumped into the Roanoke River. The waters in the vicinity of Salem are no better off, being at the mercy of spillage of chemical wastes, urbanization, and channelization. Although water quality has improved since the Clean Water Act was passed, the river will not completely recover without strictly enforced protective measures.

A channelization project has been proposed to control the Roanoke's occasional floods. Channelization usually involves major alterations of the stream channel. Simply stated, the river is widened, straightened, and the bottom is made very uniform by a great deal of bulldozing and dredging. The banks of the river are cleared of all trees and leveed up as well. By reducing the resistance the water encounters as it flows, the chances of flooding are lessened in the channelized area, but flooding downstream is increased. Unfortunately, channelizing a river for flood control purposes drastically alters the habitats of the aquatic animals occupying the affected area. Because the Upper Roanoke River basin is full of fish species and home for two threatened endemic species, extreme caution must be exercised before tampering with the environment. The populations of both the Roanoke logperch and the orangefin madtom live in generally the same kind of habitat within the Upper Roanoke River system; a single threat would probably affect both of them. Both fishes could become endangered in one fell swoop.

Biologists had known for almost a century that these two species lived in the same habitat, mainly because of the work of David Starr Jordan, a noted American ichthyologist and president of Stanford University. During his first collecting trip to the Upper Roanoke drainage basin in 1888, Jordan and some fellow collectors netted a few individuals of both the Roanoke logperch and orangefin madtom, both new to science. In keeping with the time-honored tradition of naming the species in honor of someone, Jordon named the orangefin madtom *Noturus gilberti* after his colleague, Charles H. Gilbert. The common appellation, "madtom" is given to this group of catfishes because of their seemingly inane swimming behavior. It was not until 1940 that another orangefin madtom was seen.

Like the canaries that were carried down into the dark, deep mine shafts by miners to check on the quality of the air, both the logperch and madtom are good water quality monitors as they are quite sensitive to environmental degradation. Wherever either of these endemic fishes are found, they serve as living indicators of moderate to good upland stream habitats. Both of these fishes live in moderate to large riffle-filled streams.

The best chance of finding one of these threatened fishes is to look in streams wider than thirty to forty feet, where the flowing water is somewhat cool to the touch, and there is a stony or rocky bottom, free of silt. The orangefin madtom resides beneath the rocks or within the crevices of the rockstrewn bottom. The presence of silt would eliminate these shelters for this small member of the catfish family. The logperch also uses the rocky bottom for cover, darting in and out from amongst the rocks in search of food. Unlike the madtom, however, the logperch is more active—moving about in the riffles and pools. The madtom is intolerant of sluggish, silted pools, but the logperch moves from the riffles into pools in the fall and stays there throughout winter. Neither one of these fishes will tolerate quiet, silted backwaters of ponds, impoundments, or reservoirs.

Aquatic insects are the preferred food of the madtom and logperch. Midge, blackfly, cranefly, and caddis larvae as well as stonefly and mayfly nymphs all find their way into the fishes' diets depending on what is "in season." Although the dietary requirements are the same, the manner in which each procures its food differs markedly. The orangefin madtom, like the majority of catfishes, does not search for its food by sight. Like most catfishes, the madtom's small eyes are located on the top of its head, giving the fish less than binocular visual capacities. The four pairs of "whiskers" or barbels that encircle the madtom's mouth, as well as the skin covering its fins and body, are studded with taste buds that send chemical messages back to the madtom's brain, telling it what is nearby—food, friend, or foe.

Because vision is unnecessary for the madtom in searching for food, it doesn't matter what time of day the madtom wishes to hunt. The orangefin madtom prefers to feed at night with the rationale for this nocturnal behavior being to avoid the confrontations with the visual predators that hunt during the day. The madtom's only means of defense are the dorsal and pectoral fins which are armed with spines.

The handsome Roanoke logperch, *Percina rex,* is a large-bodied darter about five inches long, which feeds on the same aquatic insects that the madtom finds so palatable, but does so in an entirely novel way. The Roanoke logperch places its long pig-like snout beneath the gravel and rocks and pushes or flips them, exposing anything that has taken shelter beneath. Then, lying patiently in wait, moving only its eyes and head side-to-side, the logperch quickly swallows the surprised aquatic insects that have momentarily lost their hiding places. Small crayfish are also captured by the logperch using this method. In order to feed in this manner, the logperch requires clear flowing water that is not laden with silt. Silt minimizes vision, and settles over the bottom, reducing the habitat for aquatic insects.

As in their respective modes of obtaining food, the spawning behavior of these two threatened species are also different. Although little is known about the reproductive biology of either of these fishes, it appears that the logperch reaches its peak spawning during the month of April in the Upper Roanoke, about the same time the madtom spawns. The madtom breeds like most of the other members of the ictalurid catfish family. A protected nest site, a cavity or other space under a rock or log or even inside a can or bottle, is carefully selected. Here the female madtom lays her large eggs, usually less than 75. The male fertilizes them and remains behind to guard the eggs. He also keeps the nest site and eggs free of silt by fanning them with his caudal fin.

The logperch, on the other hand, is a substrate spawner. The female deposits her eggs directly into the sand or gravel bottom of flowing water. After the eggs are deposited, the parents leave for good. The eggs and young logperch fry, should they make it past the egg-stage, are left to fend for themselves in a world of competition and predation which is further complicated by Man-made problems.

Black bands and spots in the fins laced with red, orange, and yellow washings against a yellowish-green body broken by dark vertical bars characterizes the coloration of the beautiful Roanoke logperch. A dark vertical bar slashes the eye and contrasts strongly with the golden iridescent background color of the side of the logperch head. The orangefin madtom, on the other hand, boasts less beauty, and in fact, its name is somewhat a misnomer. The fins are not really orange in color, but most often yellow. With an olive-brown upper body and head, and yellow-white underneath, the orangefin madtom sports the basic coloration typical of the catfish family Ictaluridae.

The Roanoke logperch and the orangefin madtom, though differing in such aspects as food-hunting strategies, spawning, and even basic body coloration, share an important factor: They live in the same habitat. And, by living in the same habitat, the two threatened species face the same Man-made habitat threats. The rapidly developing metropolitan area of Roanoke and Salem is encroaching on the river, pushing nature to the limits in maintaining the environmental quality of the Roanoke River system. Impoundments have been proposed for some of the areas currently inhabited by populations of the madtom and logperch. If the impoundments are built, the inundation of the clear swift water habitat would result in reduced populations of both species. The settling of silt into the rocky and gravelly habitat of both species would decrease the available living space and alter the feeding and spawning areas. The deposition of eggs would be severely affected by a layer of silt covering the bottom.

Unlike impoundments that hold water back, channelization projects are designed to speed the flow of water off the watershed as fast as possible. It should be pointed out that channelization projects may reduce some flooding in the channelized area, but they increase flooding in areas downstream.

A much better long term solution to the flooding problem is flood plain zoning. By moving homes and businesses out of the flood plain of streams, flood losses can be greatly reduced. The land along the stream which is periodically flooded can be used for parks and recreation. We hope this modern approach to solving flood problems through flood plain zoning can be applied in cities along the upper Roanoke River. This solution would help maintain the integrity of the Roanoke River ecosystem, protecting not only the threatened orangefin madtom and Roanoke logperch, but also the significant stream fishery which exists in this system.

# Lake Waccamaw Fishes

There are several major theories to explain the origin of the numerous oval-shaped depressions called "Carolina Bays" found scattered over the Coastal Plain from Virginia to Georgia. This name was apparently given to the depressions because of the common occurrence of the evergreen bay trees found in them. The majority of these "bays" are concentrated in the Lake Waccamaw region of southeastern North Carolina. According to some geologists, the Carolina Bays were formed relatively recently between 32,000 and 75,000 years ago, by a massive meteorite shower that literally punched out the crater-shaped depressions in one fell swoop. The theory has it that the meteorites approached the Coastal Plain from a low angle and crashed into the earth; the heat of the meteorites destroyed all surrounding vegetation. Over time, the "bays" gradually filled with water and silt from the eroding crater rims. Another school of thought simply feels that the depressions or bays were excavated by water from artesian wells in the area and then scoured out by wind and water forces.

No matter how the Carolina Bays were created, one thing is certain: These "bays" have played a major role in the historical development of the state of North Carolina. In fact, much of the history stems from one particular "bay" called Lake Waccamaw, the largest of the "bay" lakes in the state. With a surface area of about 6000 acres, this shallow lake, averaging only seven feet in depth, has been used by people in a variety of ways since the time of the Waccamaw Indians, one of five tribes inhabiting the Cape Fear River. Not only did the Waccamaw Indians fish and hunt along the banks of Lake Waccamaw, but they also successfully capitalized on the turpentine and saw milling market that accompanied the arrival of white man. Still another piece of Indian lore has it that the chieftain, Osceola, who led the Seminoles into war against the United States government during the early 1800s, was presumably born on the banks of Lake Waccamaw.

An entrepreneur by the name of Charles Oscar Beers noted that splendid cypress swamps surrounded the land around Lake Waccamaw. This casual observation led to the formation of the shingle industry in early 1869. Cypress shingles were quite profitable at the turn of the century. "Shingle-laden" barges regularly crossed Lake Waccamaw from the south side to awaiting mule-drawn rail cars that would take the goods to the train depot.

Although Lake Waccamaw and its surrounding area have had a tremendous impact on the history of this section of the Atlantic Coast, this Carolina Bay is special in another way. Certain lakes scattered around the world are regarded as centers for rapid and extensive evolutionary change in species. These lakes are virtual gold mines for the study of evolutionary processes in nature because they provide the biologist with a glimpse of how natural selection works in a confined area often at an accelerated pace. For example, in the geologically young lakes of Victoria, Malawi, and Tanganyika in Africa, the numerous species of cichlid fishes have evolved in a relatively short period of time. Some biologists have called this "explosive evolution." The extensive and rapid rate of speciation of fishes has also occurred in Lake Lanao in the Philippine Islands.

The extremely high diversity of fish species including three endemic fishes as well as several endemic invertebrates within this young body of water makes Lake Waccamaw unique among Atlantic coast drainages and one of the rare centers for rapid evolutionary change. The high number of fish species in Lake Waccamaw may be attributed to the geologic past when the Waccamaw system drained a much larger area than now. As the drainage area steadily shrank over the years, the existing species had to compete for less available food and space resources. The constriction of these competing fishes into tighter quarters may have resulted in unique adaptations and specializations of these species. This may explain the high species diversity in Lake Waccamaw.

Unlike the endemic fishes in African and Philippine lakes that evolved unique adaptations as a result of the vast number of widely differing habitats, the three endemic fishes of Lake Waccamaw faced a relatively uniform environment where the water was extremely clear and the lake bottom was uninterestingly flat. The Lake Waccamaw endemics were isolated in the lake environment and separated from their relatives downstream. In these clear open waters, a special premium was likely placed on fishes that could escape from the sharp-sighted predators patrolling the clear expanses of water. Consequently, the endemic darter, killifish, and silverside all have become streamlined for speed, an adaptation which contributed to their survival in Lake Waccamaw.

Of the 44 species of fishes that have been found in Lake Waccamaw, the Waccamaw darter, *Etheostoma perlongum,* the Waccamaw killifish, *Fundulus waccamensis,* and the Waccamaw silverside, *Menidia extensa* are endemic to the clear waters of the bay lake. All three face identical threats, though their lifestyles differ remarkably.

# Waccamaw Killifish
## *Fundulus waccamensis*

Known locally as the "sand shiner," the Waccamaw killifish has been a perennial favorite among fishermen in the area who use the small three-inch fish as bait. The Waccamaw killifish is hardy and easily obtained, making it an excellent bait minnow. Because Waccamaw killifish tend to travel in large schools especially near shoals or around the shoreline, the fishermen can easily fill their bait buckets for the day simply by making one pass along the shoreline with a seine. The killifishes are especially plentiful in the shallow waters along Lake Waccamaw from early March through August when spawning occurs.

Male killifishes patrol circular territories on the lake bottom, about five feet in diameter, keeping other male killifishes outside of the territory and pursuing female killifishes that enter the territory. Unlike the male Waccamaw darter that carefully chooses a nest site, the male killifish spawns with a female killifish on the sandy bottom within the circular territory. The eggs are then buried in the sand. Upon hatching, the young are left on their own without parental protection or care.

Although a native of Lake Waccamaw, the killifish is also found in another similarly clear, shallow North Carolina lake called Phelps Lake. Biologists are not certain whether this particular population of killifish was introduced at some point by Man from the Lake Waccamaw population, or if it represents a relict distribution pattern dating back thousands of years. Because the two populations show only slight variations, some scientists believe that this was originally a single population. Deterioration of the habitat similar to that faced in Lake Waccamaw also affects the killifish population of Phelps Lake. Land developers are clearing and draining the land surrounding the lake for agriculture and housing, causing loads of silt and nutrient-rich organic matter to settle on the lake bottom. Besides leading to the eventual eutrophication of the lake, the silt might bury aquatic insect larvae emerging from the bottom and consequently wipe out a major food source for the killifish. The silt could also suffocate the developing killifish larvae as they hatch out and emerge from their sandy birthplace.

Ultimately, without the killifish—one link in the food chain of the game-fishes—fewer gamefishes would be left to roam the waters of Lake Waccamaw. The integral part played by each trophic level in the overall balance of an ecosystem has far-reaching consequences.

# Waccamaw Silverside
## *Menidia extensa*

The Waccamaw silverside is an open water surface-feeding fish that tends to travel in large schools for protection and feeding. Feeding primarily on planktivorous crustaceans such as daphnia and copepods, a silverside will capture each prey item individually. During feeding forays at the surface, the large schools of silversides frequently attract the attention of predatory fishes. The predators swim through the schools, making the silversides disperse and even jump clear out of the water to escape. Fishermen know that when they see silversides skipping across the water, large gamefishes are usually nearby. In fact, local fishermen refer to the jumping silversides as "skipjacks."

Like both the Waccamaw darter and killifish, the silverside comes close to the shoreline to spawn from March through July. However, unlike the other two species, the Waccamaw silverside spawns in open waters near the shoreline and is very sensitive to water quality conditions. Although biologists have tried to learn something about the actual spawning behavior of the Waccamaw silverside, no one has ever witnessed this in nature. All attempts to artificially fertilize the eggs have failed. The eggs, which number around 150 in an average-sized female, are externally fertilized and sink to the lake bottom without any parental care. The remarkable silverside egg has a long, coarse, thread-like, sticky filament that allows the egg to adhere to sand grains or other objects lying on the bottom. With any luck, the eggs hatch and juvenile silversides begin their lives immediately within a large school.

Like the Waccamaw killifish, the slender, almost transparent, 2½ inch long silverside plays an important natural link in the food chain of the predatory fishes. Local bait dealers know their importance economically. They will seine for the silverside and sell them frozen to fishermen who troll them for white perch, *Morone americana,* largemouth bass, *Micropterus salmoides,* and a host of other gamefishes. The abundance of silversides in the open waters of Lake Waccamaw indicates how essential this forage species is as a primary food source for the gamefishes. Any threats to the welfare of the endemic silverside could lead to the disruption of Lake Waccamaw's ecological balance.

2–2
Lake Waccamaw is the largest of the Carolina Bay Lakes. Photo by J. D. Williams.

# Waccamaw Darter
## *Etheostoma perlongum*

Of the three endemic species, the Waccamaw darter has the rather dubious distinction of being the rarest one, numbering roughly 91,000 individuals. Both the Waccamaw killifish and the silverside number around 800,000 individuals according to biologists' calculations. The darter spends most of its life on the sandy lake bottom where, like most darters, it searches for aquatic insect larvae and amphipods to satisfy its hunger pangs. The Waccamaw darter hardly reaches three inches in length when full grown, and probably lives about one year.

During the months of March through June, the normally pale adult male darters become dusky to almost black and migrate to the shallow shoreline for spawning. The males precede the females in this migration to the shallows to select choice nest sites in which to raise the young. The male will search for any submerged object like a stick or log under which he will excavate a shallow depression in the sand by fanning his tail. After the males have staked out their territories, the female darters reach the shallows and participate in a courtship ritual. The male displays and then leads the female to the nest which he shows to her by inverting his body so that he faces the underside of the submerged object. If the female accepts his offer, she will deposit forty to fifty eggs while upside-down beneath the submerged object. The eggs, each of which has an adhesive area, are deposited in a single layer onto the underside of the object that serves as the nest. After this is done, the female leaves and the male darter is left to guard the eggs.

The male, however, is not satisfied with only one female. He will immediately begin courting another and the same ritual is replayed over again. The male darter will continue to court females and willingly accept their egg deposits which he eagerly fertilizes in his communal nest. The nest will end up with around 1200 eggs.

The male darter does have his problems during the breeding season in Lake Waccamaw. A curious phenomenon known as the "pseudo-female, sneaky male" plagues the nest-guarding male darter. Although two or more willing females may be near the nest at any one time, the male can only spawn with one female at a time. When the nest-guarding male leaves the nest unattended, a small female-marked male Waccamaw darter suddenly enters the vacated nest. This "new" male begins to spawn with available females until he is chased away by the return of the nest-guarding male. Because of their female-like markings, these male darters have occasionally spawned without being noticed by the nest-guarding male. The communal nest will be guarded by the male anywhere from 13 to 36 days during which time the young hatch out and leave the nest.

The migration into the shallows is vital to the Waccamaw darter's breeding season. Any difficulties such as waste run-offs or heavy siltation that prevent the darter from making its one-time effort into the shallows could seriously effect the species. Excessive siltation is known to be lethal to fertilized eggs and larvae of many fishes.

\* \* \*

These three fishes are threatened primarily by the increasing popularity of Lake Waccamaw as a recreational park. No modern waste disposal system services the area. The seasonal resident and tourist populations tax the existing sewage system and waste seeps through the sandy soil into the lake. Lake Waccamaw's waters are further enriched by garden fertilizer run-offs from local residents' yards. Land developers, sensing large real estate profits, have excavated drainage canals on the lake's northern and eastern shorelines. Erosion from these canals are causing silt to empty into the lake, gradually but most assuredly making the shallow lake even shallower.

What concerns biologists most about the infusion of nutrients into Lake Waccamaw is the possibility that the water will become more suitable for massive algal blooms that could lead to rapid eutrophication. Being stripped of its dissolved oxygen, the lake waters would certainly endanger the very existences of the darter, killifish, and silverside as well as other sensitive fishes. The fragile Lake Waccamaw ecosystem would become little more than an eutrophic lake and not the attractive recreational site that it is.

The choice now is not between continued development and recreational use of the lake, or no development and recreational use. The choice is between careful planning and development considering the lake ecosystem, or uncontrolled development of the Lake Waccamaw area. We hope, for the unique fish fauna as well as for the people who live near the lake, the direction will be one of planned development of the area that will maintain or improve the existing conditions in and around the lake. This approach may involve installing waste treatment plants for the existing development and redirecting some of the drainage ditches around the lake. This is the only way to maintain this unique, attractive natural resource for future generations to enjoy and to protect the threatened fishes of Lake Waccamaw.

2-3
Open water over a clean sandy bottom and shallow, weedy areas along the shores of Lake Waccamaw are important habitats for its endemic fishes. Photo by J. D. Williams.

# Okaloosa Darter
## *Etheostoma okaloosae*

For most Americans, Eglin Air Force Base conjures up images of a makeshift city that served as the first American home for the southeast Asian boat people and the Cuban refugees. Few Americans realize that Eglin Air Force Base, in the northwestern corner of Florida, is the permanent home of the endangered Okaloosa darter. This small fish was discovered in 1939 when Francis Harper, an early naturalist and explorer of the southeastern United States and the Okefenokee swamp region in particular, netted a single specimen during a collecting trip to Okaloosa County's Little Rocky Creek. Harper's specimen eventually came to the attention of an ichthyologist at the Academy of Natural Sciences of Philadelphia, Henry W. Fowler, who described this two-inch fish and named it *Etheostoma okaloosae,* after the county in which it was first captured.

The Okaloosa darter is native only to six small tributaries of Choctawhatchee Bay in Okaloosa and Walton counties of the Florida panhandle. The streams, with their tea-colored water, are generally fast-flowing with temperatures ranging from 45° to 50° F in winter to about 70° F in summer, and have a total length of 186 miles. Eglin Air Force Base occupies 90 percent of the 113,000 acres of land within the watersheds that feed the darter's streams, with the remaining 10 percent located on private property. The watershed lands consist of tall sandhills reaching elevations of about three hundred feet and covered with pine trees and scrub oak.

Little is known about the Okaloosa darter's ecology and reproductive biology. The relatively pollution-free darter streams are about five feet deep and shaded over most of their course. The fishes live in the areas where aquatic vegetation such as the bulrush, *Scirpus,* and the spike-rush, *Eleocharis,* cover a clean sandy stream bed. Biologists studying the ecology of the darter believe that the vegetation provides cover, protecting the darters from predators and at the same time support populations of aquatic insects and crustaceans for food. The vegetation also may act as a physical barrier to strong currents, which otherwise might sweep the darters away from the sixteen inch square territories. While the Okaloosa darter appears to prefer protected areas, it will not tolerate an environment where the water is stagnant and slow-moving, or impoundments and ponds created by damming streams. When the Okaloosa darter breeding season begins in late April or early May, male darters zealously begin to clear their territories of any other males. A female entering the territory slowly swims back and forth through the rushes, followed closely by the male. When she is ready to spawn, the female buries the anterior third of her body in a clump of rushes and waits for the male to move alongside her. Both fishes then swim deeper into the vegetation and come to rest just above the sandy bottom, where the female inclines her body to bring her genital opening close to the male's. After the female lays her eggs, attaching each egg to the stalk of a rush, she swims away. A large yolk almost fills the three millimeter-diameter eggs, which hatch in five to six days. The darter fry grow rapidly, reaching sexual maturity in about one year, and live a maximum of about two years, dying shortly after spawning the second year.

As early as 1964, ichthyologists who were concerned over the status of the

Okaloosa darter's population, noticed that a relative, the brown darter, *Etheostoma edwini,* was appearing with increasing frequency in samples collected within the Okaloosa darter's range. By 1980, brown darters occupied about 32 percent of the Okaloosa darter's historic range, and they could outcompete the Okaloosa darter for habitat, and ultimately for survival in streams where both species are present. Ichthyologists and ecologists are uncertain whether the two darters compete for space, food, or breeding sites, but they know that the brown darter can better tolerate less-than-ideal habitats and extreme environmental conditions such as floods. The brown darter also spawns about four to eight weeks earlier than the Okaloosa darter, possibly using the Okaloosa darter's limited breeding sites.

The Okaloosa darter's limited geographic range and the loss and deterioration of its habitat due to impoundments, road construction, and siltation from land clearing, prompted the U.S. Fish and Wildlife Service to place this fish on the endangered species list on June 4, 1973. The U.S. Fish and Wildlife Service subsequently established a recovery team to determine what factors are contributing to the rapid decline in the Okaloosa darter's population. The team developed an Okaloosa darter recovery plan, which the Fish and Wildlife Service approved in October 1981, to protect and increase the existing population of Okaloosa darters, and reestablish the species throughout its natural range. Under the plan, biologists will determine possible hazards to the Okaloosa darter, such as pesticide and herbicide use, land development, industrial and urban effluents, stream impoundments, and the introduction of exotic predators and competitors. The plan also calls for additional research studies to supplement the currently limited information available on the Okaloosa darter's biology, distribution, population size, and habitat preference. After these studies are completed, the U.S. Fish and Wildlife Service and the state of Florida will develop a comprehensive management plan for the Okaloosa darter's limited habitat. In the meantime, biologists from the state of Florida monitor populations of the Okaloosa darter to ensure its well being.

# III.

# Great Lakes Fishes

About 12,000 years ago the glaciers of the Pleistocene Epoch retreated, leaving behind a great chain of lakes in eastern North America. Sandwiched between the United States and Canada, the five Great Lakes (Superior, Michigan, Huron, Ontario, and Erie) form a single vast drainage system that flows west to east, terminating in the St. Lawrence River. These lakes contain 65 trillion gallons of water, one-fifth of the world's surface supply of freshwater. They send such a huge volume through the St. Lawrence River that every ten minutes of flow produces enough water to supply New York City for an entire day. Ranging in depths from 200 to 1300 feet, the Great Lakes stretch over 1200 miles and have a total U.S. coastline of 4500 miles—longer than the U.S. Atlantic and Gulf Coasts combined. With an area of 126,000 square miles, the Great Lakes drainage area represents one of the largest fresh water systems in the world. Rainfall and stream inflows recharge these vast inland seas, which then empty their waters into the Atlantic Ocean via the St. Lawrence River—whose outflow is exceeded in the U.S. only by the Columbia and Mississippi rivers.

Being so accessible to the shipping trade, the Great Lakes vicinity became a thriving business center. Inexpensive transportation and a seemingly infinite source of high quality water gave birth to the automobile, paper, steel, and a host of other industries in this region of North America. And along with the industries came the people. Today about one-fifth of the U.S. population and seven million Canadians reside in the Great Lakes basin.

While the Great Lakes have an impressive capability of absorbing the punishing onslaught of Man's activities, the overutilization of the lakes' resources has grown at astronomical rates, further testing the lakes' ability to recover.

3–1
Industrial development on river tributaries to the Great Lakes eliminated stream habitat and contributed to the pollution of the lakes. Photo by J. D. Williams.

Heavy metal pollutants and chlorinated organic compounds produced by industries find their way into the lakes. Agricultural pesticides and fertilizers run off the fields into the lakes as well, promoting eutrophic conditions. Land developers have destroyed much of the shallow water habitat of fishes by dredging and filling areas of the Great Lakes to alter the shorelines for new houses, factories, and recreational facilities. The destruction of habitats resulting from land development has eliminated much of the wetlands area many species use as spawning and nursery grounds. The combined effects of chemical pollution and physical alterations have had a tremendous negative impact on water quality and productivity of the Great Lakes.

The introduction of non-native fish species has had an enormous impact on the native fishes of the Great Lakes as well. The sea lamprey entered the Great Lakes via the man-made Welland Canal in the early 1800s. The population explosion of the sea lamprey during the late 1930s and 1940s resulted in a dramatic decrease in the native lake trout population. The lamprey parasitized the trout and other fishes by firmly attaching themselves to the sides of their prey, using their circular sucker-like mouths. Once secured, the rasplike teeth within the mouth of the sea lamprey would rasp through the trout's skin and suck the body fluids for nutrition. The weakened lake trout would either die fairly quickly from shock or succumb to disease shortly thereafter. Because the sea lamprey population multiplied at such an astounding rate, the lake trout came to the brink of extinction in the Great Lakes system. The disappearance of the deepwater cisco and blackfin cisco from Lakes Michigan and Huron in the 1950s and 1960s has been partially blamed on the introduction of the sea lamprey.

The alewife, a member of the herring family, was an accidental introdction into the Great Lakes. These fishes quickly managed to establish themselves in great abundance, and subsequently displaced the native ciscoes. It was Lake Michigan's most abundant species of fish by the 1960s, but is now reduced in numbers.

28

A species of Pacific salmon called the pink salmon, *Oncorhynchus gorbuscha*, was mistakenly released into Lake Superior in the 1950s. The species easily established itself in many spawning streams within the lake. Today the non-native salmon has dispersed into the remaining Great Lakes and the St. Lawrence River. The pink salmon's impact on the commercial and sport fishery is still not clear.

Biologists all agree that to expect the Great Lakes to return to their original conditions with their native fishes intact is asking for a miracle. It does appear, however, that the continued sound management of the Great Lakes depends upon the combined efforts of the states within the Great Lakes drainage, and the governments of the United States and Canada. Programs in several university, state, and federal laboratories are making promising strides towards ensuring the future of the lakes through pioneering research efforts and public education programs.

The three species of Great Lakes fishes portrayed in this section are all facing similar threats. Stories of their struggle for survival reveal the essence of living in one of the world's largest freshwater systems with a large human population along its shores.

# Lake Sturgeon
## *Acipenser fulvescens*

The sturgeon has been intimately linked with Man throughout history. In ancient Rome, this large fish was served at lavish banquets and crowned with flowers. King Edward II of England, who assumed the royal throne in 1307, took a fancy to the sturgeon and issued an edict to his British subjects: "The King shall have the wreck of the sea throughout the realm, whales and great sturgeons." At one point, any sturgeon captured above London Bridge belonged to the Lord Mayor of London, but all others belonged to the king by royal decree. Henry I is said to have banned the eating of the primitive fish at any table except his own. While some of these laws appear to be politically unjust by our standards today, they unwittingly provided some protection against overexploitation.

About 25 species of sturgeon belong to the family, Ascipenseridae; seven of which inhabit North America. Of these seven species, four are anadromous spending most of their life in marine or estuarine waters and the remaining three species live only in freshwater. The sturgeon is a primitive fish whose massive elongated body is partly covered by five longitudinal rows of heavy, bony plates or scutes arranged two rows on either side and one along the back. Its sharp, conical, snout is outfitted with four fleshy barbels studded with taste buds for finding food on the bottom. The sturgeon is a relict species that has retained a cartilaginous skeletal system and shark-like caudal fin since the Devonian period some 300 million years ago.

Whether tracing the Anglo-Saxon word "stiriga" meaning a stirrer, the Swedish word "stora" meaning to stir, or the German word "storen" meaning to poke or rummage around, it is easy to see how the name sturgeon came about. The sturgeon's name reflects its manner of feeding on the bottom of lakes and rivers. Possessing only small beady eyes, the sturgeon uses its barbels beneath its snout to brush over the lake or river bottom to detect prey by taste. Well-adapted with a highly protrusible and toothless mouth, the stugeon rapidly sucks up crustaceans, aquatic insect larvae, molluscs, and even fish eggs. The sturgeon efficiently retains food items by filtering them from other soft bottom materials which are eliminated through the gills.

Unlike the endangered shortnose sturgeon, *Acipenser brevirostrum*, which is anadromous, the threatened lake sturgeon, *Acipenser fulvescens*, is confined to freshwater habitats. Historically the sturgeon occurred east of the Rocky Mountains and west of the Appalachians from south central and southeastern Canada south to Arkansas and Alabama. Based on fishery reports from the late 1800s, the lake sturgeon was more commonly encountered in the northern portion of its range. Formerly an abundant species in the Great Lakes, especially Lake Erie, the populations of lake sturgeon have steadily declined since the turn of the century. Although greatly reduced in numbers, today the lake sturgeon can be found in southern Canada, portions of the Great Lakes, the St. Lawrence River drainage, and the upper Mississippi River drainage.

Depending on where the lake sturgeon is found, a variety of common names have been given to this giant of inland freshwater fishes: bull-nosed, rock, stone, red, ruddy, and shell-bark sturgeon, among others. The lake sturgeon ranges from an olive-yellow to reddish to bluish-gray coloration dorsally. The variation in hues may be the result of local conditions in which the fish resides. Its scientific name, *Acipenser fulvescens*, actually means "reddish-yellow or tawny colored sturgeon." Juvenile lake sturgeons under about twenty inches long possess four dusky blotches, one on each side of the back behind the nape, and one on each side of the back below the dorsal fin. These blotches disappear with age.

While those lake sturgeons usually seen are 20 to 55 inches long and weigh between two and sixty pounds, some individuals have measured in around eight feet long and up to three hundred pounds! Females tend to outlive their male counterparts and attain larger sizes. Forty year old lake sturgeons are not unusual with some particularly long-lived individuals reaching the century mark. A lake sturgeon caught in 1953 was reputed to have been 152 years old! The age of a sturgeon is determined by cutting through the leading fin ray of one of its pectoral fins. An ultra-thin cross-section of the fin ray viewed with a microscope shows opaque bands alternating with narrow clear bands. This alternating pattern gives the researcher the age of a sturgeon much as the concentric rings of a tree trunk are counted to age a tree.

The lake sturgeon usually inhabits waters cooler than 75° and less than fifty feet deep. Found on the bottom of large rivers and in the shallow waters of large lakes, the lake sturgeon is rarely in the lakes that are not connected with one or more relatively large tributaries. It avoids areas where there is a soft, muddy bottom, but prefers clean substrates composed of sand and gravel, or rocks for feeding and especially for spawning.

Growth is slow for the lake sturgeon. The females become sexually mature and capable of breeding when they are fifteen to twenty years old. At this age they are approximately thirty inches long and weigh only twenty to thirty pounds. Unlike most other fishes that breed annually upon reaching sexual maturity, the female lake sturgeon spawns intermittently, about every four to seven years after becoming sexually mature.

During May and June, sexually mature adult lake sturgeons migrate to areas of rocky rapids in rivers or shoals in lakes with strong wave action to spawn. In waters two to fifteen feet deep spawning begins when a ripe female enters the confines of a group of three to six males. Several of the males attend to the female by swimming alongside the female in the same direction against the current. Eggs and milt are released simultaneously during the spawning act which lasts for only about five seconds. A large female lake sturgeon can deposit anywhere from 50,000 to 700,000 adhesive eggs onto the shallow, gravel riffles or rocky shoals. In about a week's time the eggs will hatch. Occasionally during spawning, the lake sturgeons will make spectacular leaps known as "breachings" clear out of the water. The reason behind this behavior is uncertain.

The spawning group of males and female will aimlessly drift about after the spawning act or swim either downstream or out into deeper waters; then return to spawn again, usually in the same spot. The average female spawns from five to eight hours up to as much as several days until completely spent of eggs. Neither the eggs nor young sturgeon fry receive any parental care.

The story of the lake sturgeon over the last 125 years in North America amply illustrates the rise and fall of the commercial sturgeon industry. Prior to 1855, despite the fact that the lake sturgeon was said to have been a food source just as important to the eastern forest indian tribes as the bison was to the western plains indian tribes, the U.S. was not commercially interested in this species. Considered a nuisance by commercial fishermen because the heavily armored and abundant lake sturgeon constantly damaged the fishing nets with their rough skins and lateral scutes, fishermen made deliberate efforts to reduce the lake sturgeon's numbers. Some fishermen retaliated for their damaged nets by leaving the disentangled sturgeons on the beach to die slowly, or they fed them to hogs. Other sturgeons were used as kindling to fuel bonfires! Special barges were constructed to haul the beached sturgeons away from the choice fishing grounds.

Then in 1855, caviar made from the roe of the lake sturgeon caught the attention of the public. Smoked sturgeon also became a good substitute for smoked halibut. By 1860, a new fishing industry was born in Sandusky, Ohio. By 1880, the lake sturgeon industry was thriving in the Great Lakes and Canada. Besides roe and the firm, coarse sturgeon meat which was now prepared baked, fried, dried, pickled, boiled, and smoked, the lake sturgeon's swimbladder was in high demand for isinglass, a gelatinous derivative made from this organ. Isinglass has a variety of uses from clarifying wines and beers to making a stiffener for jams and jellies. In addition, the sturgeon's oil and skin had become valuable.

For the next several years the lake sturgeon was the most important commercial species in the St. Lawrence River and was particularly abundant in Lake Erie. Lake of the Woods which straddles Minnesota and Ontario was described before the turn of the century as the greatest sturgeon pond in the world. Before 1900, the greatest annual production of lake sturgeons came out of Lake Erie with 4.7 million pounds. Lakes St. Clair and Huron were the next closest in annual production, each contributing one million pounds. Lakes Michigan, Ontario, and Superior all produced less than a million pounds of lake sturgeon during this period.

Declines in the annual production of lake sturgeons began by 1890. By 1910, the commercial sturgeon industry had become relatively unimportant, a mere shadow of its former self. Over fifty years later in 1968, nearly the entire 41,000 pounds of the total Great Lakes production was taken from the Canadian waters of Lake St. Clair and North Bay, Lake Huron.

There are several reasons why the lake sturgeon declined so dramatically and quickly. The wanton destruction of vast numbers of lake sturgeons during the 1800s when these fishes were considered little more than nuisances by the commercial fishing operations and the later intense efforts to catch them when the sturgeon had become a viable commercial species greatly reduced future spawning populations. The overexploitation of such a long-lived species as the lake sturgeon, one that has both slow growth and a long period of sexual immaturity, surely left scars on the ability of this species to bounce back from depletion.

In addition, dams constructed across rivers and tributaries of lakes have blocked adult lake sturgeon from reaching their spawning grounds. Expansion of human settlements into choice breeding sites threatens the sturgeon eggs and fry with siltation. Eroding soils smother the clean gravel and sand that the eggs adhere to and eliminate the various bottom dwelling organisms on which the lake sturgeon feeds. By dredging and filling marshlands bordering on lakes, the available spawning and feeding areas for sturgeon are greatly reduced. Industrial developments pollute these waters, further degrading the habitat.

Preservation of habitat is the single most important factor to ensure that populations of sturgeon grow, reproduce, and survive. All of the above threats to the lake sturgeon have long-lasting effects because growth is slow and sexual maturity is not reached for several years. As such, most of the sturgeons today are the products of environmental conditions that existed twenty to forty years ago. Management efforts to maintain and preserve the lake sturgeon's habitat today must be viewed as a long-range plan, where results will come only after several years of hard work, patience, and hope.

Recently lake sturgeon young have been raised by artificial propagation. Some biologists believe that sturgeon aquaculture could be the wave of the future because cultured sturgeon grow two to three times faster than their counterparts in the wild. They feel that at that rate a commercial operation could have a marketable product in only three to six years.

In most regions of the U.S. and Canada commercial fishing efforts have either been completely banned or highly restricted. Sportsfishing also comes under rigidly enforced regulations. Levels of removal of the lake sturgeon from most of its range are controlled by closed seasons, limits to numbers of sturgeon taken seasonally, gear and size restrictions. Without these restrictions, the lake sturgeon would most certainly be wiped out at least in the United States. Such restrictions on the taking of lake sturgeon would have seemed ludicrous to early commercial fishermen who considered the lake sturgeon to be a nuisance.

# Shortnose Cisco and Shortjaw Cisco
## *Coregonus reighardi* and *Coregonus zenithicus*

(Color plate 3.)

*The ciscoes of the Great Lakes probably represent the most significantly endangered fishery, the most significantly endangered fish populations, and the most significantly endangered combination of fish species in the freshwaters of the United States.*

*The eight species of ciscoes in the coregonine group (family, Salmonidae; subfamily, Coregoninae) once were the dominant commercial fish of the Great Lakes, and the dominant forage fish for lake trout and other piscivores. Now the ciscoes are virtually extinct in Lakes Erie and Ontario, are restricted largely to Georgian Bay in Lake Huron, and are rapidly diminishing in abundance in Lakes Michigan and Superior.*

> *From a report released on August 2, 1974*
> *U.S. Fish and Wildlife Service's*
> *Great Lakes Fishery Laboratory in*
> *Ann Arbor, Michigan.*

In 1927, the ichthyologist Walter Koelz published the most comprehensive taxonomic study of the Great Lakes ciscoes, a group of silvery white fishes that constitute one of the three genera in the coregonine subfamily of the family Salmonidae. Koelz believed that the Great Lakes coregonines differentiated before the Great Lakes had attained their present form about 20,000 years ago. As a result of his study, Koelz established the criteria for identifying and classifying the ciscoes of the Great Lakes and described nine species including four new ones. Although biological and morphological differences do exist among the Great Lakes cisco species, they all look very similar. In addition, the ciscoes inhabit all the Great Lakes—even the deeper waters below the thermocline. During the 56 years that have followed Koelz's study, biologists have continually discovered specimens of ciscoes that do not conform to Koelz's criteria, and this has led to a reexamination of the cisco taxonomy with the realization that the ciscoes are a remarkably adaptable and variable group of fishes.

The difficulty in establishing the criteria that define a particular species of cisco is that morphologically the fishes vary considerably from lake to lake as the environment influences these characteristics. The shape, size, growth rate, and numbers of scales and gill rakers that characterize a species of cisco in one lake may therefore be different from the same species in another lake. Taxonomists disagree on how many species are in the genus *Coregonus,* and the number of species reported have ranged between eight and fourteen. Some biologists believe that the problem of cisco identification has been compounded by introgressive hybridization. As some species of cisco become increasingly rare, they lack mates of their own species and instead breed with closely related species. The individual that results is a hybrid and exhibits some characteristics of both parents.

Despite the uncertainty such morphological variation causes, taxonomists have managed to identify at least five species of ciscoes that are endemic to the Great Lakes: the deep water cisco, *Coregonus johannae;* the longjaw cisco, *Coregonus alpenae;* the shortnose cisco, *Coregonus reighardi;* the kiyi, *Coregonus kiyi;* and the bloater, *Coregonus hoyi.* Three other species of cisco not endemic to the Great Lakes are the lake herring, *Coregonus artedii;* the blackfin cisco, *Coregonus nigripinnis;* and the shortjaw cisco, *Coregonus zenithicus.* All of these species, except the lake herring, inhabit the deepwater habitats of the lakes and are known collectively as "chubs."

Since the late nineteenth century, the Great Lakes have supported a large chub fishing industry in the United States and Canada which in turn supplied a significant smoked fish market. Years ago fishermen set gillnets with 4.5-inch meshes in the deepwater regions of the lakes to catch the chubs. They discarded the smaller species of cisco and sold the larger blackfin, deepwater, and longjaw ciscoes. Even by the 1920s, the larger cisco species were becoming rare. To maintain their annual catch, the fishermen switched to a 2.13-inch mesh size net and began to capture the intermediate-sized shortjaw and short-nose ciscoes. Between 1930 and 1960, these species also declined while the populations of small bloaters increased dramatically, partially because the lake trout that had preyed on the bloaters were gone.

3–2
The Great Lakes have suffered from pollution for many years, but efforts to reduce or eliminate contaminants entering the lakes are underway. Photo by J. D. Williams.

For years, the bloater population has maintained what remains of the Great Lakes chub fishery and traditional smoked fish market, but recently even the bloater catch has declined. The alewife, a species of herring that was introduced into the Great Lakes as early as the 1870s, may have competed for food and habitat with the bloaters and fed on the bloaters' eggs. Industrial and urban pollutants have put additional pressure on the embattled bloater population.

By the early 1970s, three cisco species in the Great Lakes were extinct: the blackfin cisco, the longjaw cisco, and the deepwater cisco. The shortnose cisco and shortjaw cisco are endangered, and the kiyi is threatened. "It was naïve," wrote one biologist, "to expect that any population of organisms could withstand such continuous and intense exploitation at the same time that the habitat was being destroyed by such activities as gravel removal, gas well drilling, and sewage discharge."

The endangered shortnose cisco, *Coregonus reighardi,* inhabited the deeper waters of Lake Michigan, Lake Huron, and Lake Ontario at depths between 30 and 480 feet. The genus name *Coregonus* was coined from the Greek language by Petrus Artedi, considered by many to be the "Father of Ichthyology," describing this group of fishes' uniquely angled pupils. The species name *"reighardi"* honors Jacob Reighard, an ichthyologist from the University of Michigan. One of the intermediate-sized Great Lakes ciscoes, the shortnose cisco reached lengths of six to ten inches and weighed about a pound. Females generally outlived males by two years, often living for as many as eight years. The shortnose cisco was the only cisco species in Lakes Michigan, Huron, and Ontario that spawned in the spring, during May and June. The adults fed almost exclusively on two species of freshwater shrimp, *Mysis relicta* and *Pontoporea affinis,* but ate copepods, aquatic insect larvae, and some clams. Although shortnose ciscos were taken for a commercial fishery for nearly forty years, biologists still know very little about the life history and biology of this species.

The shortnose cisco was last found in Lake Michigan in 1972 and has disappeared from Lake Ontario since 1964. Its distribution in Lake Huron is limited to Georgian Bay on the lake's Canadian shore.

The endangered shortjaw cisco, *Coregonus zenithicus,* was named after Duluth, "the Zenith City," where hundreds of specimens of this species were seen in Booth and Company's cold-storage plant. Also a member of the intermediate-sized cisco species, the shortjaw cisco averaged about eleven inches in length, but occasionally reached sixteen inches in length. The shortjaw cisco is one of the easiest species of cisco to identify in Lake Superior, where it has a longer snout, shorter fins, and fewer and shorter gillrakers than the other species. In addition, the lower jaw of the shortjaw cisco is shorter than the upper jaw. In contrast to the shortnose cisco, the shortjaw cisco spawns in the fall and winter, from late November to January. The adult diet includes freshwater shrimp, some aquatic vegetation, insects, and occasionally other fish.

Although the complete range of the shortjaw cisco is not known, it was once common in waters 65 to 600 feet deep in the Great Lakes, except possibly Lake Ontario. The last shortjaw cisco specimen taken in Lake Michigan was in 1975, and one was in Lake Huron in 1982. Both probably represent strays from Lake Superior. Fishery biologists now believe that the shortjaw cisco occurs only in Lake Superior and Lake Nippigon, a large body of water immediately north of Thunder Bay in Lake Superior.

Today, the Great Lakes Fishery Laboratory and the University of Michigan in Ann Arbor, Michigan, are conducting long-range taxonomic and biological research on the Great Lakes ciscoes. They are helping state fishery managers identify the abundance, distribution, and status of the various cisco species that remain in the Great Lakes to develop regulations and quotas protecting the ciscoes from continued overfishing. The biologists support managing local stocks, or populations, of Great Lakes ciscoes, but not widespread populations. This lake-by-lake management should prevent fishermen from converging on any one of the remaining cisco species in the belief that the species' populations in the other lakes would keep the species viable. Management of local stocks and clean-up and protection of habitat are essential if we are to prevent the shortjaw cisco from becoming an extinct species.

"Without an early increase in the quantity of input into cisco research," the Great Lakes Fishery laboratory reported in 1974, "the situation will be so nebulous that the regulations covering the capture, possession, or disposition of endangered ciscoes in the Great Lakes by anyone, as described in the Endangered Species Act of 1973, will be unenforceable."

# IV.

# Pacific Coast Freshwater Fishes

Unlike the Atlantic seaboard, most of the Pacific Coast is mountainous. The mountains that stretch from Alaska to Baja California are young and still growing. Extending eastward to the deserts of the Basin and Range Province in Mexico and the southwest U.S., the Columbia-Snake River Plateau in the northwest U.S., and to the Rocky Mountains and Intermontane Plateaus of western Canada, the mountains of the Pacific Coast comprise roughly 360,000 square miles. The desert conditions of the southwest are the result of these mountains capturing the moisture from air moving inland from the Pacific Ocean.

Steep bluffs characterize much of the Pacific coastline from California north to Washington. These are the results of non-resistant coastal geologic formations that are easily eroded by the wind and surf. The Los Angeles basin in the south is unusual in that a coastal plain slopes from the foot of the mountains to the sea. Looking north to Puget Trough, however, only about a half-dozen plains can be found; all of them small and at the mouths of broad valleys.

Coastal rivers, alpine lakes, mountain streams, desert pools, and forest ponds are all found along the Pacific Coast region. The climate varies from warm and dry, cold and wet, temperate and wet, and cold and dry. The altitudinal range can go from sea level to over 14,000 feet. These great differences reflect the vast length of the Pacific Coast, stretching more than 26 degrees latitude. Because of this geologic and climatic variability, no wonder a great diversity of aquatic habitats can be found in the vast region of the Pacific Coast.

In general, the threats to aquatic habitats in the states of Washington, Oregon, and California are based on the loss of water, introduction of exotic fishes, destruction of habitat, and pollution. Habitat alterations have been the major problem for endangered and threatened fishes living in the Pacific Coast freshwater ecosystems. Dams have impounded the fast-flowing waters of streams and rivers. Therefore, fishes adapted to swift waters have been eliminated, while exotic fishes more adapted to slower moving reservoir waters have flourished. Almost every major stream appears to have been dammed to catch the runoff and send it through canals for industrial, domestic, or agricultural purposes. This de-watering of streams for various purposes greatly reduces water levels downstream. Channelization of streams has lead to the demise of one of the highlighted fishes in this section and contributed to the extinction of the thicktail chub, *Gila crassicauda,* in the early 1950s.

The native fishes of the Pacific Coast are silently disappearing from the low elevation regions where man's impact has had the greatest influence. The widespread introduction of non-native fishes has seriously affected the survival of many of the native fishes. By some estimates, close to 40 percent of the fish species now present in the aquatic habitats of California are the result of introductions—no less than 33 species from eastern North America. These introductions have occurred for a variety of reasons including: (1) to improve sport and commercial fishing; (2) to provide forage for gamefishes or bait for fishermen; (3) to control insects and weeds. Also, some introductions are accidental. In many areas, the introduced, non-native fish species are the most abundant fishes in the California waterways.

From a river in the northeastern corner of California to the Los Angeles basin in southern California, and from a mineralized lake in a remote and arid section of Oregon to a thermal lake in southeastern Oregon come accounts of four Pacific Coast freshwater fishes whose stories illustrate the varied problems they face.

## Borax Lake Chub
### *Gila boraxobius*

Most of us can still remember a television commercial that boasted of a household cleaning compound that was as strong as a twenty-mule-team: *Boraxo. Boraxo* was the trade name for the generic chemical, sodium borate, an odorless white substance commonly known as borax. Besides its use as a cleaning agent, borax was also used in the tanning, curing, and preservation of skins; fireproofing fabrics and wood; manufacturing enamels and glazes; and even "artificially aging wood." Furthermore, the world of medicine had found value for borax as a mild antiseptic.

Sodium borate is an inorganic chemical compound that occurs naturally in some of the mineral-rich waters of the western United States. During the early 1900s, the mineral-laden waters of one such body of water, aptly named Borax Lake, was heavily used for borax extraction. Even today there are remnants of the former mining operation along the shoreline of Borax Lake. Two huge metal evaporating tubs used to extract the borax and a tiny adobe shack the miners used for shelter are still visible.

Borax Lake is a small ten acre lake in the sparsely populated Alvord Basin of south-central Oregon. It is a shallow, crater-shaped, warm water lake with

4-1

Borax Lake, northeast of Fields, Harney County, Oregon is the only habitat of the Borax Lake chub. Photo by J. D. Williams.

a silty bottom that is fed by several thermal springs. Little aquatic vegetation grows in the lake except for algae and some small clumps of grasses along its margin. Near the center of the lake thermal spring water rises to the lake bottom from a fault line that extends along the valley floor. Water flowing into the lake is about 104°F, resulting in water temperatures around the margin of the lake frequently above 86°F. Thousands of years of mineral salt "build up" has formed a thick crust of borax and raised the lake's edges thirty feet above the rest of the valley floor.

At ten acres in total size, Borax Lake is the largest thermal lake in Oregon and the warmest environment where fish of any species occur in the entire state. The Alvord Basin, located in one of the most arid and remote regions in Oregon, is peppered with numerous hot springs, among them Borax Lake. Few paved roads exist in the Alvord Basin, and the closest incorporated town is over one hundred miles away. The fifty or so individuals that do live in the basin are either owners or employees of cattle ranches.

The outflow from Borax Lake leads to an adjacent body of water called the Lower Borax Lake—probably created during the diversion of the borate-rich waters in the borax extraction operation of the last one hundred years. The shallow Lower Borax Lake, whose highly alkaline waters overlie a mudflat, often goes completely dry during the summer. The thermal waters of the Borax Lake area is one of the few places in the entire Alvord Basin that remains ice-free during the winter. This feature has made it an unusual habitat for a diverse assemblage of wildlife. Migrating and resident birds including shore-birds, song birds, raptors, and waterfowl nest, rest, and feed in this refuge.

Within the shallow reaches of Borax Lake, and occasionally Lower Borax Lake when not completely dried, lives a lone species of fish appropriately called the Borax Lake chub, *Gila boraxobius*. This dwarf member of the minnow family, Cyprinidae, was isolated from the surrounding watershed by the lake's elevated position above the valley floor as a result of the mineral salt precipitation. The Borax Lake chub measures only one to two inches long but has a large head complete with large eyes and a long jaw. Males are readily distinguished from the females of the species which appear to be longer than the males, but their fins are proportionately smaller than the males. Despite the relatively depauperate fauna and flora in the lake itself, the dark olive-green minnow with the purplish iridescent sides is an opportunistic feeder fond of aquatic invertebrates. It will primarily pick up food from the soft lake bottom or from rocks strewn across the bottom and will eat throughout the day. During the fall the chub will eat terrestrial insects that have become stranded in the water. Diatoms, microscopic algal cells encased in siliceous boxes, and microcrustaceans are also important food items during the winter when the choicer aquatic invertebrate food is scarce. Little is really known about the biology of the Borax Lake chub including how it can live in such borate-concentrated waters. Studies of how the kidneys of this minnow species eliminate the high concentration of sodium borate would be intriguing. They might even provide biomedical insights into devising more efficient kidney dialysis machines.

Because of the lake's physical position above the valley floor, the fragile Borax Lake ecosystem is susceptible to threats by humans. The Borax Lake ecosystem is threatened by diversion of water from the lake for irrigation and development of the area for geothermal energy. The diversion could affect the lake ecosystem drastically by decreasing the area of the lake and adjacent marsh habitat. Any significant decrease in water volume in the lake basin would increase the water temperature, posing a mortal threat to the Borax Lake chub. The impact from geothermal energy development could likewise render the habitat untenable for the Borax Lake chub.

The entire Alvord Basin is considered to be a Known Geothermal Resource Area (KGRA), by having a high potential for geothermal energy development. Much of the area is owned by the federal government but there are private lands scattered throughout the area. The Bureau of Land Management has already leased rights for geothermal exploration to a private energy company, the Anadarko Production Company, despite protests from a long list of conservation organizations. Conservation groups felt so strongly about the leasing that they considered filing a lawsuit against the Bureau of Land Management. In the eyes of the Bureau of Land Management, the leasing would not significantly affect the environment if safeguards are in place.

The Anadarko Production Company holds leases surrounding a portion of Borax Lake and plans to drill three deep geothermal wells (down to 8000 feet) to determine whether a potential commercial geothermal resource exists. In compliance with the leasing agreements drawn up between the Bureau of Land Management and the Anadarko Production Company, the company cannot drill within one-half mile of the lake and must institute a monitoring program designed to protect Borax Lake. Along with this program is a stipulation that drilling must be stopped as soon as there is any change in either the water

40

quality, including temperature, or level in Borax Lake resulting from drilling efforts. The exploratory drilling activity in the valley floor could accidently puncture the thermal aquifers that provide the warm waters to Borax Lake and the surrounding wildlife habitats, altering the pressure and temperature levels of the thermal spring waters flowing into the lake. Equally possible, the drilling could create a system of interconnecting aquifers or springs, draining the lifeblood of Borax Lake.

Oddsmakers claim that at best, the odds are one in four that the company will actually locate the geothermal reservoir. At worst, there is a one chance in twenty . . . Anadarko estimates it may take several years to determine whether the geothermal source is large enough to develop economically. It has been estimated that the Borax Lake area has the potential of producing 91 megawatts of electricity for thirty years according to a study released by the U.S. Geological Survey. Translated into real economic terms, this is equivalent to literally millions of dollars each year.

Borax Lake itself is on private land owned by Mrs. J.E. Calderwood, owner of over one-third of the entire Borax Lake area. The lake is fenced and no one is allowed access without first receiving Mrs. Calderwood's permission. Permission has been granted to biologists, and as a result, Borax Lake has been the focus of several scientific studies. For some time now groups such as the Nature Conservancy, Bureau of Land Management, and the U.S. Fish and Wildlife Service have desperately tried to purchase or exchange land for Borax Lake, but no such deal could be made. Now, in addition to the exploratory drilling in search of geothermal energy by the Anadarko Production Company, the Getty Oil Company has leased the mineral rights on the Calderwood property for exploration. The Getty Oil Company lease is for forty years. The Getty Oil Company is aware of the unique ecosystem represented by the Borax Lake area.

The U.S. Fish and Wildlife published a final ruling, effective November 4, 1982, listing the Borax Lake chub as an endangered species. This action was taken because the Borax Lake chub is only found in Borax Lake, its outflow, and Lower Borax Lake (when there is water in the shallow marsh), as well as the threats posed by geothermal development in the area. In this ruling, critical habitat for the Borax Lake chub was also delineated to include the Borax Lake area and 640 acres around the lake—both federal lands and Mrs. Calderwood's land.

The critical habitat designation, contrary to what is often believed, does not mean that the Borax Lake area is to become a wildlife sanctuary, automatically closed for most uses. The geothermal exploratory drilling can proceed within certain guidelines agreed upon among the U.S. Fish and Wildlife Service, the Bureau of Land Management, and the geothermal companies. Should successful wells be found, then chances are good that other energy companies would want to "hop on the bandwagon" and begin drilling elsewhere in the Alvord Basin. This additional exploration would place greater stress on both the water supply and air quality in the Alvord Basin.

The question becomes how much longer can the Borax Lake chub endure and survive in the face of America's increasing energy demands? Only time will tell.

*     *     *

41

As this book was going to press we received some encouraging news about the Borax Lake chub and its unique habitat. The Nature Conservancy and Mrs. Calderwood are discussing a long-term lease agreement, with an option to purchase Borax Lake and the surrounding land. If the Nature Conservancy successfully negotiates the lease, the Borax Lake chub will literally have a new lease on life.

# Warner Sucker
## *Catostomus warnerensis*

During the Pleistocene Epoch, a period in the earth's history some 12,000 to 3 million years ago, continental ice sheets advanced and retreated over much of North America. This period was also characterized by a slight increase in rainfall which created vast Pleistocene lakes such as Lakes Bonneville, Lahontan, and Warner. Gradually, with warmer and drier climate, the glaciers receded. At the same time the water levels of the lakes began to drop due to evaporation. The lands in which these once large freshwater lakes existed, with their banks lined by trees and luxuriant grasses, are now seemingly barren semi-deserts. The familiar Bonneville salt flats, used today for test driving high-speed vehicles, and the Great Salt Lake are all that remain from Pleistocene Lake Bonneville.

Like Lake Bonneville, Lake Warner used to cover a vast expanse of western U.S. topography, having a surface area of over five hundred square miles and reaching depths of over three hundred feet. Lake Warner's water level dropped continually during the shift to warmer and drier environments. As the evaporation lowered the water level in this large inland sea, the basin was splintered by a string of offshore bars into the eleven shallow lakes on the basin floor. These eleven lakes spread out across the flat floor of the Warner Basin and average only six to ten feet deep. Water to the lakes is supplied almost solely through streams flowing down from the well-timbered Warner Mountains on the western flank of the basin. Water in all of these lakes is alkaline and supports a limited biota.

Of the eleven lakes, only the three in southern Warner Valley are consistently fed with waters from inflowing streams. Their eight counterparts in northern Warner Valley all periodically dry up. Crump, Hart, and Pelican lakes with their larger tributary streams make up the entire known habitat of the threatened endemic Warner sucker, *Catostomus warnerensis*. First discovered by the naturalist, Edward D. Cope in 1883, the Warner sucker was formally recognized as a new species in 1908 by J.O. Snyder—based on twelve preserved specimens.

This greenish-gray fish, known locally as the "red horse" because of the bright vermilion color that the male Warner suckers wear during the spring breeding season, prefers to inhabit slow-moving sections of creeks and lakes. This species also occurs in some of the larger irrigation canals that form long networks across the flat valley floor. In its lake and stream habitat, the tiny-eyed Warner sucker searches the bottom more by smell than sight for a variety of aquatic insect larvae and crustaceans. As its name implies, the Warner sucker picks up food with its fleshy lips which are well-supplied with taste-buds. As in most species of suckers, the mouth is positioned ventrally on the head. When the spring breeding season comes around, the three to four year old mature Warner sucker begins the trek in search of gravelly-bottomed creeks, essential for egg deposition and for a nursery site. The young live for several months in these creeks before moving to one of the lakes.

The Warner sucker is a potadromous spring spawner that is having great difficulty in making its run into the creeks. Local residents claim that up until the late 1930s, spawning runs of thousands of Warner suckers would ascend the creeks in the spring. Since that time, a spreading labyrinth of irrigation ditches, dams, diversions, and channelized canals has blocked the major creeks that feed the Warner Valley lakes. With access between the spawning grounds and lakes blocked by these obstacles, mature suckers cannot ascend the creeks, and if they do, the young may be diverted into the irrigation canals of nearby cultivated fields as they try to get to the lakes. The alteration of the southern Warner Valley habitat for the Warner sucker is so drastic that the irrigation canals appear to be the most available habitat for them. The modifications to the southern Warner Valley environment has been, and continues to be, the major reason for the decline and threatened status of this endemic fish.

Of the three southern Warner Valley Pleistocene remnant lakes, Pelican Lake is the smallest. This weed-choked shallow lake provides shelter to a large diversity of shore birds from egrets to grebes. Feeding on the plentiful aquatic vegetation and schools of the tui chub, *Gila bicolor,* several of the birds, including a colony of white pelicans, nest on two tiny islands that poke up from the lake. In the past, Deep Creek, one of the valley's larger creeks, provided water to Pelican and Crump Lakes. As the area was developed for agriculture, Deep Creek was diverted directly into Crump Lake. Pelican Lake is currently fed by the ground water originating from irrigation water combined with the water supply from some small springs.

Situated between Pelican and Hart Lakes is Crump Lake. Reputed to have the greatest water storage capacity of the three lakes, Crump Lake has never gone dry. Two creeks, Deep Creek and Twentymile Creek, supply water to the lake during those years with normal or above normal precipitation. However, during dry spells in the region, the entire water supply from the two feeder creeks is diverted into the canals to irrigate fields. Regardless of the amount of rainfall, Crump Lake always has some water and acts as a haven for birds as well as fishing grounds for introduced gamefishes.

During periods of high inflow, Crump Lake drains through a small narrow channel called "The Narrows", into the most abused of the three southern lakes, Hart Lake. The flow from Crump Lake, in addition to a water supply from Honey Creek, provides Hart Lake with a renewable source of water. In the early 1930s Hart Lake almost went dry during a drought due to natural evaporation and reduced flow from tributary streams. Only a small segment at the southern end of the lake remained under the water. The rest of the fertile lake bottom was made into farmland. In the past large pumps have been placed along the banks of Hart Lake with the sole purpose of drying the lake to reclaim the rich soil for farming. This land reclamation is being implemented even though Hart Lake probably holds the largest population of endemic Warner suckers in the valley.

Most of the land that once comprised the bottom of Pleistocene Lake Warner has been dramatically transformed into cultivated fields of alfalfa, grass hay, and small grains. Cattle, first introduced into Warner Valley in 1869, graze on the forage crops throughout the year, especially during the winter when they are coaxed down from the high country. The fields where the cattle graze receive their water supply via irrigation canals that tap three principal tributaries to the lakes in southern Warner Valley.

Deep Creek is the largest of the three perennial creeks flowing into Warner Valley. Six irrigation diversions have been placed along its length removing most of the creek's water even in a year of normal rainfall. These diversions not only channel water into the cultivated fields, but also prevent the Warner sucker from migrating upstream to the gravel beds to spawn.

The headwaters of Honey Creek originate 6000 feet above sea level and travel almost thirty miles due east before running right into Hart Lake. Between the three miles from the higher altitude entrance into southern Warner Valley to the end in Hart Lake, thirteen diversions for irrigation of Lake Warner's fertile bottom terrain have been installed over the years. As in Deep

4–2
Warner Valley Lakes and their tributary streams in south-central Oregon are habitat for the Warner sucker. Photo by J. D. Williams.

Creek, the Warner sucker is discouraged from using most of the length of Honey Creek for spawning.

Twentymile Creek, the third perennial source of water into the southern Warner Valley has a diversion structure that funnels most of its water into the irrigation canal system. Any excess water flows past the diversion, following an artificially built channel until it reaches Crump Lake.

All of these creeks will probably have their waters diverted to irrigate the adjacent cultivated fields depending on the amount of precipitation that falls in the southern Warner Valley basin during any given year. This maze of irrigation canals and its drastic modification of the Warner sucker's habitat is the primary threat to the sucker's population. But the possible geothermal development in Warner Valley could bring new problems. A portion of the basin is a Known Geothermal Resource Area (KGRA) and there have been recent geothermal investigations. Even explorations by private companies to develop Warner Valley for its geothermal resources could adversely affect the Warner sucker's future. Geothermal development would demand more of the finite waters and change the water temperature with hot waste water effluents. New geothermal development might spell the end for a fish that we know little about.

And finally, introduced fishes such as catfishes may prey upon the young Warner suckers as they travel the hazardous route back into the lakes. This problem needs additional research to determine just how seriously the Warner sucker population is affected by the exotic fishes.

Though greatly reduced since its discovery one hundred years ago, the Warner sucker appears to be holding its own . . . for the time being.

# Modoc Sucker
## *Catostomus microps*

High up on a western volcanic plateau some 4000 to 5000 feet above sea level in the small stream tributaries of the Pit River lives an endangered fish known as the Modoc sucker, *Catostomus microps*. This dwarf member of the sucker family reachers only seven inches in length when fully grown. Its common name appears to come from a local indian tribe, Moatakni maklaks, meaning the "People of the Moatak" or "People of Tule Lake." Both the tiny gray to greenish-brown sucker that inhabits the river and the plateau where the fish is found are called Modoc.

In the northeastern corner of California the Pit River originates in the Warner Mountains and flows southwesterly to the Sacramento River, draining almost 5200 square miles of California. The Modoc Plateau, which is drained by the Pit River, is bounded on the east by the Warner Mountains and on the west by the Cascade Range. This plateau resulted from volcanic activity during the Pliocene and Pleistocene periods. The extensive volcanism dramatically altered the topography of the area and the Pit River changed from its Pliocene pattern of flowing into the upper Klamath River to its present southwesterly flow into the Sacramento River. The natural diversion into the Sacramento River occurred at the beginning of the Pleistocene period when a large lava flow blocked the upper Klamath River's flow and created the deep Lake Alturas. Overflow later made Lake Alturas part of the Sacramento River Basin. These past geological events make it easier to understand why the fishes of Pit River show affinities to the fishes of both the Klamath and Sacramento River systems.

The Modoc sucker's origin in the Pit River is still a mystery, as it does not share close affinities with either the Klamath or Sacramento River fishes. Biologists don't even know when the Modoc sucker entered the Pit River. However, biologists do know that the Modoc sucker resembles a relative, the Tahoe sucker. Because of this, some biologists speculate that the Modoc sucker reached the Pit River from the nearby pluvial Lake Lahontan system. Perhaps one of Lake Lahontan's tributaries might have been captured by the Pit River system, introducing its unique biota into the Pit River.

The Modoc sucker prefers cool creeks with little water flow. In such areas the small-eyed bottom feeder can search for the detritus and algae that make up 75 percent of its diet. The Modoc sucker's mouth enables it to literally suck up substrate during its nightly foraging runs.

Biologists know that the sexually mature female Modoc sucker releases 6,400 to 12,600 eggs, but no one has witnessed spawning. Neither the male nor the female of this species seems to live longer than four years, with sexual maturity occurring in the second or third years. The Modoc sucker's dwarfed size, early maturity to reproduce, and short life-span are all adaptations evolved by this fish to cope with life in the small intermittent streams of the Pit River. Much is still unknown about the biology of this tiny fish.

Today the Modoc sucker is confined to a few small creeks in the upper Pit River where the water is moderately clear and partially shaded by tree or shrub canopies. While eight cool clear creeks currently support this rare fish, only Hulbert, Washington, and Johnson creeks have populations with genetically pure Modoc suckers. The total population is estimated to be less than 1300 fishes, but their numbers were probably never very large. The genetically pure Modoc sucker has been eliminated in other creeks because of hybridization with its larger cousin, the Sacramento sucker, *Catostomus occidentalis*. The Sacramento sucker is common in the reservoirs and larger streams, and ascends the tributaries to spawn. Extensive channelization has eliminated several natural instream barriers that prevented migration of the Sacramento sucker. Without the natural barriers, the Sacramento sucker enters the Modoc sucker creeks. Sacramento suckers hybridize with Modoc suckers because of the overlap in spawning seasons (mid-April to late May), the absence of their own mates, and the proximity of each species' spawning locations. Hybridization is a concern for the last three genetically pure populations.

Though hybridization has taken its toll eliminating pure populations of Modoc suckers throughout the Pit River system, the major threat to this fish is the overall physical habitat deterioration caused by overgrazing of livestock and channelization for land development and controlling streambank erosion. This region of northeastern California is heavily dependent upon agriculture. The banks of the Pit River have been steadily eroded away and lost into the creeks by cows and sheep trampling and overgrazing local meadow lands. To curb the erosive forces washing away the soil, channels have been built. But these channels drastically alter the Modoc sucker's preferred habitat of gentle, clear waters into long, shallow riffles with no cover or shade. During the summer months much of the water is diverted to irrigate pastures. What is left trickles through the gravel in the stream bed.

Preventing further habitat degradation and hybridization of the Modoc sucker are top priorities to protect this endangered species. Private land owners, Modoc National Forest, and the Bureau of Land Management share the 5200 acre watershed of eight creeks inhabited by the Modoc sucker. Personnel from the Modoc National Forest are protecting its Modoc sucker populations by sinking a fence along key areas of Washington and Johnson creeks to discourage livestock from entering these fragile habitats. Also, they recently constructed a fish barrier near the mouth of Tanner Creek to discourage upstream migration of the Sacramento sucker into Modoc sucker habitat. They are also carefully watching the condition of natural barriers that prevent hybridization. Only with such safeguards can the Modoc sucker continue as a viable, distinct species—one whose origins remain nebulous.

# Unarmored Threespine Stickleback
## *Gasterosteus aculeatus williamsoni*

(Color plate 4.)

*This stream, at the place where the road crosses it, flows in a broad but shallow bed, depressed about twenty feet below the general level of the plain. The vertical banks are seen to consist of horizontal, alluvial strata of sand and clay, very similar in their appearance to those of the banks of the San Joaquin and King's river. . .*

*After crossing this stream, our course was changed at an acute angle towards the southeast, in order to reach the San Fernando Pass. Our road lay for nearly four miles over a level plain, which was intersected in every direction by dusty trails made by the numerous herds of cattle. They presented a curious appearance, extending in nearly straight lines over the broad area. Owing to the absence of a well marked wagon-road, and the confusion caused by these trails, we kept too far west, and at night, reached low hills of sandstone, and were obliged to encamp without water, except a little that was skimmed from the surface of cattle tracks in a muddy spring nearby. While two of the party were engaged in collecting this water, two bears make their appearance in search of their evening drink.*

> From the journal of Lieutenant R.S.
> Williamson, Corps of Topographical
> Engineers, on the Santa Clara River, 1853.

Lieutenant Williamson wrote this passage about the Santa Clara River in Southern California while surveying the land for a Pacific railroad route in the mid-1800s. During the mapping of the river, Dr. Al Heerman, a naturalist attached to the survey group, chanced upon a number of small olive-green, spindle-shaped fishes living in the freshwater pools of the river. The naturalist carefully preserved a sample of the easily caught fishes, packed them away, and continued with his work. When the survey mission was finished, the preserved fishes were sent to an ichthyologist by the name of Dr. Charles Girard in 1854. Girard recognized the specimens were new to science and described them as a new species of stickleback. Unlike the common threespine stickleback, this California form did not have the distinguishing feature of the stickleback—it lacked the numerous armored-like plates along the sides which probably helped protect the fish from predators. Because of this unusual difference, it received the common name "unarmored threespine stickleback" over the years. Later when it was found that the unarmored form interbreeds with the armored form of the threespine sticklebacks in some areas, biologists recognized it as a subspecies instead of a full species. The subspecific name *williamsoni* was applied after Lieutenant Williamson of the survey party.

The stickleback family has a cosmopolitan distribution, being found all over Europe and northern Asia as well as in North America. This family is no stranger to the world of science. The mating and nesting behavior of *Gasterosteus aculeatus,* whose name means "spined belly-bone" for its surgically sharp ventral spines, has helped us understand animal behavior. The behavior in sticklebacks probably has been studied more carefully than that of any other group of freshwater fishes. They have been very important subjects in research involving predatory-prey interactions and are also used in evolutionary studies.

The stereotyped spawning behavior of the stickleback has long fascinated biologists. During the breeding season, the male stickleback's belly becomes bright red against its blue sides and iridescent blue or green eyes. The female stickleback transforms in color as well, but her pale pink throat and belly certainly are not as flashy as the male's colors. The male stickleback builds a nest from decaying strands of aquatic vegetation, which he cements together with a substance secreted from the kidney. This nest is usually near aquatic vegetation in pools with slow flowing waters. The first stage of courtship commences when a breeding male expresses his interest to mate by performing a zig-zag dance. A receptive female then approaches this amorous male with her head tilted upwards. The male then leads the willing female to his nest where he induces her to deposit her eggs. After fertilizing the eggs, the male assumes the responsibility of watching over and fanning the nest, providing an adequate flow of oxygenated water for the eggs.

Two features of the stickleback's habitat are essential for the survival of the young. First, a slow flow of clean water is necessary for proper development of the eggs. Sticklebacks are not found in even slightly turbid waters. Second, once feebly swimming fry emerge from the eggs, aquatic vegetation must be found along the shoreline to provide much needed cover and an abundance of microscopic food organisms. The unarmored threespine stickleback's Santa Clara River habitat is shrinking and areas that fit these two major habitat requirements are becoming increasingly difficult to find.

During the time of Lieutenant Williamson's expedition back in the mid-1800s, and even as late as 1913, the unarmored threespine stickleback had a wide distribution throughout much of the Los Angeles basin, being especially abundant in the San Gabriel, Santa Ana, and Los Angeles Rivers. These three rivers, like the Santa Clara River, are intermittent or dry for most of the year, except during the rainy winter season. These rivers course through this semi-arid region of southern California, their waters barely trickling most of the time, occasionally forming permanent clear water pools behind obstructions in the path of water. The twentieth century brought with it a number of problems for the wildlife in the canyons of the Los Angeles basin. The streams containing populations of this stickleback were modified to irrigate the citrus orchards. This ambitious project is responsible for lowering Santa Clara River's water levels. Furthermore, grazing and timber cutting eliminated the plant cover, blanketing the surrounding hillsides, sending silt from the barren, eroding hillsides straight into the river. Because clear and flowing water are two major requirements for the stickleback, siltation and irrigation diversion have rendered much of the stream uninhabitable. As the Los Angeles urban area sprawled, the unarmored threespine stickleback has been forced to seek refuge from advancing agricultural, domestic, and industrial growth and "progress." The only remaining habitat for the stickleback was in the permanent to intermittent waters of the upper Santa Clara River system. Today the unarmored threespine stickleback resides in only three small areas of the Santa Clara River drainage in Los Angeles County: a small tributary in the San Francisquito Canyon, the Santa Clara River at Soledad Canyon, and in the Del Valle area farther downstream. A fourth population of this endangered freshwater fish was recently discovered on the Vandenburg Air Force Base in San Antonio Creek, to the north of the Santa Clara River. In these last four habitats, the unarmored threespine stickleback clings to life.

Two new threats menace the stickleback in its remaining habitats. The African clawed frog *(Xenopus laevis)* a non-native frog that is commonly used in medical laboratories and found in the pet trade until it was prohibited, was found in the upper reaches of the Santa Clara River. This frog appears harmless enough, but is actually a voracious predator and probably has been preying on the sticklebacks unfortunate enough to get within its range. Remember, the endangered stickleback subspecies does not have the armored-like plates along its sides, and the fin spines are shorter and weaker than its cousins. Biologists feel that the stickleback's armor plates and fin spines are adaptations evolved as anti-predator devices to protect the feeble-swimming fish. Biologists think that this subspecies had few predators in its historic range and so had no need for the protective armor and fins. Although all of the clawed frogs were removed, reintroductions, either accidental or deliberate, would be quite simple because many are still present in laboratories and home aquariums.

Soledad Canyon, one of the last habitats for unarmored threespine sticklebacks, has been recently plagued with trail bikes. These motorized bikes tear up the vegetation and soil, leaving crisscross trails along the stream banks, increasing the silt runoff that enters the river. Crossings in the shallow pool areas of the river also destroy nest sites and vegetation along the stream margin which serves as cover for the young.

Although these two threats are problems to watch in the future, the major problem facing the unarmored threespine stickleback is urbanization and the alteration of habitat that accompany such human "progress." Associated with urbanization is the severe problem of stream desiccation by diversion or groundwater pumping. In fact, the recovery plan calls for installation of groundwater pumps to get water in selected sections of streams in an emergency. Urbanization usually increases the amount of siltation, pesticides, pollutants, and other potentially harmful substances that could degrade water quality in the Santa Clara River. Stream channelization, which frequently accompanies land development, poses a problem of a different nature. Channelization could destroy the natural barriers now separating the unarmored threespine stickleback from its closely related subspecies, the West Coast threespine stickleback, *Gasterosteus aculeatus microcephalus*, which is widespread in freshwaters of California. Without these barriers, populations of the two subspecies of sticklebacks could come together and interbreed, thus eliminating the genetic integrity of the endangered stickleback. While interbreeding with the West Coast threespine stickleback remains only a possibility, such channelization efforts would certainly eliminate the pools and shallow backwaters that constitute the stickleback's nesting habitat. The slow water flow and well-developed aquatic vegetation that is necessary to the stickleback for nest building and courtship would be destroyed. An approved recovery plan, which was developed by federal agencies, California Department of Fish and Game, and the Los Angeles County Museum, assures that efforts will be made to protect the habitat and restore the unarmored threespine stickleback to a healthy self-sustaining population. If the stickleback recovers successfully, it could be reclassified from endangered to a threatened status. We hope the recovery efforts will be sufficient to preserve one of southern California's most unique native freshwater fishes.

4-3
Irrigation of citrus orchards and other crops in the Santa Clara River Valley has reduced stream flow. Photo by J. D. Williams.

# V.

# Pyramid Lake Fishes

*Beyond, a defile between the mountains descended rapidly about 2000 feet; and, filling up all the lower space, was a sheet of green water, some twenty miles broad. It broke upon our eyes like the ocean. The waves were curling in the breeze, and their dark-green color showed it to be a body of deep water. For a long time we sat enjoying the view, for we had become fatigued with mountains, and the free expanse of moving waves was very grateful. It was set like a gem in the mountains, which from our position, seemed to enclose it almost entirely. . .*

*The next morning the snow was rapidly melting under a warm sun. Part of the morning was occupied in bringing up the gun; and, making only nine miles, we encamped on the shore, opposite a very remarkable rock in the lake, which had attracted our attention for many miles. It rose, according to our estimate, six hundred feet (actually it was less than three hundred feet out of the water at the time) above the water; and, from the point we viewed it, presented a pretty exact outline of the great pyramid of Cheops. This striking feature suggested a name for the lake; and I called it Pyramid Lake; and though it may be deemed by some a fanciful resemblance, I can undertake to say that the future traveler will find a much more striking resemblance between this rock and the pyramids of Egypt, than there is between them and the object from which they take their name. . .*

*John Charles Freemont, January 10, 1844*
*The first white man to see Pyramid Lake*

In the Great Basin area, vigorous tectonic activity took place during the Oligocene Epoch (about forty million years ago) resulting in massive fault

TUFA DOMES IN PYRAMID LAKE, NEVADA.

5–1
Pyramid Lake tufa domes. United States Geological Survey etching made in the 1880s.
Etching from *Geological History of Lake Lahontan* by I. C. Russell.

5–2
Pyramid Lake, same area today. Note water level. Photo by D. Sada.

block upheavals and valley formations creating a highly segmented system of interconnected basins. In more recent geologic time, periods of continental glaciation extended into the Great Basin during the Pleistocene Epoch which began some two million years ago. During the Pleistocene the interconnected valleys of the Great Basin filled with waters from the increased precipitation, forming extensive pluvial lakes. Like the other major lake system found in the Great Basin region of the United States, Lake Lahontan was endorheic—the lake did not have an outlet. The only water loss was by evaporation. During the Pleistocene Epoch the Lake Bonneville and Lake Lahontan system covered much of what we now know as desert in northern Nevada and northwestern Utah.

These large bodies of water found in the Great Basin were about equal in size to Lake Erie, the fifth largest freshwater lake in the world today. The Lake Lahontan drainage basin covered some 475 acres of land in the Great Basin region. Once occupying an area from west-central Nevada to the Oregon border, Lake Lahontan's only remnants today are Pyramid Lake, Walker Lake, and Honey Lake. Lake Winnemucca, a fourth lake located adjacent to Pyramid Lake, a smaller and shallower body of water, went completely dry in 1938 because of excessive diversions of water from the Truckee River for irrigation. All three of the remaining lakes are, in actuality, evaporating pans for inflowing streams. Because they are decreasing in size, they are constantly increasing in salinity and alkalinity. The well-known Great Salt Lake is a good example of an evaporating pan left from the Lake Bonneville lake system.

Located thirty miles northeast of Reno, Nevada, Pyramid Lake represents the deepest remnant body of water from Lake Lahontan. Its depth averages 180 feet and it reaches 340 feet in some spots. This lake occupies an area entirely within the confines of the Pyramid Lake Paiute Indian Reservation. It is a 25-mile long wedge-shaped lake whose waters are considered saline, though it is about one-seventh as salty as seawater. Highly alkaline, with a pH of about 9.1, Pyramid Lake is considered one of the most alkaline lakes in the world.

Inland bodies of water with high saline levels usually contain few species of flora and fauna. Not so with Pyramid Lake. Pyramid Lake is a eutrophic body of water, rich in planktonic life on which the higher forms of life subsist. Over one hundred plant and animal taxa have been collected from the lake since J.O. Snyder began his initial studies of the Pyramid Lake fishes in 1911. His pioneering efforts proved to be the engaging force that eventually made this Pleistocene lake one of the most extensively studied lakes within the Lahontan basin.

Double-breasted cormorants, white pelicans, California gulls, and a host of other shore birds find refuge on Anaho Island, the only major island in Pyramid Lake. Situated near the southern end of the lake, Anaho Island has been set aside as a National Wildlife Refuge because it boasts North America's largest breeding colony of white pelicans. Chains of smaller "islands" that poke out from Pyramid Lake are called "tufa domes." General theories have been advanced to explain the origin of these domes. These bizarre formations are calcium carbonate deposits that may have been created on the bottom of ancient Lake Lahontan, possibly by the precipitation in muds resulting from the action of hot, supersaturated waters rising from below. Some of these tufa domes are over three hundred feet tall. No matter how they were formed, the tufa domes have found their way into several local Paiute Indian legends.

At the narrower southern end of Pyramid Lake lies the entrance of its principal source of water, the Truckee River. Originating high in the Sierra Nevada Mountains of eastern California, the Truckee River flows through Lake Tahoe and descends the mountains to enter the arid Nevada lowlands. Once on the lowlands, the river flows northeast for some 120 miles; then finally ends its journey by emptying into Pyramid Lake. Pyramid Lake, which is constantly losing water through evaporation, is almost solely dependent on the Truckee River for its source of water. The average annual precipitation is only six inches and much of that is snowfall.

Because Pyramid Lake is the terminal catch basin for the Truckee-Tahoe drainage system to the west, it came as no surprise at the turn of the century for Man to tap the waters of the Truckee River for agriculture. This opportunistic attitude led to the construction of Derby Dam and the Truckee Canal in 1905. This dam and canal were constructed to transport water from the Truckee River to agricultural land along the Carson River. Water from both the Truckee and Carson Rivers combined to supply water to the "Newlands Reclamation Project," a federally-sponsored agricultural and hydroelectric power venture.

Diverting Pyramid Lake's major source of water proved to be cataclysmic. This diversion led to the complete drying of Lake Winnemucca in 1938, the same year the Pyramid Lake race of cutthroat trout became extinct. The gradual lowering of the Pyramid Lake water level coupled with insufficient springtime flows in the Truckee River during the years following construction of the

5–3
Southern end of Pyramid Lake near mouth of Truckee River. Photo by J. D. Williams.

Newlands Reclamation Project made it impossible for the trophy gamefish to ascend the mere trickle of water that flowed over the Truckee River. The fish could not migrate to their spawning grounds upstream. Without a chance to spawn, future generations of the Pyramid Lake strain of the cutthroat trout were lost. As the remaining population of trout lived out their lives entrapped in Pyramid Lake, it was only a matter of time before the last Pyramid Lake cutthroat trout would die and the secrets of a unique and valuable fishery resource would be lost.

As Derby Dam approaches its eightieth anniversary of operation, the water level in Pyramid Lake has ironically dropped a corresponding eighty feet. One foot for every year of large-scale water diversion. With Pyramid Lake becoming increasingly saline and concentrated in its dissolved solids because of the diversion of the Truckee River, the time may come when the waters will be too alkaline or filled with too much brine to support fish and other fauna. Adaptations to such conditions may prove to be too much for species to evolve under the given time constraints. The cui-ui and Lahontan cutthroat trout are two endemic species of Pyramid Lake fishes that are in danger of being eradicated unless the water resources of the Truckee River and Pyramid Lake are managed intelligently.

5–4
Derby Dam on the Truckee River east of Reno, Nevada. Water diversions behind this dam lowered the water level in Pyramid Lake by more than eighty feet. Photo by J. D. Williams.

# Lahontan Cutthroat Trout
## *Salmo clarki henshawi*

(Color plate 5.)

From the time white man first discovered Pyramid Lake, in the mid-1800s, anglers caught spectacular trophy-sized trout in this remnant of Lake Lahontan. These trout were also a staple in the diet of the indians that lived in the area for aeons before white man arrived. Once the word of this unique fish got out, sportfishermen from all over the United States clamored to Pyramid Lake's shores to test their angling skills and equipment on the Pyramid Lake cutthroat trout. Their desire to catch this large gamefish was attested by the sportfishing record established for Pyramid Lake when a local Paiute Indian caught a large trout in 1925. The behemoth fish tipped the scales at a little over 47 pounds! About one hundred years after the discovery of this race of incredible trout, it disappeared . . . never to be caught or seen again.

The Pyramid Lake cutthroat trout is more correctly referred to as the Pyramid Lake strain of the Lahontan cutthroat trout, *Salmo clarki henshawi.* During the Pleistocene the Lahontan cutthroat was widely distributed throughout the waters of the Lake Lahontan system—more than 6000 miles of suitable cold-water streams and approximately 330,000 surface acres of lake habitat. It is thought that cutthroat trout stocks originally entered the Lahontan basin of west central Nevada from the headwaters of the Snake River during a period in the Pleistocene Epoch when Lake Lahontan's level was at one of its high points. The Lahontan cutthroat trout easily dispersed itself throughout the Lahontan basin at this time. As the climate warmed and became drier, Lake Lahontan shrank. The Lahontan cutthroat survived in some streams and the various pluvial remnant lakes such as Lake Winnemucca, Lake Tahoe, and Pyramid Lake.

Because of the great diversity and isolation of habitats left within the huge Lahontan basin after the climatic changes shifted this region from an inland sea to a semi-arid desert, the Lahontan cutthroat trout began to exhibit a variety of color schemes and sizes. In general, this trout has prominent black spots uniformly scattered over its entire body, and its coloration gradually changes from dark olive above to silvery sides tinged with a pinkish stripe below. The characteristic scarlet slash running along its lower jaw denotes its cutthroat trout heritage.

*Salmo clarki henshawi* is named after two pioneers of the western frontier. The species name, *clarki,* honors Captain William Clark, the co-leader of the Lewis and Clark expedition to the Pacific Coast; the subspecies designation, *henshawi,* honors Henry W. Henshaw, a naturalist who worked with the Wheeler survey, explorers along the 100th meridian and west. Both men would probably shudder in horror at the degree of exploitation the once pristine lands that they first laid eyes on underwent in the next one hundred years.

Indians caught and ate the Lahontan cutthroat for thousands of years and did not significantly affect the standing stocks of the trout population. But in the mid to late 1800s the white man began to seriously affect the populations throughout the Lahontan basin by altering the habitat in several ways. The

Lahontan cutthroat trout population began to decline in numbers and size as water was diverted from its habitat for mining and agriculture. Adjacent fields and entire watersheds were denuded of their grass cover by livestock over-grazing the land. When rain came, the now barren soils washed into the streams and caused siltation problems. In addition, non-native gamefishes such as brook, rainbow, and brown trout were introduced over the years into many Lahontan basin streams where they vigorously compete with the Lahontan cutthroat trout for space and food resources. Also, these non-native gamefishes prey upon the juvenile cutthroat trout. Today, these non-native trouts are still a major problem facing the Lahontan cutthroat trout throughout its range. The Lahontan cutthroat currently exists in less than 5 percent of its historic stream habitat and in only 0.3 percent of its original lake habitat. What had taken 8000 years for the endemic Lahontan cutthroat trout to establish in the La-hontan basin was undone by Man's exploitation of both the fish and its habitat in a little over a century.

The large number of Lahontan cutthroat trout was so stunning when the white man first became acquainted with this region that commercial fishing ventures soon sprang up in Lake Tahoe, Pyramid Lake, and other Lahontan basin lakes. Fishing pressure became increasingly heavy from both anglers and the commercial fishing industry in the west. The large size of the Pyramid Lake cutthroat brought notoriety to the lake. For some reason, the Pyramid Lake strain was the largest-sized Lahontan cutthroat trout in any of the La-hontan bodies of water. Perhaps because Pyramid Lake is the deepest of the remnant lakes, its population of Lahontan cutthroat trout had a chance to grow in what appears to be an unlimited habitat. Most of the other lakes and streams are shallow and provide less shelter and food resources for the trout.

For nearly 75 years, Pyramid Lake provided all who came to her shores a plentiful supply of huge cutthroat trout. Captured individuals were shipped throughout the west by rail in seemingly endless carloads. Hundreds of en-terprising indian peddlers traveled the territory immediately around the lake and sold trout to local residents and ranchers. Then a surprising thing hap-pened. From all historical accounts, 1920 was the last year in which fishing for the Pyramid Lake trout was good. Never again have the numbers of Pyramid Lake trout equalled that seen during the early twentieth century. The indians began to sell fewer and fewer fish. In fact records during one three-year period, from 1935 to 1938, reveal an 85 percent reduction in the numbers of fishes available for sale. The indians no longer watched the smaller Pyramid Lake trout (three to five years old) called "tommy" (Tama-Agaih or spring trout) make spawning runs up the Truckee River from Pyramid Lake in April and early May. These runs used to follow the late fall and winter migratory spawn-ing runs of the red-hued, larger Pyramid Lake trout called "redfish" (Tomoo-Agaih or winter trout). Like the "tommy," the "redfish" runs also declined. Throughout the 1920s and 1930s a peculiar phenomenon was taking place. Not only were lower numbers of Pyramid Lake trout being taken, but of those that were caught, the average size kept increasing! In fact, Pyramid Lake trout caught in 1935 were one half the size of those caught three years later.

The progressively increasing average size of the trout gave many fishermen the feeling that fishing conditions were improving. This false impression was widespread, and the frequently mentioned observation that the Lahontan cutthroat trout in Pyramid Lake might be hovering on the verge of extinction was treated as a far-fetched myth.

In reality, the increasingly larger size of the trout being caught meant that the spawning cycle had been interrupted for some reason and no young fish were entering the population. Smaller trout were not seen in the catches simply because there were no young trout living in the lake. During periods of high precipitation in the area, the sexually mature Pyramid Lake trout would ascend the Truckee River to spawn in the gravel riffles, depositing their fertilized eggs in the gravel sediment. Upon hatching, the young fish would remain in this riverine habitat for a period of time, feeding on aquatic invertebrates and insect larvae before migrating downstream to join their parents in the depths of Pyramid Lake. It was these young fish that were not appearing in the depleted yearly catches. We can trace the disappearance of younger size classes in Pyramid Lake to the 1905 construction of Derby Dam and the Truckee Canal.

How could one small dam affect such a large body of water? Waters from the Truckee River that were destined to terminate in Pyramid Lake were diverted to supply the Newlands Reclamation Project, an agricultural enterprise sponsored by the federal government. Without its major source of water, Pyramid Lake's water level gradually lowered. Even the flows during the springtime couldn't provide enough water to maintain the water level in the lake. The mouth of the Truckee River became increasingly broad and shallow over the years following Derby Dam's construction. Finally, an impassable delta covered by just a trickle of water was formed, and fishes like the Pyramid Lake cutthroat were prevented from reaching the upstream gravel riffles necessary for their successful spawning. When this barrier was created in the early 1900s, the Pyramid Lake cutthroat trout's fate had been sealed—unrecognized by most of the fishermen who were exploiting the species. As time went on and the Pyramid Lake cutthroat trout was confined to the lake, what the fishermen continued to catch with less frequency, but larger in size, were older and older trout. By 1938 the Lahontan cutthroat trout of Pyramid Lake was extinct.

By the late 1950s, the state of Nevada began to restock Pyramid Lake with a smaller strain of Lahontan cutthroat trout from Heenan Lake. Later the Summit Lake strain was chosen because it maintained the largest self-sustaining population of this subspecies in existence. Summit Lake had not felt the recent activities of Man as severely as other bodies of water holding the Lahontan cutthroat. In addition, Summit Lake was isolated from all the other aquatic habitats in the Lahontan basin and scientists generally believed that its strain of the subspecies had been established for quite a long time. The California Department of Fish and Game, the Nevada Department of Wildlife, the Lahontan National Fish Hatchery of the U.S. Fish and Wildlife Service, and both the Pyramid Lake and Summit Lake tribes of the Paiute Indians, have all developed hatchery propagation techniques that produce young Lahontan cutthroat trout. These fish are generally maintained for stocking into habitats unable to support self-sustaining populations of the trout.

Originally listed as an endangered species in 1970, the status of the Lahontan cutthroat trout has been downgraded to threatened because of the successful

61

5–5
Ladder at entrance to the Pyramid Lake fishway. Photo by J. D. Williams.

propagation and reintroduction of this fish into some of its original range. Though not of pure Pyramid Lake cutthroat stock—that stock being lost forever—these hatchery fish have helped the Lahontan cutthroat trout to once again thrive and become the third most abundant fish in Pyramid Lake today.

The completion of the Marble Bluff Fishway in 1976 provided migrating trout access to the Truckee River, but little recruitment of the Lahontan cutthroat trout has actually taken place. Problems vary from poor survival of the eggs deposited in the lower Truckee's gravel beds to numerous unscreened water diversions that carry the young trout fry into agricultural fields where they eventually die as the water evaporates.

While the demise of the Pyramid Lake strain of the Lahontan cutthroat trout is a sad tale, fortunately all was not lost and we have a chance to conserve the remaining Lahontan cutthroat trout. For the present, this subspecies will continue to be listed as a threatened species because it no longer inhabits much of its historic range and the problems of deteriorating water quality and non-native fishes continue to threaten this fish. However, with the success of the restocking program so far, the ongoing efforts to prevent introduced brook, brown, and rainbow trout populations from replacing the Lahontan cutthroats, and efforts to improve water quality, the outlook is encouraging for healthy, self-sustaining populations to become reestablished and secure.

# Cui-ui
## *Chasmistes cujus*

*. . . In the meantime spawning had begun and was progressing with great activity. On April 24, the first females were seen depositing eggs. However, several ripe males and females were secured a little earlier. By May 5, every suitable bar or gravel bed was occupied by spawning fishes, whose activities entirely ceased before the 16th.*

*At times cui-ui appeared in such large and densely packed schools that consid-*
*erable numbers were crowded out of the water in shallow places, especially on the*
*gently sloping river bars. Once several hundred were observed stranded near the*
*mouth of the river. In some places they were jammed together in masses two or*
*three deep. Some were crowded entirely out and dead, while others were in water*
*a foot deep, yet pushing close to the main group in a perfectly demoralized condition.*
*When one such conditionally free individual was carried some distance away and*
*headed upstream, it passed on its way with great speed, but if removed a short*
*distance only it returned to the mass like an iron to the magnet. It was impossible*
*to separate any number and get them started away from the stranded school.*

> *John O. Snyder, first biologist to*
> *publish on the biology of the cui-ui*
> *Lahontan system, Spring, 1913.*

Could the supply of cui-ui (pronounced kwee-wee), an endemic sucker (family Catostomidae) found exclusively in pluvial Pyramid Lake, ever become so depleted that the species would border on extinction? Awestruck by the steady stream of spawning cui-ui moving doggedly up the Truckee River, Pyramid Lake's major inflow of water, John Snyder could never have comprehended in 1913 that a mere 54 years later, this fish was to become a federally listed endangered species and still remain in that status today.

Long revered as food and a commodity to be traded with other tribes by the Paiute Indians, the cui-ui is a rather large and cumbersome-looking fish with tiny eyes and large rounded gill covers. The genus name of the cui-ui, *Chasmistes,* means "one who yawns." The fish was such an integral part of Paiute life that their tribal name comes, in part, from the cui-ui. The Pyramid Lake Paiute Indians named themselves, Kuyuidokato or Ku-yu-wi-kut-teh which literally means "sucker or cui-ui eaters." In addition, Pyramid Lake itself is known to the Paiutes as Lake Coo-yu-ee-pah or "home of the cui-ui."

The spring coming of the cui-ui marked the event of the year for the Paiutes who used to set up camps near the mouth of the Truckee River in anticipation of the thousands of sexually mature male and female cui-ui that would have to pass them on their way upstream to their shallow, gravel bottom spawning grounds. These camps were located strategically, based on the Paiute knowledge that the cui-ui has a habit of resting in schools in quiet water. The willow racks used by the indians to dry the captured fishes were located near such areas. As the dense schools of cui-ui migrated past the make-shift camps, the Paiute Indians readied improvised gaffs and dragged them through the roily waters, easily hooking cui-ui after cui-ui.

The catch of cui-ui would be eaten fresh or smoked while others would be spread on the willow drying racks and allowed to dry in the Nevada sun. The dried flanks of fish would be used by the Paiutes as food for themselves or bartered for a variety of goods with other tribes. Cui-ui reached a length of more than two feet—a single fish would have made a formidable trading item for the Paiute Indian entrepreneur.

For years this Paiute tribal ritual left no marks on the populations of long-lived cui-ui. Man and fish lived in peaceful co-existence in this region of the former Pleistocene Lake Lahontan drainage system. When non-indian immigrants began to settle in the Lahontan Basin in the latter part of the nineteenth century, this situation began to change. Many of the new residents of the Pyramid Lake region joined in with the Paiutes to harvest the seemingly inexhaustible supply of cui-ui found at the mouth of the Truckee River. The enterprising white man not only sold the cui-ui in the immediate vicinity, but also shipped them throughout the region.

This added influx of new settlers to the region affected the area in other ways besides the increased harvest of cui-ui from Pyramid Lake. As the number of immigrants to the region increased, so too did the demands for water to irrigate crops planted in the nearby fields. The demand for water from the Truckee River grew in such proportions that Derby Dam was constructed on the Truckee River at the turn of the century. Instead of flowing into Pyramid Lake, much of the Truckee River was diverted to supply the federally-sponsored agricultural venture called the "Newlands Reclamation Project" in the adjacent Carson River basin. Also, the Truckee's waters were used on a small scale for hydroelectric power.

Diverting the waters of the Truckee River away from Pyramid Lake is directly responsible for the death of Lake Winnemucca, a sister lake to Pyramid Lake, that completely dried up in 1938. Sharing a common drainage system with Pyramid Lake, but separated from it by a narrow band of mountains, Lake Winnemucca was much smaller and shallower than its sister lake. But, it held the only other population of cui-ui anywhere in the world. The diversion of river water has also affected the water level in Pyramid Lake, currently some eighty feet lower than its "pre-Derby Dam" days. Not only is the lake level down, but the level of dissolved solids in the remaining waters continues to increase. The river's entrance to the lake has also been affected. Before Derby Dam was built the river was several feet deep at its entrance to the lake. After the dam was in place the water level dropped to a trickle flowing across a wide silty delta at the mouth of the river.

Before the mouth of the Truckee River was a barrier to migration, vast numbers of sexually mature cui-ui would ascend the river to get to the gravelly beds found upstream. Not only is the gravel substrate necessary for the eggs to hatch, but developing cui-ui eggs cannot tolerate the salt water of Pyramid Lake. The eggs require the freshwater of the Truckee River. In the relatively shallow waters of the Truckee River where the flow is fairly rapid, the adults complete the spawning in three to five days. The average adult cui-ui spawns many times during these few days. A particular male cui-ui appeared to have spawned over three hundred times during one season! Two, three, or even more male cui-uis attend a single female during the actual mating.

The sexes are often easily separated by color, but some have been observed to be about the same color. The male usually has a dense black stripe on its side which runs from the gill covers to the tail, slate blue fins, and a noticeable red streak on its back above the black stripe. The female on the other hand has a general dark brownish-black luster on its back—some locals call the female a "black sucker." The reddish-colored male escorts wriggle and thrash around the female in efforts to spawn. The act of spawning itself only lasts between three and six seconds.

After the spring spawning the adults return to Pyramid Lake where they disappear into deeper waters until the next spring again beckons them to make the upstream journey. In the meantime, the young hatch, wriggle free from the gravel nursery grounds, and begin their journey downstream to the lake. The young have a well-developed yolk sac which serves as a food source until they are about ten days old, about the time they reach the lake. In the lake they begin feeding on zooplankton, a source of nutrition for their twenty-year lifespan. Shortly after the young cui-ui return to the lake they are not seen again for approximately four years when they enter the spawning run themselves.

Although the upper reaches of the Truckee River are blocked, the cui-ui has managed to hang on precipitously by spawning in Pyramid Lake gravel beds near the mouths of perennial streams connected to the saline lake. But even a salinity count as low as 1.8 parts per thousand caused a 70 percent hatching failure of the cui-ui eggs. This problem, plus the threat of the tui chub preying on the lake-spawned eggs poses high mortality rates on these eggs. About once every ten years the cui-ui did make successful spawning runs in the Truckee River when there was high rainfall and water levels, giving them access to spawning areas. This has probably contributed to their survival.

The Paiute Indians of Pyramid Lake have worked to preserve the legendary fish. In the 1940s they set a daily bag limit of five cui-ui per day, plus a fee of $1 per day, or $3 per calendar year. In 1967 the Paiutes enforced regulations by prohibiting non-indians from fishing for cui-ui at all. That was the year the cui-ui was officially recognized as an endangered species. In 1979, even the indians were not allowed to fish for the cui-ui.

While the Paiute Indians were diligently taking steps to protect the cui-ui in Pyramid Lake, between 1973 and 1976 the U.S. Fish and Wildlife Service began two preservation projects of its own. Techniques for artificially propagating young cui-ui to the stage where they could swim on their own were being perfected. Almost 7.5 million cui-ui fry were released into the lower

5–6
Pyramid Lake fishway, necessitated by the lower lake level, allows Lahontan cutthroat trout and cui-ui on spawning runs to reach the Truckee River. Photo by J. D. Williams.

Truckee River and Pyramid Lake during those three years. The Paiute Indians were trained in the propagation techniques and taught the proper way to net and transport the cui-ui fry from hatchery to lake. In this manner the Paiutes could assume direct control and responsibility over their natural resource. Today they manage the entire hatchery operation.

The U.S. Fish and Wildlife Service and Bureau of Reclamation then built the Pyramid Lake fishway, an eight mile long bypass across the impassable Truckee River delta region for both the cui-ui and the threatened Lahontan cutthroat trout. While the Lahontan cutthroat began to use the fishway immediately, the cui-ui could not negotiate the particular fish ladder design. Modifications of the ladder design were made in 1978 and 1981 and cui-ui have successfully entered the lower Truckee River to spawn during the last four springs.

It is still too early to judge whether the cui-ui will be removed from the endangered classification in the near future. The restoration of the cui-ui to a non-endangered status must be the top priority for all concerned. More studies must be initiated to understand the biology of this fish so that a viable reproducing population can be maintained. With the dedication and perseverance shown by the Paiute tribe, state, and federal agencies, the cui-ui has a very good shot at coming back, provided the water quality of the Truckee River and Pyramid Lake can be improved . . . or at least protected from further degradation.

5–7
Spawning cui-ui at the upper end of the fishway are captured and released into the Truckee River to continue their spawning run. Photo from U.S. Fish and Wildlife Service.

# VI.

# Desert Spring and Pool Fishes

Seventy percent of the fishes currently on the federal list of endangered and threatened species live in desert environments. Most of the aquatic ecosystems in the desert southwest are limited to rather small areas with restricted amounts of surface water. The water found in these habitats comes from two different sources: (1) springs in which the groundwater coming from a fairly distant source moves through an aquifer that runs along geological faults or within solution channels until surfacing in a marsh or a spring pool; and (2) creeks and rivers that arise in mountain ranges from spring runoff of snow melt supplying water for these desert streams.

All of the fishes we will discuss in this section live in spring pools. While there are generally few species of fishes in these desert habitats, an amazing number are endemic. As an illustration, more than twenty species and subspecies of fishes inhabit the small desert pools of North America and almost all of them are native to only a single location. The pupfishes, Cyprinodontidae, join the minnows, Cyprinidae, the suckers, Catostomidae, and the livebearers, Poeciliidae in dominating the desert aquatic habitats. This differs dramatically from springs in the eastern U.S. which are inhabited by a variety of fishes belonging to several families.

The high degree of isolation of desert spring fishes living in such specialized habitats is remarkably similar to species living on an island. An organism living in such a restricted habitat is subject to extirpation by a single catastrophic event that might destroy its entire habitat. While natural catastrophic events do occur, they are infrequent and rarely bring about the extinction of species. Unlike natural catastrophies, those induced by Man are frequent in occurrence and often result in extinction. Physical habitat alteration by Man has been disastrous for many fishes isolated in aquatic islands in the sea of desert. Perhaps the most insidious problem for any island species is the introduction of non-native species which become established and compete for food and space or prey upon it.

The harsh aquatic ecosystems of the southwest desert and their unique fish fauna may be the most threatened in North America. What does it take for a fish species to survive in such a harsh environment? Most of the fishes have evolved an array of impressive morphological, physiological, and behavioral adaptations to cope with waters that are unusually high in dissolved solids and often have high temperatures because of the geothermal gradients they pass through. These desert spring and pool fishes generally have stubby, robust bodies complete with broad rounded fins for maintaining their positions in the slowly flowing waters. On the whole, these species are omnivorous feeders, using the few dominant food items that might be present. A typical desert spring fish lives about one year but has an extended breeding season. It produces few offspring per brood, but makes an attentive parent that cares for the privileged few.

Unfortunately, the rapidly growing human population coupled with the increasing demands for agricultural and industrial development are outpacing the limited water resources in these arid environments. The heaviest demand for the water resources of the southwest desert comes from the large metropolitan areas like Las Vegas, Phoenix, and Los Angeles. The most serious threat facing the fragile desert aquatic habitats is the practice of pumping large quantities of groundwater which lowers the water table. This demand for water, which is used primarily for agriculture, has led to pumping of groundwater supplies from large underground aquifers that cover thousands of square miles. This "mining" of water seriously lowers the water table under the desert because the volume of groundwater removed from the aquifer exceeds its recharge. In some areas the lowered water table causes the aquifer to collapse, reducing or eliminating its ability to hold or transport water. The excessive use of groundwater has turned several lush desert spring pools into little more than dust bowls.

Not only is the groundwater to the desert pool systematically removed by pumping, the surface waters are also subject to Man's thirst to manipulate his environment. These waters are dammed into small reservoirs that are diverted into canals to irrigate adjacent fields. Pesticides and other toxic materials that run off agricultural lands can destroy the small spring pools. Livestock feeding near spring pools overgraze the land, allowing soil to erode and wash into the pools causing severe siltation problems. These small pools are also susceptible to the introduction of non-native fishes such as the mosquitofish, *Gambusia affinis*, which has the potential of easily replacing the endemic fishes. Some 36 species of non-native fishes have either reduced or replaced several of the native desert fishes through predation, competition, and hybridization.

Prior to the colonization by white settlers during the middle of the nineteenth century, Man's effects on the original desert fish fauna were negligible. With the consequent habitat modifications made over the last 125 years, however, the southwest desert aquatic ecosystems are among the most altered environments in North America.

# Desert Dace
## *Eremichthys acros*

Old-timers vividly recall when the spring waters of Soldier Meadows were so hot that you could hardboil an egg in them! As fantastic as it may sound, no one really doubted that some of the spring waters in this remote section of northwestern Nevada were hot enough to perform this feat. Biochemists tell us that to hardboil an egg, you have to heat the water sufficiently to "denature the proteins of the egg." Most proteins will denature when heated to a temperature of 122° to 140° F, well within the thermal range of warm springs.

What would have amazed these old-timers even more is that in some of those thermal spring outflows in Soldier Meadows lives an amazing olive-green colored fish that has evolved the ability to survive water temperatures upwards of 100.4° F. Known as the desert dace, *Eremichthys acros*, or the "Soldier Meadows desertfish," this member of the minnow family now survives in only eight of the twenty thermal springs that percolate throughout the six square miles of Soldier Meadows.

Soldier Meadows is a rounded basin, over 4500 feet high, and flanked by the Calico Mountains on its western boundary and by the Black Rock Range on its eastern boundary in Humbolt County, Nevada. This isolated desert region is part of the spectacular Lake Lahontan drainage system. Twenty thermal hot springs bubble to the surface from a fault in the earth and form a marshy environment. The general climate is rough with hot, dry summers and bitter, snow-filled winters.

Legend has it that Soldier Meadows got its name from nearby Camp McGarry, a Civil War military outpost on the shores of Summit Lake in the Black Rock Range. Summit Lake itself is the etymological origin of the species name, "acros" meaning summit. In 1890, the camp was abandoned. The Bureau of Land Management currently controls most of the remote surrounding area, but the immediate Soldier Meadows section itself, with its thermal springs and outflow creeks which support the desert dace, is privately owned. The Soldier Meadows Ranch uses the area for cattle grazing.

The desert dace was discovered by Robert Rush Miller on July 5, 1939. Among cyprinid fishes in the west, this tiny 2½ inch fish holds the record for surviving in the hottest waters, even though it prefers waters that range from 73° to 84° F. Besides this unusual ability to tolerate such high water temperatures, the desert dace has another unique feature that distinguishes it from all other members of the cyprinid family. A close inspection of the dace's ventrally positioned mouth reveals fleshy lips that extend beyond the borders of the jaws and enclose prominent horny sheaths. These sheaths extend across most of the upper and lower jaws. Scientists have suggested that this jaw is an evolutionary adaptation designed for herbivorous grazing on the spring bottom. The desert dace generally eats mostly filamentous algae, diatoms, and other forms of aquatic vegetation, although snails and aquatic insect larvae are eaten as nourishing supplements.

The quantity and quality of the thermal spring water in the pools and outflow streams of Soldier Meadows is the most crucial conservation factor for the

6–1

Soldier Meadows in western Humboldt County, Nevada. Thermal springs in this valley are the only habitat of the desert dace. Photo by J. D. Williams.

desert dace. Soldier Meadows Ranch has diverted water from these natural sources into man-made drainage ditches, drastically altering much of this fish's habitat. Because the desert dace cannot tolerate water temperatures much above 100°F, losing the valuable water through drainage ditches in spring systems where the spring headpool waters exceeds this temperature is exceptionally perilous. In such cases, the desert dace can only live in the cooler spring outflow creeks. Should the water in the outflow creeks evaporate during an unusually dry period, the dace would be trapped between the hot headpool waters and the drying creek. The desert dace population would certainly perish.

There are two additional threats that may complicate life for the desert dace. Two reservoirs were recently constructed on the north and south ends of Soldier Meadows approximately three miles from the springs and their outflow creeks. One of the reservoirs received an introduction of bass and catfish. Because of the proximity of this reservoir to the Soldier Meadows springs and outflows, it is possible that these non-native fish species could move into the choice desert dace habitats. The catfish and bass would compete with or prey on the dace, as well as introduce diseases and parasites unknown to the endemic Soldier Meadows dace.

Besides the lingering threat of non-native fish introductions into Soldier Meadows via the reservoir, this desert region is geologically described as a Known Geothermal Resource Area (KGRA). Several years ago, explorations began in the Soldier Meadows area to pinpoint geothermal energy sources, but these efforts were later abandoned. Should the energy-seeking companies resume their searches, Soldier Meadows risks losing water from the aquifers that flow into the thermal springs.

70

Because of the restricted nature of the desert dace's habitat and the potential threats that could extinguish the species, the U.S. Fish and Wildlife Service is considering the possibility of listing the desert dace as a threatened species. With only a one year lifespan and its single February to May breeding season, the desert dace is extremely vulnerable. One major catastrophe could easily eradicate the species.

Unlike the many bodies of water sheltering endangered or threatened fishes near metropolitan or developing areas, Soldier Meadows is situated in a very isolated and undeveloped region of Nevada. Real estate developers pose no immediate problems for the Soldier Meadows area—so at present the available water resources are relatively safe. These desert lands have only been used commercially as range country for cattle. But this does not license future irresponsibility. The source of water supplying Soldier Meadows should be carefully monitored. In fact, the actual landscape is practically the same as when Charles Fremont, the first explorer to the area in 1843, made his initial trek through it. It's even been said that one could take his diary of the journey, the first written record of the area, and still use it as a travel guide around these lands. Traveling on New Year's Eve, 1843 and New Year's Day, 1844, Charles Fremont vividly described the sheer beauty and wildness of the Soldier Meadows area:

*December 31, 1843 . . . After an hour's ride this morning, our hopes were once more destroyed. The valley opened out, and before us again lay one of the dry basins (High Rock Lake). After some search, we discovered a high-water outlet (Fly Creek Canyon), which brought us in a few miles, and by a descent of several feet, into another long broad basin, in which we found the bed of a stream (Mud Meadow Creek), and obtained sufficient water by cutting the ice. The grass on the bottoms was salt and unpalatable . . .*

*New Year's Day 1844 . . . We continued down the valley, between a dry-looking black ridge on the left (Black Rock Range) and a more snowy and high one on the right (Calico Mountains). Our road was bad along the bottom, being broken by gullies and impeded by sage, and sandy on the hills, where there is not a blade of grass, nor does any appear on the mountains. The soil in many places consists of a fine powdery sand, covered with a saline efflorescence; and the general character of the country is desert (Black Rock Desert). During the day we directed our course towards a black cape (Black Rock), at the foot of which a column of smoke indicated hot springs (Great Boiling Spring).*

*Charles Fremont, A Report of the Exploring Expedition to Oregon and North California in the Years 1843–1844*

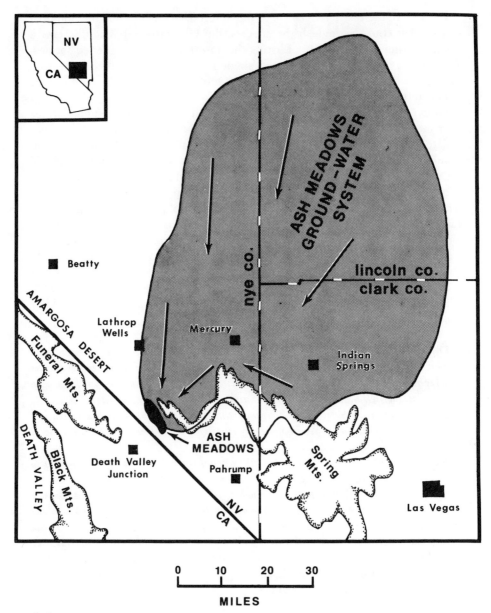

**MILES**

6–2
Ash Meadows groundwater system. Arrows indicate the direction of groundwater flow into Ash Meadows. Map by R. D. Ono.

# Ash Meadows Fishes

During the last century weary travelers riding horseback or in horsedrawn wagons found Ash Meadows, a desert wetland in one of the most arid regions of the world, a welcome relief from the sunbeaten trails. In this large and lush oasis, the horses were watered and the traveler found shelter, food, and water. The history books do not cite a definite origin of the name, "Ash Meadows," for this desert wetland. Some believe the name reflects the ashy color of the alkaline soil while others are convinced that Ash Meadows refers to the many groves of velvet ash trees surrounding this desert oasis. The origin of the name will probably remain uncertain. The controversy over the origin of the name is rather trivial and unimportant, but Ash Meadows has played an important role in the general history of desert life. With dozens of springs fed by an extensive groundwater system, the desert wetlands of Ash Meadows supports hundreds of plant and animal species, with more than twenty species endemic to this oasis.

The many plant and animal species that have congregated in this arid section of Nye County, Nevada, where the average rainfall barely reaches 2½ inches per year, are the result of the gradual evaporation during the Pleistocene Epoch. During the Pleistocene, much of the American southwest was under large inland lakes, but about 12,000 years ago, the climate warmed, the precipitation decreased, and the area began to dry out. Lakes and rivers began to disappear, as did many of their resident populations of flora and fauna. The bodies of water that remained were connected to springs or other sources of replenishing water which allowed some plant and animal species to survive this geologic event.

Because this evaporative process transformed the watery American southwest into a desert relatively fast in geologic time, the springs in Ash Meadows became a series of "evolutionary islands." Here the surviving stranded plant and animal species evolved specialized morphological or physiological adaptations to survive in the rapidly changing environment on these isolated "islands." Those that didn't adapt were doomed.

Until the twentieth century Ash Meadows remained relatively pristine and undisturbed by Man. Only a small group settled in the desert wetlands, from 1910 to 1930, to mine peat and clay. Enough mining families were present to warrant a tiny one room school house near School Spring, one of the major springs in Ash Meadows. Aside from this incidental business venture, Ash Meadows only sporadically supported a few small farming and ranching enterprises. When homesteaders first saw the area, they had great expectations for farming the area because of the vast amount of freeflowing spring water and the plainlike topography of this desert valley. The poor quality of the soil, however, completely destroyed the dream of converting the area into farmlands.

It wasn't until the 1950s that Ash Meadows began to feel the negative impact of Man's activities. Several of the springs suffered because exotic species (mosquitofish, mollies, platyfish, and bullfrogs) were introduced into the Ash Meadows habitat. Hard as it may be to fathom, an illegally operated tropical fish farm located at Forest Spring in the early 1960s introduced an even greater variety of exotic species, among them the arawana, a predacious South American fish. This large predator must have feasted on the tiny native pupfish and dace species that once populated the vast spring system. Introduced species compete with and prey on the native fishes in the habitat once they become established, spelling danger for the native species. A few non-native species established themselves in most of the large springs in Ash Meadows, leading to the extinction of the Ash Meadows killifish, *Empetrichthys merriami*.

While exotic species were outcompeting the native species in Ash Meadows, major physical changes to this oasis began in the 1960s when a marsh area known as Carson Slough was drained and mined for peat. A large population of Ash Meadows Amargosa pupfish and a large migratory waterfowl habitat were destroyed by this draining operation. By the late 1960s and early 1970s, agricultural interest in Ash Meadows was rekindled and habitat was altered on a much larger scale than the Carson Slough incident. Large scale irrigation ditches were installed for the first time and groundwater pumping systems peppered the land around Ash Meadows. What had taken aeons for nature to assemble, Man was to wreck in a few years.

## Devils Hole Pupfish
## *Cyprinodon diabolis*

(Color plate 6.)

Within the streams and pools of the arid Death Valley and Ash Meadows area in the southwestern United States live several unique members of the family Cyprinodontidae, commonly known as pupfishes. These fishes have evolved remarkable adaptations, all in a geologic "second" (about 10,000 years), that enable them to survive in small desert spring pools. One species of *Cyprinodon*, for example, evolved the ability to withstand temperatures ranging from near freezing to more than 100° F; another can live in water six times as saline as seawater. Still another species inhabits spring water containing high concentrations of borates. Other species have evolved the ability to hibernate within the mud bottoms of springs and creeks during freezing weather.

Although the Cyprinodontidae have a worldwide distribution, the Death Valley group, referred to as the desert pupfishes because of their playful, tenacious, and fiesty nature, are the stars of the family. While the pupfishes are not important as food or forage fishes, they are valuable keys to the evolution puzzle. The pupfishes of the Death Valley system are quite similar to Darwin's finches of the Galapagos Islands because they, too, have managed to evolve remarkable adaptations rather quickly in geologic time. Each species has managed to adapt to its own set of local, desert conditions such as high temperatures, high salinity, and low oxygen concentrations. Uncovering these secrets of adaptation could have practical implications for medicine, animal husbandry, and space travel. Just one physiological adaptation, how the pupfish

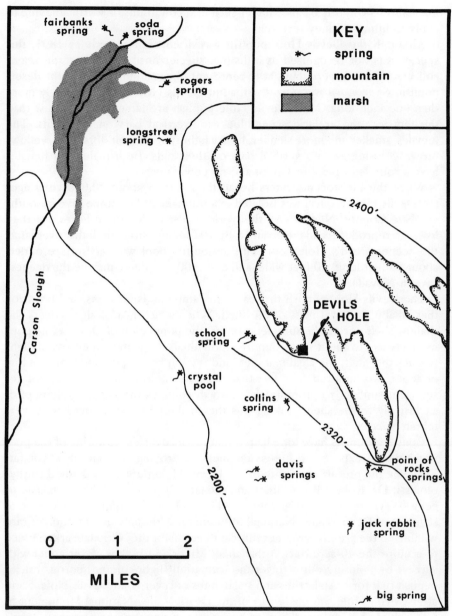

6–3
Ash Meadows Springs in relation to elevation in the area. Map by R. D. Ono.

maintains its osmotic balance under such arid conditions, is worth studying to apply to human kidney research.

Although the Devils Hole pupfish was discovered as early as 1891, this species was not recognized as a distinct species until 1930. The specimens collected in 1891 were thought to represent unusual individuals of the desert pupfish, *Cyprinodon macularius*. An adult Devils Hole pupfish is rarely more than one inch long. Male Devils Hole pupfish are larger, more robust than the females, and are iridescent blue with vertical bars on their tails. The females, smaller and more slender, have a light spot on their dorsal fins, yellow-brown coloring and no vertical bars on their tails. Both males and females have a rounded caudal or tail fin and no pelvic fins.

When the Pleistocene waters began their retreat about 20,000 years ago, the Devils Hole pupfish was isolated in a water-filled limestone cave in southern Nye County, Nevada. All the world is a stage for these fishes, for they live, eat, reproduce, and die on an 18-by-10 foot limestone shelf that overhangs the deeper Devil's Hole pool. This spring-fed pool with no surface outlet, about 55 feet long, 10 feet wide, and over 300 feet deep, may be the deepest cave in Nevada.

The Devils Hole pupfish thrives on the amphipods, diatoms, and protozoa that inhabit the algal mats of the shelf. When a rich mat of algae covers the shallow shelf during the summer months, the population of Devils Hole pupfish increases to about seven hundred individuals. In winter, when less sunlight reaches the shelf, the algal mat dies, and the pupfish population dips to a low of about two hundred. The fact that the water below the shelf does not get sufficient sunlight to promote algal growth confines the Devils Hole pupfish exclusively to the shelf, making this the smallest habitat of any known vertebrate species.

Convervationists have long feared that the inadvertent lowering of the pool water would expose the life-giving shelf, destroying the pupfishes' habitat. Realizing the precarious nature of the Devils Hole pupfish, two noted ichthyologists, Dr. Robert Rush Miller and the late Dr. Carl L. Hubbs, managed to get a 40-acre tract of land surrounding Devil's Hole incorporated as a separate segment of Death Valley National Monument. Although identification of rare wildlife on the premises was not sufficient reason for the National Parks Service to acquire the 40-acre tract at that time, Miller and Hubbs cleverly met with success by pointing out a travertine formation (light-colored, porous calcite deposit that forms stalactites and stalagmites of caverns) in Devil's Hole. Soon after Devil's Hole was made part of the Death Valley National Monument in 1952, the U.S. Geological Survey began monitoring the water level of Devil's Hole.

A three foot drop in water level, exposing the highest parts of the rocky shelf, could mean destruction of a significant portion of the life-giving algal mat. By 1962, a copper washer had been installed on the wall of Devil's Hole as a reference point to monitor the water level. The following year, the U.S. Geological Survey noted no apparent change in water level, but warned that any removal of groundwater from Devil's Hole would affect the water level with serious consequences. Moreover, in 1967, the U.S. Department of Interior declared the Devils Hole pupfish an endangered species because of its unique qualities and restricted habitat. Neither the U.S. Geological Survey

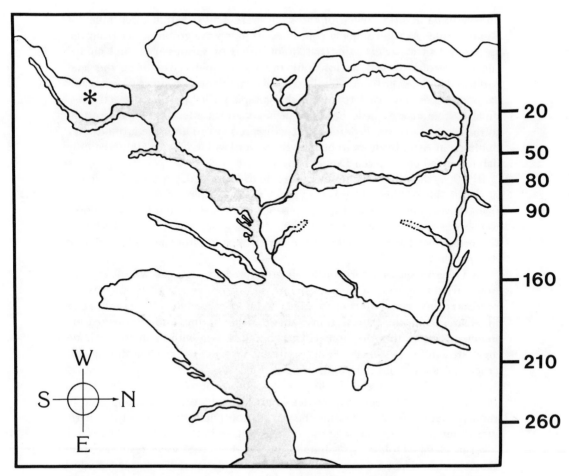

6–4
Cross section view of Devil's Hole. The shelf is indicated by the star and water depth, in feet, along the right margin. The Devils Hole pupfish is restricted to the water around the shelf area. Illustration by R. D. Ono.

water monitoring efforts nor the U.S. Department of Interior's declaration, however, prevented the pupfish-threatening chain of events that began in 1968.

During a flurry of renewed agricultural interest in Ash Meadows, the Bureau of Land Management (BLM) made a very serious mistake. The Bureau of Land Management, which controlled most of the 40,000 acres of land encompassing Ash Meadows, exchanged 5,645 acres of Ash Meadows land to Spring Meadows, Inc., a private company, for 5,400 acres in the Osgood Mountains. Spring Meadows, Inc., which was owned by F. L. Cappaert, a farming entrepreneur from Mississippi, planned to use the land to grow forage crops to feed large numbers of cattle. Attempting to gain the majority rights to the area's water supply, Spring Meadows, Inc. successfully purchased 12,000 additional acres from private landowners.

Spring Meadows, Inc. began operation almost immediately, sinking well after well into the desert wetlands to tap the life-giving water in the deep underground aquifer. Seven of the wells were drilled within three miles of Devil's Hole. As the company continued to pump the groundwater from the spring system to irrigate the land, populations of various plant and animal species were destroyed by lowering the water table and altering the land surface. The U.S. Fish and Wildlife Service and various conservation organizations desperately tried to curtail the company's habitat-altering activities. Finally, after making little headway in negotiations, the matter was brought to the attention of the Federal Court with a request to limit the groundwater pumping in Ash Meadows to protect the water level in Devil's Hole, the only habitat of the endangered Devils Hole pupfish.

By 1969, the water level in Devil's Hole had dropped, exposing 60 percent of the life-giving shelf. That same year, a small group of concerned scientists from universities, state, and federal agencies, formed the Pupfish Task Force to coordinate pupfish-saving efforts. Out of this group came the Desert Fishes Council, which has made significant contributions towards the conservation of desert fishes.

As Department of Interior officials attempted to negotiate with Cappaert, others tried to introduce the pupfish into desert springs devoid of other fishes, predators, and competitors in the Nevada desert . . . and to culture the species in aquaria. Both the pupfish transplants to other springs and pupfish rearing in aquaria met with little success. The fiberglass shelf with lights to stimulate algal growth in the Devil's Hole pool that researchers installed during this crucial period did aid the pupfish population.

Then in 1971 the Devils Hole pupfish went to court. The case was tried in July of 1972, in the Federal District Court and the decision was appealed to the U.S. Supreme Court. During the various court deliberations, nature nearly wiped out the pupfish population. An earthquake in Alaska caused the water level in Devil's Hole to rise dramatically. A three foot wave resulting from that uprising crashed down onto the shelf and destroyed some of the algal growth covering it. Two months later, severe thunderstorms destroyed most of the remaining algal mats and littered rocky debris over much of the shelf. The complete extermination of the most highly evolved species of fish in the Death Valley system seemed inevitable.

The decision that gave the Devils Hole pupfish the right to survive was finally handed down in June of 1976. The U.S. Supreme Court justices decided to limit the amount of water that could be pumped from the basin supplying the Devil's Hole National Monument. According to this ruling, the forty acre segment of the Death Valley National Monument was formed specifically to guarantee the existence of the pupfish, and any operation threatening that existence violated federal law. For the first time in its history, the U.S. Supreme Court decided the fate of an entire species.

Shortly after this court ruling was handed down, Spring Meadows, Inc. determined that the amount of groundwater that they could legally pump was not adequate for their irrigation purposes and they offered their lands for sale. Spring Meadows, Inc. initially offered to sell the land to the U.S. Fish and Wildlife Service for one million dollars. Incredibly, the U.S. Fish and Wildlife Service declined to purchase the lands because the heads of the agency felt that the Supreme Court decision was sufficient to prevent or limit development in Ash Meadows. They shortsightedly failed to recognize that other land de-

6–5
Closeup of Devil's Hole with light and artificial shelf installed in an attempt to increase pupfish habitat after the water level dropped, exposing a portion of the natural shelf in Devil's Hole. Photo by C. H. Lostetter, U.S. Fish and Wildlife Service.

velopment threats besides the pumping of groundwater loomed inevitably in the future and might irreparably alter the Ash Meadows habitat. The Nevada Department of Wildlife even offered to share in the cost of purchasing the Spring Meadows, Inc. land, but the U.S. Fish and Wildlife Service still refused to make the purchase. The Nevada Department of Wildlife felt that the Ash Meadows area could become an excellent wildlife management area beginning with the restoration of the destroyed wetland areas as a winter haven for migratory waterfowl.

At this point the future of Ash Meadows was up for grabs and time was running out. It was already too late for other members of the Cyprinodontidae family. During the last 35 years, one species and two subspecies of pupfish had become extinct. The obituaries included the 1948 death of the Ash Meadows killifish, *Empetrichthys merriami*, through the introduction of exotic species such as mosquitofish, mollies, crayfish, and bullfrogs into its habitat. In 1955 the Raycraft Ranch killifish, *Empetrichthys latos concavus,* and the Pahrump Ranch killifish, *Empetrichthys latos pahrump*, became extinct due to destruction of their habitats in Pahrump Valley, Nye County, Nevada. Still, biologists were hopeful that the lessons learned from these three tragedies, as well as the nearly catastrophic Cappaert incident, would lessen the probability of extinction of the five species and six subspecies of Cyprinodontidae remaining in Death Valley-Ash Meadows area.

In 1977, shortly after the initial offer to the U.S. Fish and Wildlife Service, a Las Vegas based real estate development company, the Preferred Equities Corporation, purchased 14,000 acres of land in Ash Meadows from Spring Meadows, Inc. By 1980, it had purchased all of the land and water rights Spring Meadows had owned. An additional 5,000 acres of land were acquired from private landowners. Preferred Equities Corporation was not going to simply pump groundwater from the underground spring system, but intended to develop residential, recreational, and industrial projects collectively known as Cal Vada Lakes. The plans called for facilities to accommodate a population of 76,314 persons. The entire Ash Meadows area now only supports a residence of twenty or thirty people! Already roads have been cut into the area and several springs have been excavated. These projects will certainly demand vast amounts of water and destroy much of the habitat considered vital to the welfare of the endemic forms of life in Ash Meadows.

Besides the Preferred Equities Corporation, the Anaconda Copper Company purchased 1,200 acres in 1980 with hopes of mining zeolite, a substance associated with volcanic rocks that has tremendous filtering properties. Anaconda has no plans at present to begin its mining operations.

# Ash Meadows Speckled Dace and Ash Meadows Amargosa Pupfish
## *Rhinichthys osculus nevadensis* and *Cyprinodon nevadensis mionectes*

In light of the threats commercial development pose for the Ash Meadows fishes, as well as the continued harassment by introduced exotic species, the U.S. Fish and Wildlife Service on May 10, 1982, placed two additional fishes endemic to Ash Meadows on the endangered species list by emergency action. These two fishes, the Ash Meadows Amargosa pupfish, *Cyprinodon nevadensis mionectes*, and the Ash Meadows speckled dace, *Rhinichthys osculus nevadensis*, join the other two endangered Ash Meadows fishes, the celebrated Devils Hole pupfish and the Warm Springs pupfish on the federal list of endangered species.

All of the spring waters that course through Ash Meadows are interconnected and equally affected by groundwater pumping. Because the Preferred Equities Corporation owns most of the water rights to Ash Meadows, and the U.S. Fish and Wildlife Service, the state of Nevada, and conservationists have not succeeded in negotiating for a comprehensive protective plan, it was vitally important to officially declare those two fishes as endangered. Protecting the Ash Meadows Amargosa pupfish and speckled dace, which live in springs at a low elevation level, essentially protects the entire fragile Ash Meadows spring network. Because of the intimate interconnections of the underground spring system, protection of the springs at the lowest level also protects springs and groundwater levels at higher elevations, including Devil's Hole, the highest aquatic ecosystem in Ash Meadows.

6–6
Big Spring in Ash Meadows, habitat for the Ash Meadows speckled dace and Ash Meadows Amargosa pupfish. Photo by J. D. Williams.

While the Ash Meadows pupfish lives in more habitats and is found in far greater numbers than any other native fish in Ash Meadows, its present range represents only a small fraction of what it was historically. This endemic species has been eliminated from at least eleven of the twenty major springs providing water to Ash Meadows as well as from thirteen miles of spring outflow because of competition with introduced exotic species and severe reductions in spring flows resulting from uncontrolled groundwater pumping. Draining Carson Slough for peat mining eliminated 2000 acres of valuable marshlands that were considered prime territory for this tiny desert fish. Consequently, this species of pupfish has been reduced over the last several years to reside in the source pools of only nine springs.

It goes without saying that the Ash Meadows speckled dace, whose historic range closely matches that of the Ash Meadows pupfish, is also facing the same shrinkage of habitat. Though the geographic range of the speckled dace is similar to that of the pupfish, the speckled dace prefers to inhabit the riffles and the pools of spring outflow channels rather than the source pools so fancied by the pupfish. Here in the riffles and outflow channels, the speckled dace, which rarely exceeds three inches in length, spawns once early in the spring and again in late summer—providing that the summer's rains have substantially increased the stream flow during this time. The spawning dace will lay a large number of tiny eggs which are fertilized and hatch within a few days. Of this large number of fry, only a fraction of them survive to adulthood to continue the species.

The Ash Meadows pupfish population, on the other hand, breeds throughout the year with peak spawning periods in the spring and early summer. Males participating in the spawning activity can be recognized by the brilliant iridescent silver-blue sheen of their flanks.

How many more generations of the Ash Meadows pupfish and speckled dace will swim in the spring pools and riffles unperturbed by the rapid development that is threatening this oasis? Ash Meadows is one of only two extensive desert spring ecosystems with large numbers of endemic species remaining on the North American continent. The other is the Cuatro Ciénegas basin in Coahuila Mexico. Ash Meadows has the more unique native plants and animals than any other comparably-sized region within the United States. Steps are being taken to help preserve this lush desert wetlands. Recently a bill has been introduced in the U.S. Senate to establish Ash Meadows as a national wildlife refuge, something that should have been done years ago. In addition, the Desert Fishes Council has formed a committee to help plan the protection of Ash Meadows. Finally, the Nevada Sierra Club, Northern Nevada Native Plant Society, Nature Conservancy, Nevada Audubon Society, and the Nevada Chapter of the National Wildlife Federation have joined forces to make certain that Ash Meadows will remain an unique ecosystem.

The large oasis which has provided food and shelter for so many species of flora and fauna, including Man, throughout its history, now needs help to ensure its own survival.

\*     \*     \*

As this book was going to press, the Preferred Equities Corporation had expressed interest in exchanging all of their lands and water rights in Ash Meadows for Bureau of Land Management lands near Las Vegas. Unfortunately, the Bureau of Land Management indicated that it did not wish to exchange any lands for Ash Meadows.

# Pahrump Killifish
## *Empetrichthys latos latos*

The original plan for deploying the MX Missile system would have pitted the Department of Defense against a small desert fish called the Pahrump killifish. The reason? One of the installations of the proposed MX Missile System was slated to occur at Shoshone Ponds near Ely, Nevada. Shoshone Ponds just happens to be one of two remaining refugia for this endangered killifish.

This tiny desert fish with the upturned mouth and bright orange-yellow fins used to live in an isolated pocket of southern Nevada known as Pahrump Valley. The Pahrump killifish, *Empetrichthys latos*, is the only native fish in this valley. The valley is a moderate-sized drainage basin on the western edge of Spring Mountains, separated from Ash Meadows to the northwest and the Amargosa River drainage to the southwest by hills ranging from 148 to over 2640 feet in elevation. Several warm springs rise in the valley floor along the margins of Pahrump Valley. All within 7.5 miles of one another, three separate springs systems flowed into the Pahrump Valley for a short distance before disappearing into the desert floor. Each spring had its own peculiar subspecies of the Pahrump killifish: Raycraft Ranch killifish, Pahrump Ranch killifish, and the Pahrump killifish. All three of the Pahrump killifish subspecies were once extremely abundant in the springs of this valley because of the lack of predators and a fast generation time that allowed them to reproduce safely and quickly.

This situation ended abruptly when groundwater pumping for irrigation dried virtually all of the springs in Pahrump Valley. One of them, the Pahrump Ranch Spring which supported the largest population of Pahrump killifishes, went completely dry between 1955 and 1957. The Pahrump Ranch subspecies, *Empetrichthys latos pahrump,* was completely eliminated. A second subspecies, the Raycraft Ranch killifish, *Empetrichthys latos concavus*, became extinct in 1955 after its habitat was bulldozed and blasted over by developers simply to divert the water flow to other areas of Pahrump Valley for agricultural use.

The third subspecies, the Pahrump killifish, *Empetrichthys latos latos*, from Manse Spring managed to survive the 1950 groundwater pumping. But the continuing threats of pumping and introduced species leave biologists unsure of the Pahrump killifish's potential in this valley. Groundwater was and continues to be mined at the unbelieveable average annual rate of about 20,000 acre–feet per year! Wisely, biologists decided to transplant much of the existing population from Manse Spring to refuge sites, among them, Shoshone Ponds. The Nevada Department of Wildlife transplanted the Pahrump killifish from Manse Spring to Corn Creek a small spring on the U.S. Fish and Wildlife Service Desert Game Range near Las Vegas, in 1971. Shoshone Ponds received transplants of the Pahrump killifish in 1972, thanks to the Bureau of

6–7
Point of Rocks Spring in Ash Meadows before "development." Photo by D. Sada.

6–8
Point of Rocks Spring after "development." Photo by D. Sada.

Land Management and the Nevada Department of Wildlife. The foresight to take these precautions was fortunate because Manse Spring, the large densely vegetated spring, was pumped completely dry in June, 1975. It would have been the end of the last subspecies of the Pahrump killifish as well as the entire genus *Empetrichthys*.

The Pahrump killifish currently lives on, but only in artificially maintained refugia at Corn Creek and Shoshone Ponds. While they survive in these transplanted habitats, the remaining few hundred individuals of the Pahrump killifish face the threats of bullfrogs and introduced exotic fishes such as the shortfin molly, *Poecilia mexicana*; mosquitofish, *Gambusia affinis*; and even the goldfish, *Carassius auratus*. A third artificial refugium set up in Ash Meadows no longer supports the transplant. It died out in 1977.

Unfortunately, transplanted fishes in refugia are not truly representative of the endemic native species. No matter how closely the refugium appears to match the species' original habitat, they will never be identical. Different selection pressures will be placed on the species, resulting in an evolutionary trend toward adapting the species to the refugium. The gene pool of the native species will then be altered. Transplantation of a species should only be done as a last resort when the species faces certain extinction as when its last natural habitat is on the verge of being destroyed. Ideally, the transplanted species should be allowed to only live in the refugia for a couple of generations with the understanding that as soon as stocks are built up, the species will be reintroduced into native habitats, if such an option exists. Unfortunately, as

6–9
Manse Spring. Former habitat of the Pahrump killifish. Photo by D. Sada.

with its close relative the Devils Hole pupfish, aquarists have had little success propagating the Pahrump killifish.

Very little is known about the life history of the Pahrump killifish. We do know that it spawns from January through July, peaking in April. The larger, mottled, greenish-brown male is not particularly interested in protecting a territory, and shows no interest whatsoever in raising its offspring. The smaller, silver-blue female spawns several times during a season and shows no more parental care for the young than the male. The energy to reproduce and grow appears to come from a variety of food items, especially snails which are commonly eaten by the Pahrump killifish.

With only two refugia left to provide suitable habitats for survival, the Pahrump killifish is far from being safe. A resident population of bullfrogs, a fierce fish predator, threatens the Corn Creek population. If the MX Missile System should end up near Shoshone Ponds refugium this population would, in all likelihood, be forced to find a new home. In the meantime, the small remaining band of the Pahrump killifish, *Empetrichthys latos latos*, lives perilously close to the edge.

6–10
Desert development uses large quantities of groundwater, reducing or eliminating spring flow. Photo by J. D. Williams.

# VII.

# Colorado River System Fishes

Over a hundred million years ago the ancient sea that inundated a large portion of the American West began to recede, gradually exposing the Rocky Mountains and the Colorado Plateau. Giant lakes formed in the northern part of the Colorado Plateau and acted as reservoirs for the drainage from the newly emerged Rocky Mountains. As the lakes filled with sediments, the plateau began to tilt toward the northeast. By the Oligocene Epoch, 25–40 million years ago, the lakes overflowed and the Colorado River was born. The new river collected water from the many tributaries that formed along its course, channeled its way south, eroding a path through lava deposits, detouring mountain upheavals, and veering westward over part of its course as the plateau continued to tilt. By the end of the Miocene Epoch, about 10 million years ago, the Colorado River and a major tributary, the Green River, had cut a 1700 mile course from the Rocky Mountains in southwest Wyoming and north central Colorado through Utah, Arizona, Nevada, and southern California to empty into the Gulf of California in northern Mexico.

In its original state the Colorado River represented a formidable habitat. Dropping a total of two miles in elevation on its run from the mountains to the gulf, the river reached the Colorado Plateau with enough force to carve mile deep canyons out of the bedrock. The river's flow ranged from extreme lows of .66 cubic yards per second in late summer, to floodwater highs of 9175 cubic yards per second in the winter and spring. During peak flow the river is reported to have carried over 175 million cubic yards of silt per day.

Despite these extreme conditions, sixteen species of fishes evolved in the Colorado River system, adapting to the radical, often rapid fluctuations in its chemical and physical properties. Biologists estimate that the endemic species comprise 70 percent of all the fishes found in the Colorado River system, and that this high degree of endemism is the result of the species' geographical isolation from other drainage systems in the region. Fishes living in swift water often evolve suckerlike organs to attach to river bottoms, but the instability of the Colorado River substrate dictated that the endemic fishes develop instead streamlined bodies and wing-like fins for maintaining headway in strong currents. Some of the fishes developed humped backs with enlarged muscle masses that apparently act as stabilizers for swimming in turbulent waters. The endemic species also developed flat, sloping heads that tended to push the fishes downward, helping them hold the bottom while pointing upstream into the current.

After surviving the Colorado River's harsh environment through millions of years of evolution, these highly specialized endemic fishes have not been able to adapt to the profound changes that Man has brought to the river. The American Indians' careful stewardship of the Colorado River basin ended when the Spanish explorers arrived. The Spaniards called the river "colorado" because of its predominantly red color. Once the river was put on the map, the Spaniards were followed by fur trappers and eventually Mormon missionaries who established cotton settlements and brought cattle to the region. After the Civil War, four U.S. government surveys, and the writing of explorer John Wesley Powell, geologist Clarence Dutton, and historian F. S. Dellenbaugh, among others, the grandeur of the American West and the Colorado River was brought to the public eye. By the early 1900s the river and its canyons had become tourist attractions, attracting notable visitors including Presidents Warren G. Harding and Theodore Roosevelt.

Following the development of farming and cattle ranching in the Colorado River basin, the river was changed both abruptly and gradually. All the changes were cumulative. The most abrupt and possibly the most severe change for the endemic fishes resulted from the construction of more than twenty dams on the Colorado mainstream and its principal tributaries. Hoover (formerly Boulder) Dam, built on the Arizona/Nevada border in the 1930s, was the first large dam on the mainstem of the Colorado River. It created a large reservoir, Lake Mead, which extends into northwestern Arizona. To the south, four dams impound the mainstream from Hoover Dam all the way to the U.S.–Mexico border. All totaled, the five dams impound more than three hundred miles of the Colorado River. The last dam constructed on the mainstem of the Colorado River was Glen Canyon Dam, which was closed in 1963. Located in Arizona near the Arizona/Utah border, this high dam impounds water more than one hundred miles into southeastern Utah.

Damming drastically altered many of the river's features upstream and downstream from the dams. Silt and debris settled out of the turbid impoundment waters, which became much colder near the bottom of the reservoir. For most of the year the dam tailwaters that formed the downstream flow were much colder than the water that originally flowed there, and forced the native fishes away from their usual habitats. When the dams periodically released water to produce power or irrigate during the summer growing season, the downstream areas were suddenly flooded with cold, clear water—disrupting the natural temperature regime. The releases also reversed the river's natural flood regime, causing peak flows in the summer instead of the winter and spring. The spawn-

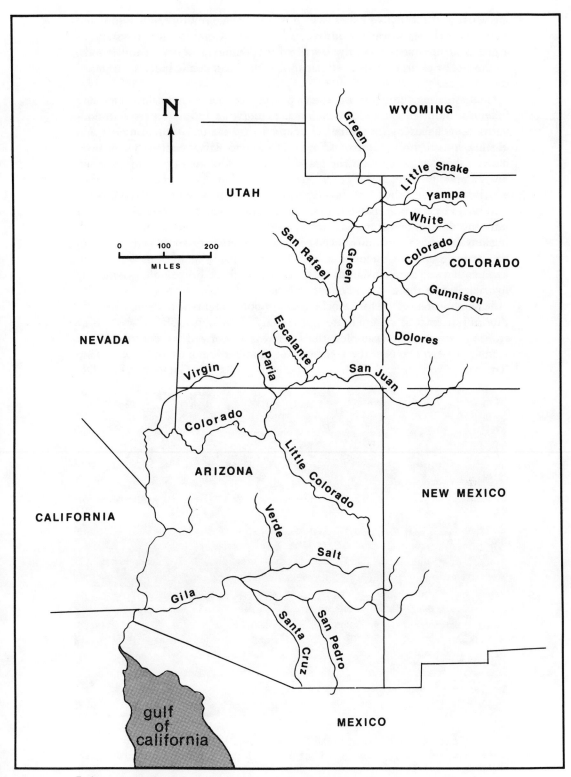

7–1
Colorado River system. Map by R. D. Ono.

ing activity of the native fishes, which is often triggered by temperature and water level changes, was seriously disrupted. The Colorado River system, as a group of biologists recently described it, became "a series of mill ponds, connected by clear, cold trout streams," leaving the endemic species "strangely out of place."

Compounding the damaging effect of dams on the native fishes, state and federal authorities stocked the man-made reservoirs and tailwaters with non-native gamefishes that were better adapted to the altered environment and quickly spread throughout most of the Colorado River system. These non-native fishes competed with the native fishes for food and breeding sites and preyed upon the eggs and fry of the native fishes. Parasites and diseases against which the native fishes had developed no resistance were introduced to the waterways by the non-native fishes. Some non-native fishes were accidentally introduced, such as certain species of baitfish that escaped from fishermen's buckets. These smaller introduced species competed for space and food with the juveniles of the endemic fishes. The man-made alterations of riverine habitats allowed native fishes to cross into each others' breeding areas, making hybridization a threat to the endemic fishes.

In some instances, before stocking the impoundments with gamefishes, authorities attempted to eradicate the endemic non-game fishes, "trash fish," from the waters. For example, after Congress authorized the construction of Flaming Gorge Dam on the Green River, a major tributary of the Colorado River in Wyoming and Utah, the Wyoming and Utah Game and Fish De-

7–2

Mouth of Little Colorado River in the Grand Canyon. Dark water in the foreground is the clear, cold water from Glen Canyon Dam located upstream. Photo by J. D. Williams.

partments, in conjunction with federal agencies, decided to clear the river of non-game fishes. This was done to establish a trout fishery in the impoundment waters following the closing of the dam. In September 1962, the authorities released the powerful fish killing chemical, rotenone, along 445 miles of the Green River and its tributaries upstream from the dam site. The rotenone treatment almost killed off several of the endemic fishes from the Green River system.

Water depletion in the Colorado River system, which resulted from agricultural diversions, urban demands, and reservoir evaporation, is the second most abrupt and severe change that Man has brought to the river. Between 1914 and 1975, the virgin water supply in the upper Colorado River system averaged 24.6 billion cubic yards per year. Records indicate that in 1965, 5.8 billion cubic yards of water per year were consumed in the region; 3.2 billion cubic yards of this went to irrigation. Reservoir evaporation represents a major loss of water from the Colorado basin—some reservoirs lose more than five feet each year. Scientists estimate that by the year 2020, consumption in the upper Colorado River system will have increased to 10.7 billion cubic yards annually. The depletion has been so extreme in the entire system that in some years no water reaches the Gulf of California in northern Mexico. The effects of water depletion on fishes are numerous: The habitat and available space diminishes, the dissolved oxygen content of the remaining water decreases (minimizing the degree of substrate aeration that is vital to fish egg development), the temperature changes, and streambanks cut away and erode, resulting in even more water runoff from channel-cutting.

Gradual but cumulative changes in the river system are harder to document or quantify. The long range effects accumulating from industrial, urban, and agricultural pollutants such as mining wastes, sewage, and fertilizers; bank erosion from the loss of stabilizing bank vegetation due to overgrazing by cattle; and the effects of non-native species introductions may not be documented for years. According to a 1976 U.S. Department of the Interior document, "if further habitat degradation occurs, the native Colorado River fish fauna may have the unique distinction of being the first major fauna to undergo mass extinction."

7–3
The Green River in eastern Utah is critical to the survival of the endangered and threatened Colorado River fishes. Photo by J. D. Williams.

# Humpback Chub
## *Gila cypha*

(Color plate 7.)

In May 1914, Emery and Ellsworth Kolb took a camping trip through the Grand Canyon and later described their experience in an article published by *National Geographic* magazine. The Kolbs wrote that one evening as they were setting up camp at the mouth of the Little Colorado River, they heard odd noises coming from the river. The Kolbs approached a pool where the noises were coming from and discovered a school of spawning fish. "The fins and tails of numerous fish could be seen above the water," they wrote. "The striking of their tails had caused the noise we had heard." The brothers described the "silvery white" schooling fishes as rarely over sixteen inches long with a "small flat head somewhat like a pike, the body swells behind it to a large hump."

The fishes that the Kolb brothers described in their article were humpback chubs, *Gila cypha,* which inhabit inaccessible regions of the Colorado River system and were not recognized as a species until 1946. Like the razorback sucker, another Colorado River endemic species, the humpback chub has a distinctive dorsal hump that rises at a steep angle directly behind the slightly concave surface of their skulls. The hump, which probably acts as a keel to stabilize the humpback chub's body in the strong currents, has a pronounced groove on each side that leads downward toward the gill openings. Biologists believe that the grooves may channel water over the gills when the humpback chub hugs the bottom of the river. The horizontal mouth is overhung by a slightly protruding fleshy snout which, in combination with the channeling action of the hump grooves, protects the mouth from onrushing water and may allow the fish to feed while swimming in strong currents. This chub with its strange humpback rates as one of the most bizarre freshwater fishes in North America.

The humpback chub has many features that are common to fishes living in the turbid, silty Colorado River waters. The eyes are fairly small, indicating that the fish probably relies on other senses such as taste or smell (chemoreception), or pressure awareness (mechanoreception), to locate food and navigate. Its scales are small and deeply embedded in the skin, minimizing the frictional surface exposed to the swift waters. Some areas of the humpback chub's body lack scales.

"Almost nothing is known of the biology of this fish," wrote ichthyologist W. L. Minckley in 1973, "principally because of the difficulties in collecting in its presumed habitat, and its resulting rarity in collections." The humpback chub seldom weighs more than two pounds and is usually found in the deep canyons of the Colorado River basin's larger rivers, where the restricted flows cut deep, fast channels. The lower Little Colorado River constitutes the major spawning area of the surviving humpback chub population in the Grand Canyon. Spawning takes place in May and June in the Little Colorado River, June and July in the upper reaches of the Green River. Water temperatures during spawning range from 65°F to 70°F. Spawning males acquire breeding colors, turning red-orange on the lower sides below the silvery-dusky body pigment and around the base of the pectoral and anal fins. The cheek below the eye becomes bright yellow and the iris pink-orange. The females turn light orange along the lower half of their flanks and at the base of the anal fin. The females lay yellowish eggs that average 2.7 millimeters in diameter. The average four-teen inch female lays about 2500 eggs.

The humpback chub's original distribution probably included all of the large river habitats in the upper Colorado River basin in addition to the canyon regions in most of the lower basin. The remains of humpback chubs found in ancient indian ruins in the lower Colorado basin, before it was flooded by Hoover Dam, indicate that the species may have been abundant in prehistoric times. Today there are no humpback chubs in the Colorado River system below the Grand Canyon. We do not have much specific information on the species' past abundance, but they were probably common over most of their range. Recent reports indicate that the humpback chub has been extirpated from the Green River system above the mouth of the Yampa River in Colorado. A small population of humpback chubs disappeared from the upper Green River in Wyoming following the closure of the Flaming Gorge Dam and the subsequent impoundment of the river in the Flaming Gorge Reservoir.

In the upper Colorado River basin humpback chubs are currently found in restricted sections of the Green and Colorado rivers and a few major tributaries. In the Green River a recent survey found humpback chubs in the Yampa River, a tributary of the Green River in northwestern Colorado, and several deep canyon areas along the Green River in eastern Utah above Lake Powell, the impoundment formed by Glen Canyon Dam. In the Colorado River the largest populations were found in the Black Rocks and Westwater Canyon areas where the river crosses the Colorado/Utah state line. Above and below these areas biologists found a few individuals in widely separated areas, perhaps strays from the Black Rocks and Westwater Canyon areas. Habitat alteration, additional impoundments and diversions, and the competition and predation problems non-native fishes present threaten the humpback chub in the Green and Colorado rivers.

Downstream, the humpback chub is limited to the Grand Canyon in northern Arizona. This population is isolated by Glen Canyon Dam upstream and reservoir waters of Lake Mead downstream. The major spawning site for the Grand Canyon population is the lower portion of the Little Colorado River, the largest stream tributary to the Colorado River in the canyon. Extremely cold water sporadically released from the Glen Canyon Dam on the Colorado River above the mouth of the Little Colorado River drastically reduces spawning habitat in the mainstream. Cool tailwater released into the warmer river waters probably disrupts or impairs the humpback chub's spawning behavior, although this has not been documented. Introduced species of game and bait-fishes are present in the Grand Canyon, but the extent to which they prey on and compete with the humpback chub is not known. The major threat to the Grand Canyon population is the proposed operational changes for Glen Canyon Dam. These changes would result in an exaggeration of the flow beyond present extreme limits.

In 1977, a pair of ichthyologists studying the humpback chub wrote, "The future of the humpback chub population in the Grand Canyon area is questionable . . . The extreme man-manipulated flow patterns of the main Colorado

River can only be viewed as detrimental to the survival of the species." A recovery team has been established to develop and maintain a minimum of five self-sustaining populations of humpback chubs in the Colorado River by 1990. In the meantime, biologists fear that the humpback chub may become extinct before its biology is understood. Only through protection of its limited habitat will the humpback chub be saved from this fate.

# Bonytail Chub
## *Gila elegans*

(Color plate 8.)

According to the U.S. Fish and Wildlife Service, the bonytail chub, *Gila elegans,* "has experienced the most abrupt decline of any of the fishes native to the mainstreams of the Colorado River system." Explorers conducting expeditions through the Colorado River basin between 1875 and 1904, reported collecting bonytail chubs relatively easily and in considerable numbers, but the fish became rare and eventually vanished from almost all of the lower Colorado River basin between 1926 and 1950. A similar decline in the bonytail population occurred in the upper basin. A group of researchers conducting a two-year study from 1964 to 1966, on the Green and Yampa rivers in Dinosaur National Monument, a reserve in northeastern Utah and northwestern Colorado, collected only 67 bonytails. Two years later, another team of researchers studying the same area found that the bonytails were even less common and reported that no evidence of bonytail reproduction could be found in any of the sampling areas.

The bonytail chub, like the other endemic Colorado River basin fishes, has evolved several morphological adaptations for life in the turbulent rivers. The bonytail's eyes are small and it probably relies on other senses for direction in the silty waters. The scales are small and are deeply embedded in the skin to minimize the body's surface resistance to the friction created by the swift currents in the water. The bonytail chub's popular name arose as a description of the fish's distinctive pencil-thin tail which terminates in a large, deeply forked caudal fin. The reduced circumference of the tail and the deep "V" of the fin reduce the drag on the bonytail chub during swimming, particularly against a current, and increase the efficiency of propulsion. The bonytail chub's head is somewhat flattened and dorsally concave; the rest of the back rises at a gradual, sloping angle from the back of the head to produce a slight hump. The bonytail's hump is much less pronounced than the humps of the razorback sucker and the humpback chub.

Eating mostly terrestrial insects, plant debris, and algae, the bonytail chub is an omnivorous feeder and grows to an average length of about twelve inches and weighs about one pound. During the spawning season the male bonytails become orange-red on their lower sides and belly, which normally appear silvery white. The females retain their typical coloration, which is silver over most of the body with a light greenish tinge along the back. The bonytail chubs spawn in schools, where dozens of individuals swim over a gravelly or rocky bottom. Each female is escorted by three to five males and the eggs are fertilized externally as the female scatters them over the gravel to which they adhere. A single female can deposit as many as 10,000 eggs. The bonytail chub does not spawn in water temperatures below 65°F, possibly an important factor contributing to its decline.

The bonytail chub disappeared from most of its original range throughout the Colorado River basin primarily because of the many dam impoundments and water diversions that destroyed most of its habitat as well as the introduction of non-native fishes. Although a few bonytail chubs may still exist in the Colorado River in Utah and Colorado, they have been extirpated from the Green, Gunnison, and Yampa rivers where they were once common. They disappeared from the Green River in Wyoming when Flaming Gorge Dam transformed the warm river into the cold, clear reservoir. In the lower Col-

7–4
Hoover Dam is one of several large dams in the Colorado River system that have contributed to the decline of native fishes. Photo by J. D. Williams.

orado River basin diversions from the Salt and Gila rivers for irrigation lowered the mainstream flow or completely dried the streams, eliminating the bonytail chub. As the Colorado River along the Nevada/Arizona and California/Arizona borders became a series of reservoirs, a few populations of bonytail chubs remained in the impounded rivers and have persisted in the reservoirs. Currently only one of these reservoirs, Lake Mohave, supports a population of bonytails.

The Lake Mohave population of bonytail chubs currently consists of old individuals and no juveniles have been reported for years. The remaining adult bonytail chub population is preyed on and must compete for food and living space with several non-native fishes that are better adapted for life in a lake environment. The few juveniles produced by surviving bonytail chubs in the unimpounded Colorado River regions have stiff competition from the non-native red shiner and redside shiner, two baitfishes that entered the river system after escaping from the buckets of fishermen. The shiners tend to prefer the same habitats as the juvenile bonytail chubs, where they compete for space and food resources.

The bonytail chub was proposed for classification as an endangered species in 1978, but did not obtain that status until 1980. Of the four fishes endemic to large rivers of the Colorado River basin, the bonytail chub is the most critically endangered. Considerable effort by state and federal agencies will be required during the next decade to prevent the extinction of the bonytail chub.

## Colorado Squawfish
## *Ptychocheilus lucius*

(Color plate 7.)

*The air was balmy, no wind blew, and a universal quiet prevailed when suddenly Jack uttered several exclamations not entirely in harmony with the moment. He thought his precious hook was caught on a snag. Pulling gently in order not to break his line, the snag lifted with it and presently he was astonished to see not the branch of a tree or a water-logged stick, but the head of an enormous fish appear above the surface. Had there been some splashing he would have been prepared for the extraordinary sight, but the monster came with barely a wiggle as if it did not know that it was about to be caught. He was successfully landed in the middle cabin of the boat, which was empty except for some water, and lay there unhurt as if it were the natural place for him. Casting again another of the same kind came fourth, and then a third. The longest appeared to be the length of the cabin, as he floated in the water, and that was four feet. He was at least 30 to 36 inches with a circumference of 15 inches. These fish are called Colorado River salmon. The flesh was white and they seemed to us good eating.*

*Account by historian F.S. Dellenbaugh of
a fishing trip on the Colorado River
mainstream in August, 1872*

The endangered Colorado squawfish, which Dellenbaugh described as the Colorado River salmon, was also known to early western settlers as "white salmon" due to its salmon-like spawning migrations, its delicate flesh, and—unlike the torpid behavior of Dellenbaugh's specimens—its spirited fight when hooked. The Colorado squawfish, *Ptychocheilus lucius,* however, is not a salmon but a minnow. Most minnows are small enough to fit on a hook and are commonly used as baitfish, but the squawfish can grow to five feet long and weigh fifty to eighty pounds. Although individuals in the currently depleted squawfish populations rarely exceed fifteen pounds, the squawfish is the largest minnow in North America.

Until their rapid decline in the 1930s, squawfish were a significant source of food in the Colorado River region. Archaeologists have found squawfish remains in the trash heaps and kitchen ruins of indian civilizations dating between 1000 and 1700 A.D. The indians caught the squawfish with nets made out of webbing stretched between two sticks. When the settlers arrived, squawfish were still so abundant in the lower Colorado River's Gila, Salt, and Verde river tributaries that they swarmed into the irrigation ditches that the farmers dug away from the river. According to historic documents, the farmers often stood on the banks of the ditches with pitchforks and removed hundreds of huge fishes for fertilizer. Ironically, the commercially important "white salmon" were also used to supplement the diets of the survey and construction crews building the dams that destroyed the squawfishes' habitat and contributed to their decline.

Once found throughout all the large streams and tributaries of the Colorado River basin in Wyoming, Colorado, Utah, New Mexico, Arizona, Nevada, California, and Mexico, the squawfish is now found only in the Colorado River and its tributary the Green River above Lake Powell Reservoir in eastern Utah, and western Colorado. The current distribution of the squawfish has been difficult to document due to the difficulty in sampling the turbulent, turbid, and isolated portions of the rivers it now inhabits.

At present biologists believe the region of most consistent reproductive success for the squawfish is in the Utah segment of the Green River. This area is the longest and least altered stretch of large river habitat remaining in the Colorado River basin. The 1962 release of the fish poison rotenone into 445 miles of the Green River above Flaming Gorge Dam on the Wyoming/Utah border eradicated the squawfish from the Wyoming segment of the Green River and depressed population levels in northeastern Utah. There are no squawfish in the cold, clear tailwaters below Flaming Gorge Dam in northeastern Utah either.

The squawfish gradually disappeared from the lower Colorado River basin following the 1935 closure of Hoover Dam. As one report notes, "changing the Colorado River into two reservoirs, Lakes Mead and Mohave, along the Nevada border seems to have effectively eliminated this interesting fish." The squawfish were poorly adapted for life in the reservoirs that formed above the dams, and the non-native game and baitfishes introduced into the reservoirs subjected the squawfish to additional stress. The squawfish's own voracious appetite may have contributed to its decline. Swallowing whole individuals of the introduced channel catfish, *Ictalurus punctatus,* some adult squawfish died of suffocation when the catfish's fin spines lodged in their throats. Other squawfish succumbed instead to the parasites they picked up from the non-native fishes. Many of the introduced non-native species traveled upstream from the reservoirs, forcing the juvenile squawfish out of the remaining river habitat. Below the reservoirs, alterations of the rivers' daily and seasonal flow patterns and the reduction of the water's natural turbidity and temperature fluctuations disrupted and depressed squawfish reproduction.

Dams and non-native fishes have not been the sole contributors to the squawfish's demise. A 1904 field biologist wrote in his notes that, in the late 1800s, squawfish were abundant in the Gila River tributary of the Colorado River in southern Arizona. The Gila River had pools deep enough for men to swim in and the "salmon" in the pools grew to 35 pounds. By the early 1900s the Gila River was virtually dry over most of its course and the "salmon" were gone from the little water that remained, apparently poisoned by the strong mineral pollutants that trickled downstream from the agricultural and mining works along the river. The severe depletion of the Colorado River basin water supply in recent years has continued to reduce the rivers' volumes, concentrating suspended solids and pollutants alike and further stressing the already hard-pressed squawfish.

Fossil records indicate that the squawfish, which have the flattened heads, streamlined bodies, and large, forked tails of fish adapted for life in river currents, were present during the Pleistocene Epoch around 2½ million years ago. The scientific name of the squawfish, *Ptychocheilus lucius,* means "folded lip pike," after the squawfish's well-defined lips and pike-like body. Biologists know little about this species' biology. Most of the published information is

7–5

Colorado River in the Grand Canyon once supported populations of endangered and threatened Colorado River fishes. Photo by J. D. Williams.

in the form of anecdotes and field observations that provide glimpses into the natural history of the squawfish. Such anecdotes indicate that before the dams were built, the squawfish moved upstream in large salmon-like spawning runs that biologists believe were triggered by increases in water temperature and river levels. The larger fishes apparently migrated over longer distances. Recent tagging studies indicate movements of some adult squawfish for a distance of one to two hundred miles. The migration triggers of water flow and temperature were obliterated by the damming, and the squawfish's movements and behavior have, most likely, been altered.

The spawning of the squawfish has never been observed in nature, and the fishes' preferences with respect to substrate, current velocity, and water quality remain unknown. Data from captive individuals in hatcheries indicate that the squawfish reach sexual maturity at six years of age, and begin to spawn after water temperatures have been at 65° to 75° F for about a month. Females lay their eggs, which are about two millimeters in diameter, over the bottom in low-current backwaters where the eggs adhere to the gravelly substrate. After two to five days of incubation, depending on water temperature, the fry emerge and subsist on small crustaceans, insect larvae, and aquatic insects. As the squawfish grow, the voracious appetite that made these fishes the top carnivores in the Colorado River basin asserts itself and juveniles begin to feed on other fishes. Adult squawfish appear to eat seasonally, feeding frequently during the spring pre-spawning period and infrequently during the winter. Adults have been observed to ingest not only other fishes, but even small mammals and birds that fall into the river.

The Colorado squawfish was first placed on the Endangered Species List in 1967, and came under the full protection of the 1973 Endangered Species Act in January 1974. In 1978, the U.S. Fish and Wildlife Service organized the Colorado River Fishes Recovery Team. A group of biologists from state and federal agencies, and universities have examined the plight of squawfish and proposed a recovery plan whose principal goal is the establishment and maintenance of self-sustaining populations of squawfish in part of the species' historic range. The populations were to be established through an artificial propagation and stocking program set up at the Willow Beach National Fish Hatchery in Arizona. The propagation program was dealt a setback in November 1980, when three men from Las Vegas stole 14 of the 27 adult squawfish from the hatchery. Twelve of the stolen squawfish were females. Their loss depleted the hatchery's 1980 wild-captured broodstock of fishes brought in each year to supply new genetic material and thereby ensure the development of a healthy population. A federal grand jury indicted the men on felony charges of theft of government property, interstate transportation of stolen goods, and possession of an endangered species. The thieves evidently took the valuable fish to eat.

Biologist Karl Seethaler, in his 1978 thesis prepared at Utah State University, summed up the plight of the Colorado squawfish in the following statement: "The Colorado squawfish has long been a perplexing riddle: Usually misclassified, never properly understood, so prominent, and yet so elusive even to the most dedicated investigators. Its value appears to wax as its numbers wane, as ignorance yields to enlightenment. As an endangered species, it has been catapulted into renown in recent years because of public awareness and concern for vanishing wildlife. The squawfish is a dramatic symbol of the changes in the Colorado River ecosystem."

## Razorback Sucker
### *Xyrauchen texanus*

(Color plate 8.)

Like the humpback chub, *Gila cypha,* the razorback sucker, *Xyrauchen texanus* is among the oddest-looking freshwater fishes found in North America. Also known as the humpback sucker, the razorback was given the name *"Xyrauchen,"* or "razor nape," because of the prominent keel along the midline of its back in front of the dorsal fin. Rising at a steep angle from behind the head, this bony, sharp-edged hump or keel stabilizes the razorback in the turbulent waters and strong currents. Over millions of years the razorback's distinctive dorsal keel evolved from the elongation and expansion of the vertical spines on the vertebrae behind the head. Muscles which apparently give the razorback additional control for swimming in currents are attached at the bony keel. Another adaptation to river life is the razorback's flat, sloping head, which steadies the fish against the bottom as it feeds and offers little resistance to the on-coming currents. Paradoxically, despite these fast-water adaptations, the razorback sucker is often found in deep, low-current pools or eddies lateral to the main currents. The razorback's adaptations to swift water may have evolved aeons ago when there was greater flow and swifter waters in the channel of the Colorado River.

The razorback sucker probably evolved from the same ancestral stock that gave rise to the widespread sucker genus *Catostomus.* Because of the distinctive morphology of the razorback sucker, it is the only species in the genus *Xyrauchen.* The razorback is one of the largest suckers in North America, growing to three feet long and weighing between ten and fourteen pounds. The scientist who first described the species in 1860 thought that his specimens had come from the Colorado River in southern and central Texas, so he mistakenly named the fish *"texanus."* The razorback, however, is endemic to the Colorado River from Wyoming to Mexico, and was historically distributed throughout the river's mainstream and its major tributaries. The razorback now survives only in isolated segments of the Green and Colorado rivers in the upper basin and in portions of two reservoirs in the lower basin.

Once abundant in the Gila and Salt rivers and their tributaries in southern Arizona, razorback suckers were a staple of the Mohave Indians' diet until the 1900s. The white settlers in this area sold the razorbacks as "buffalo fish" during the early 1900s, and fisheries records show that as recently as 1949, one fisherman caught 7000 pounds of razorback suckers in Saguaro Lake below the Roosevelt dam on the Salt River. There were so many razorbacks that the fisherman took the entire catch in one season by dragging grab hooks through spawning schools of the fish. When Saguaro Lake was drained in 1966, not a single razorback remained. Razorbacks have also been extirpated from the

Gila River drainage in Arizona, where it once occupied all of the larger streams. Diverting water from many of the Gila River's tributaries dried up the Gila for much of the year, eliminating the razorback. Similar problems exist on larger tributaries throughout the Colorado River basin.

Researchers believe that high dams along the main channel of the Colorado River and some of its major tributaries, with the subsequent creation of a series of deep, cold reservoirs, killed off the razorback sucker from much of its original range. Razorbacks disappeared from the upper Green River after rotenone was released into 445 miles of the river and its tributaries just before Flaming Gorge Dam was closed in 1962. There are no razorbacks in the Flaming Gorge Reservoir created by the dam, or in the cold tailwaters below the dam.

The razorback suckers preferred habitat is warm flowing water, over sand, gravel or rocky bottom. However, they have been observed in some of the lower Colorado River basin reservoirs feeding along the shorelines where the wave action produces a current-like action. They feed on algae and insect larvae brought to the surface of the gravel or sand by the current action. Studies published in the late 1970s indicate that the razorback suckers were still fairly abundant in the lower basin reservoirs of Lakes Mead, Mohave, and Havasu; yet despite sitings of spawning razorback suckers in these lakes, no juvenile suckers have been found there. The razorback's lifespan can reach thirty years, and scientists fear that as the older fish die, even these remaining populations will disappear. Based on recent surveys, it appears that the population in Lake Mead has disappeared.

Before the dams were built, the razorback suckers made extensive spawning migrations in the early spring when water temperatures averaged between 54° and 68°F. The disruption that the dams have caused in this spawning behavior may account in part for the decline in the species' reproductive success. Dams are not the sole cause of the razorback sucker's decline. The species has also disappeared from areas like the Salt River canyon west of Phoenix, Arizona, even though there has been no physical alteration of the area. Non-native game and sport fishes such as largemouth bass, *Micropterus salmoides*, and channel catfish, *Ictalurus punctatus,* introduced into the reservoirs, as well as baitfishes like the red shiner, *Notropis lutrensis,* may impair the razorbacks' reproductive success further by preying upon the razorbacks' fry.

Hybridization has further depleted the already low razorback sucker populations in the Colorado River system. Razorback hybridization with native flannelmouth suckers, *Catostomus latipinnis,* is a well-documented occurrence, reported as early as the late 1800s. While hybrids occur throughout the basin, they are most frequently encountered in disturbed habitats such as below dams and areas of drastically reduced flow. The threat of the extinction of local populations by hybridization is magnified by the continued loss of habitat the razorbacks have suffered.

The Colorado River Fishes Recovery Team has begun a life history study of the razorbacks in Lake Mohave to fill in some of the gaps in our knowledge of this unique fish. In the upper Colorado River basin, biologists are surveying remote sections of the river to determine population levels of the razorback. The team also developed an artificial propagation program at the Willow Beach

National Fish Hatchery in Arizona, and the Dexter National Fish Hatchery in New Mexico which has produced thousands of razorback suckers for restocking suitable habitats in the lower Colorado River basin. The team researchers acknowledge that little or nothing can be done to restore the Colorado River system to its original state: That would require reversing the conditions that have so adversely affected the razorback suckers and other endemic fishes. Efforts should be made throughout the Colorado Basin to maintain the existing habitat and renovate former habitat. Captive propagation could be a critical factor in the razorback's survival. The team hopes that the reintroduction of the razorbacks into the least altered of their former habitats will establish several self-sustaining populations.

# Woundfin
## *Plagopterus argentissimus*

An ichthyologist once called the woundfin an "anteriorly-depressed, stream-lined torpedo," aptly describing the shape of this small minnow that is so well-adapted for life in the rapidly flowing and silted streams of the lower Colorado River basin. The woundfin rarely exceeds four inches in length, and its scaleless body and flat head, propelled by large powerful fins, allows it to slice through currents with little resistance. The eyes are reduced in size and are of little value in the murky waters that the woundfin inhabits. The sense of sight is supplemented by the chemical sensory information from taste buds located on two barbels that project downward from the woundfin's lips. The woundfin drags its barbels near the sandy ripples that the current creates on the river bottom. The taste buds detect aquatic insect larvae and protozoan-covered algae, the major food items of the woundfin's diet.

Two of the woundfin's distinctive morphological features are reflected in its popular and scientific names. Tan along the back and silver on its sides and belly, the woundfin blends with the sandy bottoms over which it is commonly found. Its scientific name *"argentissimus,"* latin for "most silvery," reflects that the woundfin is one of the most silvery of all North American minnows. The popular name "woundfin" refers to the stout sharp spines that extend into the tips of the dorsal and pelvic fins. The presence of spines in the fins of minnows is most unusual and has probably discouraged would–be predators from swallowing the woundfin.

The woundfin is endemic to the lower Colorado River system. Its original range included the Colorado River mainstream and large tributary rivers from southern Arizona north through eastern California and southern Nevada to the Virgin River, a mainstream tributary that flows into the Colorado River in southern Nevada from southwestern Utah and northwestern Arizona. In the Gila River basin, a Colorado River tributary in southern Arizona, the woundfin occurred as far upstream as the Salt River near Tempe, Arizona. The last woundfin found in the Salt and Gila rivers were collected around 1915. Droughts, agricultural diversions, dams, and introduced non-native fishes have eradicated the woundfin populations in the lower basin. Peak irrigation demands typically coincide with low water periods. Consequently the water diversions have dried large areas of the tributary streams of the Colorado River, destroying the woundfin's habitat. Six major dams on the Salt and Verde rivers and two on the Gila River have effectively cut off the flow to the lower reaches of the Salt and Gila rivers, except during extreme flood stages. These alterations have eliminated all populations of the woundfin in these three rivers.

The woundfin's range is now restricted to the Virgin River, where it is the most numerous of all the native fish species. Described by a scientist as an "aquatic desert" because of the relatively few species living in its waters, the Virgin River is a harsh desert river with extremely variable water flows and high sediment loads. During the winter and summer rainy seasons, local thunderstorms produce flash floods that roar down the river's steep valleys, scouring the bottom with their abrasive sediment load. In the late summer, however, droughts reduce parts of the river to a trickle and eliminate the flow entirely along several miles of the river upstream from the springs that feed it. Temperatures in the remaining waters often reach 90°F.

In 1776, cartographers for Spanish explorers named the Virgin River the "Sulfureous River," because of the hot sulfur springs that flow into the river in the southwestern corner of Utah. The Paiute Indians called it "Pah-rush" or "water that tastes like salt" and the "Pahroos" or "dirty rushing stream." The river's final name came when traders in the 1830s anglicized the Spanish name "Rio de la Virgin." In this harsh river, which U.S. Army Captain John C. Fremont described during an 1844 expedition as "the most dreary river I have ever seen," the woundfin continues to live and reproduce. While the river is "harsh" by most standards, the native fishes are well adapted to survive its extreme conditions.

7–7
Virgin River in Washington County, Utah is excellent habitat for the endangered woundfin. Photo by J. D. Williams.

Woundfin spawning begins in April and May, apparently triggered by the low flows and increased clarity of the water. The reduced flow lessens the chance that eggs, which are deposited on the sandy bottom, will be swept away by the current, and the decreased sediment load means that the eggs will not be buried as they develop. When the eggs hatch, the young woundfins remain in the shallows along the margin of the stream, outside the swift mainstream currents that they will inhabit as adults.

The woundfin's ability to survive in a habitat that most fishes could not possibly tolerate has protected it from predation and competition pressures from most introduced species. Unfortunately the red shiner, *Notropis lutrensis,* a bait minnow, was introduced by fishermen into the lower Colorado River in the 1950s. The aggressive red shiner, which was preadapted to fluctuating, extreme environments, rapidly spread throughout the lower basin. The red shiner now equally shares the lower Virgin River with the woundfin. The woundfin's survival is in jeopardy when faced with competition from the red shiner and the continued alteration of its habitat in the Virgin River.

The Virgin River supplies water to dairy and feedlot industries that return animal waste runoffs high in bacteria. In the past, irrigation returns contaminated with pesticides, fertilizers, and other mineralized pollutants have chemically altered the Virgin River waters. Now, two Virgin River water projects proposed in the late 1970s threaten to further alter the river. The Allen-Warner Valley Energy Project, a 50 megawatt, coal-fueled power plant on the Virgin River mainstream, requires the construction of a 45,000-acre-foot Warner Valley reservoir. A 1977 report on the anticipated impact of the Allen-Warner project, the largest project ever attempted on the Virgin River, predicted that the power plant and reservoir would affect the Virgin River mainstream from Hurricane, Utah, to the river's entrance into Lake Mead on the southern Nevada border, a distance of more than 75 miles.

The project will reduce mainstream flows for the river. With a reduction in flow, the river would lose the scouring action that maintains the pool habitats, important for the woundfin and other native species, especially during periods of low flow. The project includes a desilting station that would return 25–35 percent of the suspended solids removed from the diverted waters to the depleted mainstream flow, which could not carry the excess load. The sediments would eventually be deposited in the stream bed near the plant, reducing the area and quality of habitat for the woundfin. Furthermore, the reduced flows would increase the salinity of the river during winter, thereby increasing the rate of mineral deposition on the river bottom and decreasing available habitat. Finally, at minimum low water levels, the woundfin and other fishes would be crowded into the few pools remaining along the river's intermittent course, enhancing the transmission of parasites and diseases.

A second proposed Virgin River project, the LaVerkin Springs Desalination Project, also would jeopardize the woundfin by altering its habitat. The project is designed to produce more water for the thirsty southwestern area of Utah by removing salt and other minerals from water issuing from the sulfur springs at LaVerkin, Utah. The fresh water from this project would be diverted to the towns and cities in the region, decreasing the amount of water in the Virgin River. This translates into less habitat for the woundfin.

The woundfin was first placed on the Department of Interior's Endangered Species List in 1967. Biologists attempted to transplant the woundfin into four streams in Arizona at the periphery of the woundfin's historic range, but the efforts failed. In 1979, a group of biologists sponsored by the U.S. Fish and Wildlife Service formed the Woundfin Recovery Team and developed a Woundfin Recovery Plan. The goal is to establish self-sustaining populations of the woundfin in the Virgin River and at least two other streams in the woundfin's historic range to secure the woundfin from extinction. The recovery team's success will depend to a large extent on the outcome of the proposed Virgin River energy and water projects. In the final analysis, survival of the woundfin depends on whether the Virgin River habitat is eventually upgraded and stabilized.

The reason for saving the woundfin and preventing the further deterioration of the Virgin River ecosystem is stated in the conclusion of one of the Allen-Warner project technical reports: "Irrigation projects in the southwest are generally shown to be short-lived in a geologic timescale, whereas continued productivity of a natural ecosystem is a long-term phenomenon. Therefore, we are trading a relatively short-term use of a natural resource for economic gain for long-term productivity of a natural ecosystem. Consequently, we are losing the availability of the knowledge contained in the ecosystem, a long-term benefit to man."

# Moapa Dace
## *Moapa coriacea*

The Moapa River originates from the warm outflow of more than twenty thermal springs in the northeastern part of Clark County, Nevada, and flows southward for 26 miles into the Overton Arm of Lake Mead. Before Hoover Dam was built and the Colorado River and the lower portion of the Virgin River were impounded, the Moapa River emptied into the Virgin River just above its confluence with the Colorado River. Heading south, the warm crystalline headwaters of the Moapa River cooled a little and picked up sediments, taking on the turbid appearance that earned the river its Paiute Indian name of "moapa" or muddy.

Five native fishes inhabit the Moapa River: the Moapa speckled dace, *Rhinichthys osculus moapae;* the roundtail chub, *Gila robusta;* the Moapa White River springfish, *Crenichthys baileyi moapae;* the desert sucker, *Catostomus clarki;* and the Moapa dace, *Moapa coricea.* A sixth native species, the woundfin, *Plagopterus argentissimus,* has been found in the Moapa River, but is not a permanent resident. As a result of the physical and chemical alterations of the river, the depletion of its headspring waters for commercial and domestic uses, and the introduction of exotic fish species, all of the native fishes in the Moapa River are either endangered or threatened.

The endangered Moapa dace is endemic to the headwaters of the Moapa River where the springs and their outflow maintain the water temperature between 82° and 90°F. Historically this habitat was chemically and physically very stable compared to downstream areas. The Moapa dace can tolerate the cooler temperatures and increased turbidity of the downstream waters, but is most abundant in the headwaters. In the upstream areas, it appears to prefer crystalline clear pool areas that support an abundant algal growth. The pools are three to fifteen feet wide, six inches to five feet deep, and are partially overgrown by a canopy of streambank vegetation. The gentle currents of the pools and streams flow over a substrate of gravel and pebbles, occasionally interrupted by sandy or muddy areas.

The Moapa dace, the only species of the genus *Moapa,* is among the smallest of the endangered fishes of the Colorado River basin. The Moapa dace reaches sexual maturity when only 1.3 to 3 inches long. Its small scales are deeply embedded in the skin, giving the skin the leathery texture from which the fish's scientific name *"coriacea,"* which means leathery, is derived. The Moapa dace is colored deep olive along its back and sides, with greenish brown patches on its upper sides and a wide, black stripe along the middle of its back. Its sides have a shining golden brown band that contrasts sharply with lighter colors of the sides. The Moapa dace is distinguishable from the similar roundtail chub and Moapa speckled dace by its prominent back stripe and by a black spot at the base of its tail. Virtually no detailed information exists on the life history of this tiny fish. The Moapa dace lives in schools and feeds primarily on insects. Like many warm spring desert fishes, they spawn year round, with peak spawning activities in the spring and summer.

Between 1933 and 1950 the Moapa dace was abundant in the Moapa River headwaters, and ichthyologists estimated that the species occupied 25 springs and about 10 miles of spring outflows. By 1964, the Moapa dace was rare in collections from the same area. In 1969, the International Union for Conservation of Nature and Natural Resources (IUCN) Red Data Book on the status of freshwater fishes estimated that the Moapa dace population numbered 500 to 1000 individuals. By 1977, the IUCN estimated that only "a few hundred" Moapa dace remained in the river. Current estimates indicate that the species exists in only three springs and less than two miles of outflow. Reproduction has been documented only in a one hundred yard stretch of outflow from one spring.

The dramatic decline in the Moapa dace population coincided with the introduction and establishment of at least two exotic fishes—the mosquitofish, *Gambusia affinis,* and the shortfin molly, *Poecilia mexicana*—which competed for the limited habitat resources and introduced new parasites. Ichthyologists estimate that a total of nine exotic species have been introduced into the Moapa River, seven of which have become common to abundant since the early 1970s.

The Moapa dace has also suffered from destruction of habitat. Most of the Moapa River headwater springs are on private property and have been lined with gravel or cement and channeled into irrigation canals or water conduits and chlorinated for human consumption. In addition, much of the vegetation that once formed a protective canopy over the springs and pools has been cleared, further altering the environment. The only surviving populations of the Moapa dace are found in springs on agricultural land owned by the Church of the Latter Day Saints and on a section of private land managed by the Moapa Valley Water Users District.

7–6
Thermal headwater springs and pools are prime habitat for the Moapa dace. These springs are located in the headwaters of the Moapa River. Photo by J. D. Williams.

In 1967 the U.S. Fish and Wildlife Service listed the Moapa dace as an endangered species. They later, in 1979, purchased twelve acres of land and the water rights for several headsprings and established the Moapa National Wildlife Refuge. Under the provisions of a Recovery Plan developed in 1982, the Fish and Wildlife Service will delist the Moapa dace after restoring the species to five of approximately twenty of the species' original habitats. To accomplish this goal the U.S. Fish and Wildlife Service plans to reintroduce the Moapa dace into existing spring outflows and newly constructed stream and pool habitats on the Moapa National Wildlife Refuge. The dace also will be introduced into the Upper Plummer Springs, one of the original spring habitats of the Moapa dace that is currently part of the Desert Warm Springs Resort.

# VIII.

# Western Trouts

Fishermen's attraction to trout as a superb gamefish was an important factor in the decline of native western trout populations over the years. The fishermen's influence has come about by introducing the larger non-native trout species into western waters. The introductions of brown trout, *Salmo trutta;* brook trout, *Salvelinus fontinalis;* rainbow trout, *Salmo gairdneri;* and several subspecies of cutthroat trout, *Salmo clarki,* have led to hybridization with the native trouts, resulting in the loss of genetic purity and competition for available food and space within the aquatic habitats.

Fishermen are not solely responsible for this decline, however. Because of Man's alteration and overuse of the water resources in the western aquatic ecosystems, the native western trout populations have dwindled and some species have been pushed to the brink of extinction. Habitat for western native trouts has been destroyed when water is diverted and stream flows reduced and when cattle overgraze adjacent rangeland and trample streambanks. Water quality problems resulting from timber harvesting and mining operations have reduced native trout populations in some streams.

One species that is quite prevalent in western North America is the cutthroat trout, *Salmo clarki.* Its name was first popularized by an editor of *Forest and Stream,* the leading sporting journal of the late nineteenth century. So common in the west that it was known as the "native trout," the cutthroat trout still boasts the widest distribution of any western trout species. Considered much more refined and beautiful than the rainbow trout, the cutthroat trout was revered by one of the greatest ichthyologists, David Starr Jordan. He was deadset against referring to such an elegant trout as a "cutthroat."

The classification of western trouts remains a confusing issue. All western trouts of the genus *Salmo* are genetically closely related and there are few sterility barriers to prevent hybridization. Because hybridization occurs, a whole spectrum of intermediate forms of western trout exist in some streams, making it extremely difficult to know the exact number of species and subspecies. The cutthroat trout consists of one species with fifteen subspecies. One of the western trouts featured in this section is a subspecies of cutthroat trout once thought to be extinct. Another subspecies of cutthroat trout, the Lahontan cutthroat, is featured in the Pyramid Lake chapter of this book. The remaining two species of western trout discussed in this section are closely related to each other. One is the only species of western trout still listed as endangered. Their stories reflect the problems faced by native western trouts today.

8–1
Introduced brook trout are serious competitors for most native western trouts. Photo by E. P. Haddon, U.S. Fish and Wildlife Service.

# Apache Trout
## *Salmo apache*

*There were no fish introduced into our streams between 1876 and 1917. The streams were always apparently stocked to capacity naturally. I personally remember that from 1898 to 1916 the fish were so plentiful that it was no trick for a boy to catch one hundred in a few hours or two hundred in a full afternoon. These fish were all of one kind; "Yellow Bellies" we called them. The Apache Indians did not eat fish and did not catch them. A superstition concerning them saved them for the white man. The first outside trout were brought in in 1917. We met the fish train in Holbrook, Arizona and brought them in by car in a wooden barrel. Holbrook is 96 miles north and it took all day. These were eastern brook and they were planted in the Colorado River above Greer. The next fish brought in were rainbow. When the South Fork Hatchery was built, ten miles from Springerville, in 1921, rainbow and Wyoming natives (Yellowstone cutthroat trout) were distributed to practically all the accessible streams.*

> Letter from E.C. Becker, of Springerville, Arizona,
> to Carl Hubbs, Ichthyologist, June 30, 1939

Becker and his contemporaries hardly suspected that introducing the brook trout, brown trout, and especially the rainbow trout into the waters inhabited by the native Apache trout would result in the Apache trout's becoming an endangered species less than sixty years later. Prior to the introduction of these non-native species, the Apache trout abounded throughout six hundred miles of streams in the White Mountains of Arizona. In the early nineteenth century, the western settlers, grouped into large parties for protection against the indians, would travel to the headwaters of the Salt and Little Colorado Rivers to fish for the plentiful "yellow bellies." The catch was salted in barrels and preserved for the lean winter months. The range of the Apache trout included the White and Black River drainages of the Gila River basin, the headwaters of the Little Colorado drainage, and the Blue River, a tributary of the San Francisco River drainage, all located in the White Mountains of east central Arizona.

Today, the range of Apache trout population has dwindled to 5 percent of its original distribution, and the fish occur in only thirty miles of the original six hundred miles of streams. The streams are located on the 1.6 million acres of the Fort Apache Indian Reservation and the Apache-Sitgreaves National Forest. The headwaters of the White and Black river drainages, coursing down the reservation's White Mountains from elevations as high as 7000 to 9000 feet, contain the greatest abundance, thousands of Apache trout.

Once the sole salmonid resident of these river drainages, the native Apache trout has been rapidly displaced by the introduced trout species. The brown and brook trout compete with the Apache trout for food and space, and prey upon the native trout's fry. Perhaps the greatest reason for the decline of the Apache trout population is the hybridization of the native population through breeding with the introduced rainbow trout. The breeding seasons of the rainbow and Apache trout overlap, and random mating between the two species has virtually eliminated pure Apache trout stock. The offspring of the Apache-rainbow trout matings are genetically distinct from either parent and are readily distinguishable. As successive generations of offspring mate with each other or with the more plentiful rainbow trout stock, their genetic composition diverges more widely from that of the pure Apache trout stock, and the native species becomes extinct through hybridization.

The competition for food, living space, and mates pushed the Apache trout to more protected and inaccessible habitats in the isolated, high altitude head-waters of the mountain rivers. By the late 1940s and 1950s, the only known populations of Apache trout existed on the Fort Apache Indian Reservation. Appalled at the drastic decline in the number of streams containing the non-hybridized, native trout, Ronnie Lupe, the chairman of the White Mountain Apache tribe, made the initial effort to conserve the species from extinction. On March 24, 1955 the White Mountain Apaches, working with the Arizona Game and Fish Department, banned sportfishing in all of the reservation streams thought to contain genetically pure Apache trout. These populations appeared to be untouched by rainbow trout, and the only other threat to them came from anglers.

As interest in protecting the Apache trout from extinction grew, the Arizona Game and Fish Department, the White Mountain Apaches, and the U.S. Fish and Wildlife Service, implemented a hatchery propagation program to raise non-hybridized Apache trout and transplant them into other streams. In 1962, fishery biologists netted stock of a pure strain of Apache trout from Ord Creek (which today no longer holds any of the native trout) on the Fort Apache Indian Reservation and propagated the fish at the Arizona Game and Fish Department's Sterling Springs Hatchery near Flagstaff. From 1965 to 1974, the propagated trout were released into Bear Canyon Lake and Lee Valley Lake in the Apache-Sitgreaves National Forest; Christmas Tree Lake on the Fort Apache Indian Reservation; renovated streams in the Kaibab, Tonto, and Coronado National Forests; and in Becker Lake, managed by the Arizona Game and Fish Department. The introduced trout species were removed from all of these locations so that the Apache trout stocks would have a chance at repopulating the waters without the threat of predation, competition, or hybridization.

The White Mountain Apaches and the federal and state agencies also de-veloped a management plan to reclaim the streams that once held the Apache trout. They erected fish barriers across the streams to keep out the unwanted rainbow, brown and brook trouts. Sun and Moon creeks were reclaimed through these efforts and an impoundment, Christmas Tree Lake, was created at their confluence to provide an additional breeding and feeding area for the native species. The White Mountain Apache Tribe's outstanding efforts to ensure the survival of the Apache trout earned the tribe the U.S. Department of the Interior's Conservation Service Award in 1969.

During the conservation effort, wildlife management authorities and sci-entists learned some of the details of the Apache trout's natural history. It is a very attractive trout with a dark, olive-green back, yellow-gold sides and belly, and dark spots covering the flanks and top of the head. The iris of the Apache trout's eye has a distinctive horizontal, dark band that produces a mask-like effect. The body is chunky, and has a long dorsal fin. The adults are seldom more than ten inches long. The Apache trout's relatively small size is due largely to its narrow, shallow, restricted headwater stream habitat. The food supply in the high mountain streams is sparse, but the Apache trout cannot move downstream into richer waters because of the introduced competitors. Apache trout can reach much larger sizes than the stunted size that the headwater populations indicate. In 1973, an angler fishing in Bear Canyon Lake landed a specimen that was 22 inches long and weighed 3.6 pounds, the world record for this species.

The life history and ecology of the Apache trout varies from other trout species living in similar habitats. The Apache trout spawns in March through mid-June when sexually mature females lay between 70 and 1100 eggs, depending on the female's size. The eggs are laid in "redds," shallow, disc-shaped depressions that the female digs to various depths out of gravel in areas of flowing water, usually at the downstream end of pools. As the female deposits the eggs in the redd, the male hovering beside her fertilizes them. Once the eggs are fertilized, they are covered with gravel and incubated. After five or six weeks for incubation, the fry hatch, work their way out of the gravel, and enter the pools in search of plankton. The fry's food preferences change as they grow. All size classes of the trout eat aquatic and terrestrial insects.

The Apache trout, first listed as endangered in 1967, was given additional protection under the new Endangered Species Act of 1973, The new law prohibited taking Apache trout from either the tribal or public waters, and provided for the establishment of a recovery team which was organized in 1975. After studying how successful the efforts to preserve the pure populations of Apache trout had been, the recovery team decided to make this fish one of the first endangered species to be reclassified from endangered to threatened status. Some streams were reopened to fishing for this species, but the tribal waters of the Fort Apache Indian Reservation remained closed during 1975.

Currently, the main objective of the Arizona Trout Recovery Plan is to restore the Apache trout to a non-threatened status. The recovery team's plans include establishing thirty discrete populations of pure Apache trout throughout the native species' historic range. Only after this goal is achieved will the Apache trout be taken off all lists.

# Greenback Cutthroat Trout
## *Salmo clarki stomias*

(Color plate 9.)

The small greenish-gold trout called the greenback cutthroat trout is currently listed by the U.S. Fish and Wildlife Service as a threatened species. This rare trout, native to the eastern slope of the Rocky Mountains in Colorado and extreme southeastern Wyoming, was reclassified from endangered to threatened status in 1978. In 1937, its numbers had become so depleted that it was thought to be extinct. The story of the greenback cutthroat trout's fall

8–2

Frozen beaver pond in Rocky Mountain National Park, winter habitat of the greenback cutthroat trout. Photo by J. D. Williams.

to near extinction and comeback to a stage of guarded survival is one that is fairly typical of several endemic western trouts with restricted distribution.

The first two specimens of what would later be coined the greenback cutthroat trout were brought to the attention of ichthyologists by a surgeon, Dr. W.R. Hammond, who accompanied an Army expedition under the command of Lieutenant F.T. Bryant to Fort Bridger, Wyoming from Fort Riley, Kansas and back again in 1856. All of the specimens that the amateur natural historian had diligently collected during the exedition were gathered together, simply labeled "Fort Riley, Kansas," and shipped to the Philadelphia Academy of Sciences. A noted naturalist and geologist of his day, Dr. Edward D. Cope recognized the two preserved specimens as a form of cutthroat trout, but one that he had never seen before. Sixteen years later, Cope formally described the trout that was first found on an Army expedition as a new species and named it, *Salmo stomias*.

David Starr Jordan first placed the misnomer "greenback" on this species of trout in 1891. Actually the greenback is no "greener" in color than any other cutthroat trout of which it is a subspecies. The body of the greenback cutthroat is washed in green-gold with large black spots that are particularly pronounced on the rear one-third of the body. It is the spots and not the green color that most clearly distinguish the greenback from other closely related cutthroat trout subspecies. The greenback trout also has the typical bright reddish-orange slash under the throat, an inherited trademark which gives the cutthroat trouts their name.

In the late 1880s the greenback cutthroat trout was commonly found throughout its native range of the headwaters of the South Platte and Arkansas River drainages, lying almost entirely within the state of Colorado, except for some small headwater tributaries of the South Platte in southeastern Wyoming. It was the only trout found in these waters and was very abundant. Gamefishes attract fishermen, and although never as popular as the "Big Three" in trout circles (the rainbow, brown, and brook trouts), sportsmen fished for the greenback cutthroat with regularity and took a fair share of them. Even in the 1880s the greenback cutthroat was small by most standards, hardly pushing the scales to two pounds and stretching a couple of inches beyond the limits of a twelve-inch ruler. It is easy to understand why the fishermen lost some interest in the diminutive greenback cutthroat when state and federal fishery agencies began introducing the Big Three in good trout waters throughout the country. Moreover, the Yellowstone cutthroat trout, a larger close relative of the greenback cutthroat, was considered for planting in the home waters of the Colorado native. Because of the habitat requirements of trouts, the only place to introduce the big, exotic gamefishes was in waters already inhabited by the greenback.

By the 1890s, the die had been cast. While the planting of the four non-native trouts was superficially innocent, the greenback began to severely feel the effects. These effects began to appear in two ways. The introduction of the Yellowstone cutthroat and rainbow trouts was causing the hybridization of native greenbacks and thus cutting down the number of genetically "pure" greenback stock. Like the greenback cutthroat, the urge to spawn in the Yellowstone cutthroat and rainbow trouts is closely attuned to changes in water temperature. As the days get longer and winter slips away, the rising temperature of the water stirs up the instinctual desire to begin the spawning ritual. With behavioral rituals so similar in these three trout species, hybridization or cross-breeding is almost a given. When the water temperatures are just right, the trout are not particular in selecting mates, so long as the male and female participate in similar courtship rituals. The consequence of breeding with these two trouts is a loss of identity for the greenback cutthroat. Genes are mixed and each generation passes on this genetic impurity.

Brook and brown trouts also compete with the greenback for space and food. While the brown trout poses a problem for the greenback, the brook trout populations have had a more significant effect by reducing the numbers of native greenback cutthroats. Fortunately, hybridization is not a problem with either the brook trout or brown trout because they spawn in response to the falling water temperatures of autumn. But brook trout are extremely opportunistic; monopolizing both the food and space available, especially in small headwater streams preferred by the greenback. In a survey of one Colorado creek, only ten greenback cutthroats were left among hundreds of brookies.

Aspects of the brook trout's life history enable it to successfully exploit the greenback's habitat. First, the brook trout becomes sexually mature at an earlier age than the greenback cutthroat. This, in effect, allows the brook trout to produce more offspring per lifespan than the greenback trout. When this factor is multiplied by a number of generations, it represents a swamping effect by the brook trout. Second, brook trout fry emerge earlier from their spawning gravel than the greenback cutthroat fry. What the greenback fry finds upon

8–3
Hidden Valley Creek, typical of the small stream habitat of greenback cutthroat trout in Rocky Mountain National Park, Colorado. Photo by J. D. Williams.

finally emerging from its spawning gravel are brook trout fry that are larger than the greenback fry. This size advantage conferred upon the brook trout fry because of earlier emergence gives them a competitive edge in feeding upon aquatic insects as well as added clout in winning territorial disputes with the greenback fry.

Without question, the non-native brook trout in these Colorado waters has pressured the greenback cutthroat to near extinction. The brook trout is now the dominant trout species in small, headwater tributary streams in the Rocky Mountains. In order to transplant pure greenback cutthroat trout, all other trouts must first be removed by either electroshocking or chemical treatment. While the greenback seems to be unable to successfully co-exist with the introduced trout species, it does show a greater tolerance to colder conditions than non-native trouts.

There currently appears to be only two genetically pure natural populations of greenback cutthroat trout left. One sanctuary is Como Creek, an isolated tributary of North Boulder Creek in Boulder County, Colorado, a part of Roosevelt National Forest. The second population is found in the headwaters of the South Poudre River above a barrier falls (which keeps other trout species from entering) in Larimer County, Colorado. Other pure, but introduced populations of this native trout are now found in Houglass Creek, South Fork of Huerfano Creek (although brook trout are now dominating portions of this stream); Cascade Creek (a small isolated tributary of the South Huerfano River); Black Hollow Creek; Big Thompson River; and Bear Lake in Rocky Mountain National Park. Greenback trout were transplanted to Hidden Valley Creek in Rocky Mountain National Park after chemical treatment removed the brook trout population in 1973. Propagation of the greenback looked good in the following two years, but by the fall of 1976, brook trout had somehow began to repopulate the creek. Without reduction or elimination of the brook trout, it will only be a matter of time before the greenback is once again eliminated by the brook trout in this creek.

While introduced trout species have pressured the greenback with competition and hybrid extinction, Man has also contributed directly to the demise of this rare trout with several forms of habitat destruction. Effluents from mining, industry, and human waste have had devastating effects on the greenback's habitat. The stream flows have been altered by the installation of irrigation and hydraulic power diversion structures. These streams have also been physically damaged because of improper watershed uses involved with timbering, overgrazing by domestic livestock, and land development such as constructing ski areas and highways.

We hope that some day in the not-too-distant future the greenback cutthroat trout will inhabit more of the eastern slope streams of the Rocky Mountains in Colorado. Though its current total population numbers only in the thousands, efforts are continuing to bring the greenback cutthroat back to the "good ol' days" of the late 1800s before non-native trouts were introduced into portions of its native range.

# Gila Trout
## *Salmo gilae*

Almost a century ago, the Gila trout, *Salmo gilae,* swam undaunted in the headwaters of the Gila River basin in southeastern New Mexico and central Arizona. The Gila trout was so numerous, in fact, that fishermen claimed that it was possible to catch the so-called mountain or speckled trout at a rate of one a minute. Historically this pan-sized fish reached a length of eighteen inches and weights of about two pounds. More recently, the Gila trout has been pushed into small streams with limited habitat that limits their growth. A large individual Gila trout today barely tips the scales at one-quarter of a pound. Populations of Gila trout are currently restricted to a few small headwater streams of the Gila River system in southeastern New Mexico. Conservation plans call for the reintroduction of the Gila trout into Arizona.

The heavy fishing pressure that faced the Gila trout initially seemed to be one reason for its decline within the Gila River. In addition, the alteration of its habitat in the Gila River basin pushed the Gila trout out of some tributaries. To make matters worse, non-native trout were introduced into the Gila trout's habitat.

To curb the decrease in trout numbers, a serious mistake was made, primarily because of the lack of knowledge concerning the biology of trouts. Several fish hatcheries in the area began rearing rainbow trout to replace the losses suffered by the Gila trout. The rainbow trout were introduced into the Gila River and its tributaries to the delight of New Mexico's anglers. The fishermen no longer worried as much about the Gila trout, for a new trout that grew to larger dimensions and possessed superb fighting abilities had caught their attention. To the horror of biologists, however, the introduced rainbow trout was coexisting so well with the remaining stock of Gila trout that it was also spawning with them. The non-native rainbow trout were rapidly hybridizing with the Gila trout and destroying the purity of the Gila trout's genetic background.

It was relatively easy to propagate rainbow trout, but biologists were having greater difficulty propagating the native Gila trout. Between 1923 and 1939, attempts were made to propagate the Gila trout at Jenks Cabin Hatchery in the heart of the Gila Wilderness and Glenwood Hatchery in Glenwood, New Mexico. Both hatcheries were finally abandoned because of their poor accessibility and low production of fishes, which made it economically unrealistic to continue the projects. Another attempt to rear the Gila trout was tried again at Glenwood in the late 1950s and 1960s, but once again the effort was terminated.

What began as a gradual decline in the populations of Gila trout accelerated to the point where genetically pure populations of Gila trout no longer existed where rainbow trout were present. Hybridization is considered to be the single most important reason for the endangered status of this western trout. All of the other western trouts that were designated as endangered have made progress toward recovery and have subsequently been reclassified to threatened status. While progress has been made toward its recovery, the Gila trout is the only western trout that retains the endangered classification.

The rainbow trout is not the only salmonid to bring grief to the hapless Gila trout. The Gila trout must compete with the brown trout for its food, aquatic insects, and for living space in the waters of the Gila National Forest and Gila Wilderness. By 1950, the onslaught of competition and hybridization by these non-native trouts was so extensive that only five pure populations of Gila trout remained. They were all in New Mexico in small headwater streams with physical barriers that prevented the migration of the brown and rainbow trouts into Gila trout habitat.

During this time the Gila trout, which up to this point had not had a true identity, became a full-fledged species. Robert R. Miller described the new species in 1950, based on specimens collected from Main Diamond Creek in the Gila National Forest and the Glenwood Fish Hatchery. Like the Apache or Arizona trout, its closest salmonid relative, the Gila trout has a deep, stout body. The dorsal and caudal fins are spotted and the tips of the dorsal, anal, and pelvic fins are white, much like the brook trout. The sides of the Gila trout are yellow to an olive-yellow with a faint rosy pink band running the entire length of the body in adults. This pink banding pattern and the proliferation of small, oval-shaped spots differentiated the Gila trout from the Apache trout. Originally the Gila and Apache trouts were considered to be one and the same fish.

Current estimates put the total Gila trout population at 10,000 individuals with more than half of that population residing in Main Diamond Creek. The fragments of information about the life history of this endangered native trout come from biologists who concentrated their study on the population found in Main Diamond Creek. In May and June, the female carefully deposits between 75 and 200 eggs in a redd. By early June, the young fry begin to work their way out of the gravelly substrate and spend the summer feeding in shallow, protected areas. The young Gila trout are opportunistic as they forage for the caddisfly, mayfly, and other aquatic insect larvae that inhabit the streams. The fry are not very choosy about what types of aquatic invertebrates they consume and feed on the most available organisms.

Even the opportunistic nature of the Gila trout was not enough to keep its place in the streams when the non-native trouts exerted their competitive pressure and hybridization threats. These threats, combined with habitat loss and continued fishing pressure, began to take such a toll on Gila trout, as the propagation attempts were failing, that in 1958 the New Mexico Game and Fish Commission placed a ban on fishing for the Gila trout in Main Diamond Creek. The U.S. Forest Service provided further protection of the watershed area by restricting livestock grazing near the Gila trout habitat to only every other year.

In the small protected headwater streams in the Gila National Forest, safe from the rainbow and brown trout pressures, flood, drought, and fire are the major threats to the Gila trout populations. These small headwaters must have pools with adequate cover and depth to provide shelter for the Gila trout during periods of drought and floods. Currently, the Gila trout is known to exist as genetically pure populations in five streams within the Gila National Forest. Pure populations of the New Mexico native are found in the Main Diamond and South Diamond creeks in the Black Range Primitive Area of

Gila National Forest as well as Iron, McKenna, and Spruce Creeks, which are all upper Gila River tributaries in the Gila Wilderness Area.

Gila trout from Main Diamond Creek have provided transplant populations for three additional streams. The first stream to receive transplants of the Gila trout was McKnight Creek, a very small stream without any native or introduced trouts. For additional protection, an artificial barrier was installed to thwart any future fish intrusions from downstream areas. In November, 1970, about three hundred Gila trout were transferred from Main Diamond Creek to McKnight Creek. A severe drought hit McKnight Creek in 1971, reducing the population to about twenty individuals. A second transplant of 110 Gila trout was made in April 1972. At the same time, 89 Gila trout from the Main Diamond Creek stock were transplanted into Sheep Corral Creek, an area plagued by overgrazing by livestock. Finally in 1974, Gap Creek in Prescott National Forest, Arizona received 65 Gila trout transplants. All transplanted Gila trout have been seen successfully reproducing and gradually increasing within these three streams. However, each of the streams are small and often intermittent during the summer and fall. This limits the available habitat for the Gila trout.

Though the Paiute, greenback cutthroat, Lahontan, and Apache trouts have all been reclassified from endangered to a threatened status, the Gila trout remains the only trout listed as endangered under the Endangered Species Act. This status affords the Gila trout a higher priority for recovery and a chance to survive . . . perhaps even to expand into the better habitat of its former native range, now occupied by the non-native trouts. The independent group of biologists working under the auspices of the U.S. Fish and Wildlife Service has developed the Gila Trout Recovery Plan with the goal of improving the status of the Gila trout to the point that it can be removed from the endangered and threatened species list.

# IX.

# Texas Spring Fishes

Springs have played an important role throughout the history of Texas. These pools of high quality water that flow from underground reservoirs in arid lands with little surface water have always attracted people. The Pueblo Indians used to settle near springs and irrigate their crops with the clean, clear spring waters. When white men came to Texas they clashed many times with the indians to gain possession of the springs. When a network of forts were established across the vast Texas landscape, most were situated alongside springs to obtain a constant supply of pure water.

Springs were oases to those traveling the old stagecoach roads and later served as an energy source for mills and hydroelectric power plants. By the late 1800s health or medicinal spas sprang up around the more mineralized springs—people thought the dissolved mineral contents cured many ailments. Towns relied heavily on spring water. At least two hundred towns picked up the name of the springs for their own town name.

When white explorers first arrived in the region that is now Texas, four very large springs existed. In order of decreasing size, they were Comal, San Marcos, Goodenough, and San Felipe Springs. Today only two, Comal and San Marcos, remain as very large springs. Goodenough Spring is flooded under ninety feet of water from the International Amistad Reservoir. Flow has been greatly reduced or even halted from this once very large spring which the Spanish explorer, Castano de Sosa, may have visited in 1590 during his exploration of the Rio Grande and Pecos River. The water level of San Felipe Springs in the Edwards Aquifer has fallen drastically because of well pumping in the immediate area. The springs, named in honor of the king of Spain after a mass was held there by Franciscan Fathers in 1657, is still the sole water supply for the city of Del Rio and furnishes irrigation water for the only winery in Texas.

Of the 281 major and historically significant springs scattered throughout Texas, 65 no longer exist. Springs in the western portion of the state have particularly rough conditions, as this area gets only one-seventh the precipitation that the eastern portion receives. Groundwater reservoirs get much less natural recharge, making their water level more susceptible to lowering by deep well pumping. The decline of spring flows probably began soon after Texas was first colonized by the Spaniards. Deforestation and heavy pasture grazing by livestock probably reduced the amount of recharge going back into the underground reservoirs. Drilling of wells no doubt reduced the artesian pressure on the springs. The natural "fountains" as early explorers described the springs, continue to dry up because of heavy groundwater pumping for agricultural, industrial, and residential use. Surface reservoirs, like that which swallowed Goodenough Spring, have inundated several smaller springs. Goodenough Spring was the only habitat for the Amistad gambusia, *Gambusia amistadensis,* which now exists only in captive populations.

About 50 percent of all Texas springs issue from two large underground reservoirs known as the Edwards (Balcones Fault Zone) and the Edwards-Trinity (Plateau) aquifers. The largest Texas springs are found along the Balcones Fault Zone, an area where rock faults have formed an impervious dam trapping the waters of the Edwards limestone underground reservoir. The water which is under artesian pressure usually finds its way to the surface along fault planes. The Edwards-Trinity (Plateau) aquifer produces gravity springs where the recharge water percolates downward until it reaches impervious clays. Then the water moves laterally and emerges as springs in a valley or in stream beds.

The four troubled fishes included in this chapter live in springs of either the Edwards or Edward-Trinity aquifers. Their plights illustrate the difficulties of living in a limited aquatic habitat that has attracted Man's attention for hundreds of years.

# Comanche Springs Pupfish
## *Cyprinodon elegans*

The Comanche Springs pupfish was discovered in 1853 in Comanche Springs, but has not been seen there since the headwaters went dry back in 1955. Once the flow of water from Comanche Springs was so great that as early as 1875 more than 6000 acres of farmland were irrigated. Captain William Whiting of the U.S. Calvary described the springs in 1849 as ". . .a clear gush of water which bursts from the plain, unperceived until the traveler is immediately upon it. . . abounding in fish and soft-shell turtles." In 1904, these waters from the Edwards-Trinity aquifer were used to power a cotton gin. The now dry headwaters of Comanche Springs lie within a park in the present city limits of Fort Stockton, Pecos County, Texas.

122

9–1

Much of the remaining habitat for the Comanche Springs pupfish is cement lined irrigation canals. Photo by J. D. Williams.

Nevertheless, the Comanche Springs pupfish has yet to go the way of extinction. Although it was presumed extinct for several years, it has been classified as an endangered species since 1967. One hundred twenty miles away is the only other historic locality where the Comanche Springs pupfish was found. The last individuals of this tiny pupfish survive in a system of interconnected springs in the Toyahvale-Balmorhea area of Reeves County, Texas. Within this maze of springs, the pupfish is mainly found in a system of earthen and concrete irrigation canals fed by waters from Phantom Lake Spring, and in Giffin and San Solomon Springs which together form an extensive, shallow marsh draining into Toyah Creek. The waters from this system flow into a manmade reservoir, Balmorhea Lake.

When Comanche Springs dried up, the Comanche Springs pupfish lost roughly 50 percent of its historic habitat. Even today groundwater pumping and antiquated water laws continue to jeopardize every spring in west Texas; many have already failed and the water level is dropping in others. As developers continue to mine the underground water for municipal and agricultural ends, the water table and spring flows reach new dangerously low levels. The system of irrigation canals themselves in the Toyahvale-Balmorhea area have diverted the natural spring flows into the surrounding fields causing the neighboring marshes to dry up. The thoughtless elimination of these marshy regions has undoubtedly contributed to the decline in the population size of the Comanche Springs pupfish and other native fishes.

With a strikingly speckled color pattern displayed by the male and a more streamlined body than is characteristic of the pupfishes, the Comanche Springs pupfish rates with the Devils Hole pupfish as two of the most distinctive pupfishes in the United States. Although the Comanche Springs pupfish is unique in coloration and body form, its ecological needs are rather generalized. This pupfish has broad feeding habits, breeds during most months of the year, and finds fast-flowing water and standing water equally suitable for spawning. All of these traits make the Comanche Springs pupfish opportunistic in its habitat. Unfortunately these generalized ecological needs make other co-occurring species of fishes an immediate competitor of the pupfish, because any need that the competing species has will most likely overlap the needs of the pupfish. The most serious competitive threat to the Comanche Springs pupfish comes from the sheepshead minnow, *Cyprinodon variegatus,* which was introduced during the mid-1960s from the Gulf Coast. Hybridization with the introduced sheepshead minnow poses a serious problem for the Comanche Springs pupfish. Many fishes perform elaborate mating rituals before actually breeding. These rituals consist of a sequential series of behavioral signals or displays forming a language that only an individual from one's own species can understand. Without this species specific behavior there are few barriers to prevent hybridization of closely related species. The Comanche Springs pupfish unfortunately does not have an elaborate prespawning behavior. Biologists have found that in the Comanche Springs pupfish habitat, several species of fishes have been introduced over the years. Many of the non-native fishes have come into the pupfish's territory via the "baitbucket" method of introduction—a fisherman who has a few live baitfish left after a successful day of fishing feels magnanimous and lets those remaining fishes "free."

Wherever the Comanche Springs pupfish and the introduced sheepshead minnow are found in the same habitat, they will spawn together, producing hybrids. When biologists took a close look at the hybrid offspring that was produced, they noted an intriguing fact: No less than 80 percent of the hybrids were females; what hybrid males were found were sterile. The fertile female hybrids can continue to dilute the pure genetic integrity of the Comanche Springs pupfish by what is called "backcrossing." In backcrossing, the offspring will mate with the parental stock. In this case, the hybrid females will mate with either the Comanche Springs pupfish or the sheepshead minnow males to produce another slightly different group of hybrids. With a year-round breeding potential and a lack of preference regarding the type of spawning

9–2
Phantom Cave, source of spring water for one population of Comanche Springs pupfish.
Photo by J. E. Johnson.

habitat, flowing water and stagnant ponds seem equally suitable, the threat of hybridization to the Comanche Springs pupfish is of grave proportions.

The pressures exerted by all of these threats make the survival of the Comanche Springs pupfish tenuous at best. Flow from the large artesian spring system in the Balmorhea area is decreasing. Predictions paint a bleak picture for Phantom Lake Springs, which may become dry within fifty years. In fact the entire Balmorhea spring system will eventually be permanently destroyed if mining of the deep aquifers continues at the present rate.

Biologists are not taking the situation lightly and have already taken actions to buffer the gradual demise of the Comanche Springs pupfish's habitat. A small refugium that was constructed at Balmorhea State Recreation Area in 1974 by the Texas Parks and Wildlife Department provides a stable habitat for a population that today numbers several thousand. In New Mexico, a pure genetic stock of the Comanche Springs pupfish has been maintained by the U.S. Fish and Wildlife Service within the facilities of the Dexter National Fish Hatchery. This population, propagated from an original stock of only thirty individuals collected in an irrigation ditch fed by Giffin Springs may represent the future for the Comanche Springs pupfish. These fishes, numbering in the tens of thousands during the summer months, are being held for reintroduction purposes should a major catastrophe occur. At present, research projects underway will provide additional information on the life history of this distinctive Texas pupfish and perhaps increase its chances for survival.

# Clear Creek Gambusia
## *Gambusia heterochir*

In 1953, while searching the clear waters of Wilkinson Springs on the Clear Creek Ranch outside of Menard, Texas for a particular species of darter, two ichthyologists, Clark Hubbs and Kirk Strawn, chanced upon a small two-inch fish that resembled the common pet store guppy. The fish proved to be new to the world of science and was described in 1957. Ushered in as a new species of the family Poeciliidae, which includes the guppy, the small stocky fish became appropriately known as the Clear Creek gambusia. The male of the species is distinguishable from other poeciliids by a deep notch in the dorsal margin of its pectoral fin.

Wilkinson Springs is a series of interconnected limestone springs that emanate from the Edwards Aquifer and form Clear Creek. Shortly after the Wilkinson family built the Clear Creek Ranch in 1878, a low, earth-concrete dam was constructed a short distance from the headsprings to impound the spring waters for irrigation and domestic purposes. This dam ended Clear Creek's days as a freely-flowing spring run and created a headspring pool of impounded waters. Three additional dams were built downstream along the spring stream in the 1930s to enhance the irrigation efforts.

Historically the Clear Creek gambusia was probably found one or two miles downstream from the spring, but today it is found primarily in the two acre headspring pool formed by the initial dam. Here, in the impounded spring waters, this livebearing fish with a metallic sheen enjoys the clear, shallow, warm water, filled with dense vegetation and the amphipods upon which it feeds. Below this first dam, only a few scattered Clear Creek gambusia are found. The habitat below the first dam is quite different, having a noticeable change in the water quality with greater temperature fluctuations and higher pH readings. And here in these lower Clear Creek waters the mosquitofish, *Gambusia affinis,* replaces the Clear Creek gambusia as the dominant species. As has been the case in so many other aquatic systems, the mosquitofish poses predation and competition problems for native fishes. There is also the problem of hybridization for the Clear Creek gambusia. It is likely that the initial earth-concrete dams built prior to the 1900s protected the Clear Creek gambusia from hybridization with the mosquitofish. This barrier prevented the mosquitofish from entering the warm waters of the headspring pool during the winter. However, Clark Hubbs, co-discoverer of the small endemic fish, noted that hybridization was taking place in this last haven. The reason? The mosquitofish was getting into this upper pool through a breach in the original earth-concrete dam's containment wall.

The hybrids between the Clear Creek gambusia and the closely related mosquitofish are fertile; thus the genome of the endemic Clear Creek gambusia is in constant danger of genetic contamination. Hybridization poses several threats. First, there would be a decrease in the total number of Clear Creek gambusia recruits because some females would carry hybrid offspring instead of pure offspring. Second, there would be competition for food and space between the Clear Creek gambusia and the hybrids with a high probability that the hybrids could eliminate the Clear Creek gambusia from its only habitat, the headspring pool. Additional loss of pure Clear Creek gambusia would occur through the backcrossing of hybrids with Clear Creek gambusia.

During the 1930s, poplars were planted on the initial dam to shade the fishermen who frequented the creek searching for gamefish such as the largemouth bass, *Micropterus salmoides*. Unfortunately, high winds ripped several poplars from the bank, which in turn knocked down portions of the dam's containment wall. The Wilkinson family repaired the damaged portions of the wall and in 1938 decided to raise the wall another half a yard. The added volume of water contained by the higher wall created higher water pressures, resulting in several breaches in the dam. As a final aggravation, nutria (a large South American rodent brought into the U.S. for its fur) were introduced into the area in the 1940s. The nutria immediately began tunneling into the earthen dam. The holes made by the nutria were ideal beginnings for erosive forces to take over and enlarge them, opening the way for the mosquitofish to invade the headspring.

The Wilkinson family has done a superb job protecting the Clear Creek gambusia. But despite their protective measures, the pre-1900 dam containing the impounded spring waters and the only habitat of the Clear Creek gambusia continued to deteriorate into the 1970s. The planted poplars that had survived the high winds some forty years ago, and low shrubbery had developed vast root systems that were splitting the dam's containment walls. The situation became so grave that the Clear Creek gambusia was in real jeopardy. A major commitment had to be made if this endangered fish was to be saved.

Finally in late August of 1979, extensive repairs were made to the dam's containment wall with funds from the U.S. Fish and Wildlife Service. Members of the Clear Creek gambusia recovery team rebuilt long sections of the collapsed dam and removed the woody vegetation and their root systems. The many holes dug by the nutria were plugged up. The efforts made at this time helped to reduce the incidental water flow through the dam by more than 80 percent. The large breach noticed by Clark Hubbs back in 1971 was finally closed up to prevent the mosquitofish from any further immigration. The upper headspring pool will be monitored to see how the Clear Creek gambusia recovers from the past hybridization and competition problems.

The Clear Creek Ranch is now up for sale. Whether the new owners will be as conscientious as the Wilkinson family in protecting this endangered fish remains to be seen. There was talk in the past of converting the Clear Creek Ranch into resort housing. The construction and development activities needed for such a commercial venture would surely cause the total deterioration of the tiny headspring pool through siltation, possible chemical contaminants, and eutrophication. If this should happen, the Clear Creek gambusia, an endemic Texas springfish, along with other unique spring organisms would be lost.

# San Marcos River Fishes

Within the city limits of San Marcos, Texas, a series of springs issue from the Edwards Aquifer supplying the only source of drinking water for San Marcos and San Antonio. The Edwards Aquifer stretches for 175 miles, varying anywhere from five to forty miles wide across south central Texas. The clear, slightly alkaline water issues from the aquifer in a series of artesian springs that joins to form the San Marcos River. Three miles below its origin, the San Marcos River is joined by the Blanco River, then flows 35 miles southeast to empty into the Guadalupe River near the town of Gonzales, Texas.

Ever since the San Marcos River and its headsprings were first discovered by Spanish explorers searching for treasure in 1743, they have played an important role in history. San Marcos Springs aided travelers as a crucial rest stop on the El Camino Real (Spanish for "The Royal Road"), between Nacogdoches, Texas and Mexico. The springs served the same purpose on the Chisholm Cattle Trail from 1867 to 1895. Over the years the water supply from Edwards Aquifer provided power to operate cotton gins, mills, power plants, and even an ice plant. The giant freshwater shrimp, *Macrobrachium carcinus,* was once so plentiful in the river that a shellfishing industry was supported during the late 1800s. These behemoth invertebrates reached six to nine inches in length. Currently, an amusement park called Aquarena Springs operates boat trips, nature trails, and a recreated frontier village on the San Marcos River. Many fishermen, boaters, and swimmers now enjoy the San Marcos River.

Although running 38 miles to its termination in the Guadalupe River, the first three miles of the San Marcos River represent one of the most unique aquatic ecosystems found anywhere in the world. Spring Lake, an unusual forty acre body of water formed when some of the San Marcos River spring flows were dammed, is also a part of this extraordinary three-mile stretch of river. As soon as the San Marcos River joins with the Blanco River, the uniqueness of this habitat disappears and from this point downstream the San Marcos River resembles any typical Texas stream. But in the initial three miles of San Marcos Springs and River an extraordinary assemblage of endemic forms of life have evolved.

Biologists are impressed with the large number of endemic species, plants and animals, that are present in this section of the river. From the river vegetation, to the vast numbers of insects with aquatic life stages, to the top carnivores in the trophic web, this portion of the San Marcos River holds life forms that have evolved separately from the rest of the San Marcos River. It appears that a combination of the constant physical and chemical factors found in this stretch of river provides the unique habitat that resulted in the high degree of endemism found here. The water temperature never varies more than one or two degrees throughout the year, maintaining a constant 72°F. Beside this constant water temperature, the clear, pollution-free waters of the San Marcos River flow at a steady rate through the initial three miles, typical of a large spring run. The constancy of water temperature and flow, in addition to the proximity to the lower end of the aquifer, creates an environmentally stable habitat. This portion of the San Marcos River will probably be the last to become intermittent or completely dry (which almost happened in 1958) because of the source of spring waters.

In an effort to protect this three-mile stretch of exceptional aquatic habitat from further alteration, four endemic species of plants and animals have been placed on the federal list of threatened and endangered species. One species is the San Marcos salamander, and one is a plant, the Texas wild rice. The other two species are fishes—the San Marcos gambusia and the fountain darter. Both are endangered.

# San Marcos Gambusia
## *Gambusia georgei*

The San Marcos gambusia was first described as a new species in 1969 and very little study has been done concerning the biology of this localized endemic species of fish. The lack of research is due in part to the rarity of the San Marco gambusia. Biologists fear that with an estimate of fewer than 100 individuals left alive, this tiny fish may be on its way to extinction. The last individuals of this species occupy only a one-mile muddy bottom stretch of the river practically inside the city limits of San Marcos. Surprisingly, even in this small segment of river, the U.S. Fish and Wildlife Service has not been able to collect a single individual in recent times. Decline of the San Marcos gambusia was likely caused by several problems including habitat alteration, pollution, and competition with introduced fishes. Whatever the reasons, there are far fewer San Marcos gambusia in the river.

This plainly-marked fish often has a diffuse mid-lateral strip along the length of its body, with its diagnostic lemon yellow-colored median fins. The gambusia prefers tranquil shallow areas with muddy bottoms away from the river banks and dense aquatic vegetation. Under bridges, where the shade inhibits the growth of algal mats, are optimal spots for this elusive fish. The San Marcos gambusia's spring stream is also inhabited by two other species of gambusia, the largespring gambusia, *Gambusia geiseri,* and the mosquitofish, *Gambusia affinis.* Competitive interactions between these three gambusia may be another factor that limits the abundance of the San Marcos gambusia.

The San Marcos gambusia is one of our most endangered fishes.

# Fountain Darter
## *Etheostoma fonticola*

Although equally endangered by the limited habitat and threat of pumping of the spring waters, the fountain darter is far more numerous and better studied than the San Marcos gambusia. Unlike the gambusia, the fountain darter whose species name, *"fonticola,"* literally means to inhabit a fountain, resides in the clear quiet waters of the San Marcos River where the aquatic vegetation grows close to the bottom. Here, among the rooted aquatic vegetation and algal mats, the fountain darter selectively searches for small aquatic insect larvae and minute crustaceans for nourishment.

This tiny fish rarely exceeds 1½ inches long. During the spawning season the male displays an unforgettable dorsal fin of black, red, and clear bands. The fountain darter used to inhabit the Comal River (also fed by springs from the Edwards Aquifer) at New Braunfels, Texas, approximately 25 miles from the San Marcos River. The Comal River population of the fountain darter was last seen in 1954. Several theories have been posed to explain their disappearance in this particular river. Some people claim that the fountain darter population was annihilated by a rotenone treatment given to the river in 1951. The fountain darter collected in 1954 was "just a straggler" according to this theory. Others noted that during a drought the Comal River ceased to flow for six months in 1956. An extreme temperature shift in the remaining small pools of water probably killed off the fountain darters adapted to the normally constant water temperatures. The last major catastrophe occurred in 1971 when the flood waters from Blieders Creek overflowed its banks and inundated the entire Comal River.

A stock population of fifty fountain darters was transplanted from the Dexter National Fish Hatchery in New Mexico into the Comal River in 1975 with hopes of repopulating this river and increasing the darter's restricted range. Because the fountain darter spawns all year, with peaks in August and late winter or early spring, scientists thought that a stable population could be achieved fairly quickly. Also, adult fountain darters do not care for their young and can spawn again relatively soon. Frequent surveys of the Comal River in recent years indicate that the transplant population is gradually increasing.

While the estimates of the number of fountain darters in the San Marcos River system number over 10,000 individuals, the entire habitat of this tiny darter remains uncomfortably restricted. With any small habitat that is fed by underground springs, the reliability of the source of water supply will always be questionable. Excessive withdrawal of water from the Edwards Aquifer would drastically alter the San Marcos ecosystem.

In this unusual Texas aquatic ecosystem are two more endemic forms of life facing some of the same threats as the San Marcos gambusia and the fountain darter. The Texas wild rice, *Zizania texana*, grows along the banks of both Spring Lake and in patchy locations within a one-mile length of the San Marcos River. While harrowing, cutting, and collecting the Texas wild rice has been partly responsible for the declining numbers of the existing population, biologists generally agree that because of the plant's adaptation to conditions of constant, clear water flow and stable water temperatures, changes in the flow by diversion or pumping would seriously jeopardize the survival of this endangered plant species.

For an amphibian known as the San Marcos salamander, *Eurycea nana*, whose only residence is a blanket of algae covering the bottom of Spring Lake, the threat of lowering the water levels to expose the algal mats could destroy this dwarf salamander's habitat. The recreation park, Aquarena Springs, owner of the lake, is keeping a watchful eye on the threatened San Marcos salamander to aid in its survival.

The upper San Marcos River is among the most unique ecosystems in the world. These four endemic species show how the destruction or alteration of a habitat affects more than just a single group of organisms. Found only in this ecosystem, these species depend on the quantity and quality of water issuing from the Edwards Aquifer. Pumping must be limited, for not only are the unique, native species in danger, but even the residents of the cities of San Marcos and San Antonio ultimately depend on the well-being of this limestone aquifer. Land development must be strictly regulated in the flood plain and along the banks of the upper San Marcos River as well as the Comal River. Biological and socioeconomic issues are intimately related and neither can stand alone without the other. If and when the water resources are exhausted, then so, too, will the economy in this Texas region. No matter what one feels about preserving the ecosystem and its unique inhabitants, abusing this aquifer's life-giving water supply will most certainly lessen the quality of life for humans in this region of Texas.

Based on current growth projections and the increased utilization of the Edwards Aquifer, continuous flow from San Marcos Spring could be interrupted periodically by the year 2000. Time is growing short for the San Marcos ecosystem.

# X.

# Texas Blindcats and Cavefishes

More often than not, the terrorizing creatures of science fiction movies turn out to be a race of mutants that live beneath the earth—in a subterranean world of caves.

Although not as strange as the TV monsters they supposedly house, caves are unusual environments. And strange creatures do, indeed, live within the deep, dark recesses of the subterranean world. Because the sun never shines in caves, photosynthesis cannot occur, and the green plants that are the basis of nearly all food webs cannot survive. The source of energy for the food web for cave animals must come from the outside world, and these limited energy resources strongly affect the lives of subterranean animals. The climate of caves is fairly constant, with the temperature about equal to the mean annual temperature of the region.

Water is present in many caves, and very special kinds of fishes often occur in subterranean aquatic systems. Survival of these cave adapted fishes has required a number of anatomical, physiological, and ecological adjustments to their unusual environment. For one thing, they are white—lacking or very deficient in pigmentation. For another, they lack functional eyes which, like pigments, are of no value in a world of darkness. In fact, eyes would likely be a detriment to cavefishes, because eyes would require energy to be developed and maintained, and could be damaged in darkness.

About two dozen kinds of blind, white fishes have been discovered in the underground freshwaters of the world. Most of them are restricted to a fairly limited area or a particular limestone formation or cave system. In the United States, the cavefish family, Amblyopsidae, has four species in three genera that occur only in subterranean systems of the Ozark, Cumberland, and Interior

133

Low plateaus. The catfish family, Ictaluridae, has two species in separate genera that live in the deep underground waters of the Edwards Plateau, Texas and a third species, the Mexican blindcat, *Prietella phreatophila,* that is known only in a deep aquifer in Coahuila, Mexico.

Three cavefishes in the family Amblyopsidae that occur in the Mississippi Valley have declined and are threatened. They are the northern, Ozark, and Alabama cavefishes. *"Amblyopsis"* means "insensible vision." All three have a relatively large head, largest in the Alabama cavefish, and a broadly rounded snout. In the northern and Ozark cavefishes, the mouth turns slightly upward and the protruding lower jaw gives them a pugnacious appearance. The head of the Alabama cavefish is flattened and the mouth is at the end of its long snout. All three species have a tapering body. The body is nearly colorless, except for tiny melanophores, and a pinkish hue from blood within the capillary beds which are visible through the pigmentless skin.

Although cavefishes of the family Amblyopsidae lack eyes, other sensory organs are very highly developed. Sensitive neuromasts of the lateral-line system help these fishes find their prey in the dark. To cope with the scarcity of food items, cavefishes have lower metabolic rates than do surface fishes. In addition, longer pectoral fins make cavefishes more efficient swimmers. Thus, these animals conserve energy, an important ability where food is in limited supply. Because food is so limited in cave environments, cavefishes can store some fat between muscle layers along the back and sides, and in tissues surrounding the viscera. These are reserves against the high probability of long periods of food scarcity.

Although the connection may not be immediately obvious, some species of bats are important to the survival of some populations of cavefishes. Bats that frequent caves have evolved as an integral part of the environment of many caves. If large bat populations are destroyed or prevented from using the cave, the cave ecosystem may be disrupted. Bat guano and dead bats are an important source of energy for the cave ecosystem and without it the food web might well collapse if an alternate source of energy is not available.

Meager food supplies have also led to decreased population sizes. Little energy is invested in reproduction, and very few females in a population breed in a given year. The number of females that breed is partly determined by the amount of food available. Those that breed produce few eggs, and their eggs and early fry are protected in the gill chamber. The developmental time of the young cavefish apparently varies from species to species and is longest in those species that show greatest specialization for subterranean life. Cavefishes become sexually mature at a later age, and have increased longevity, further regulating population size.

Instead of large, visible scales, these cavefishes have embedded, smooth scales that are very hard to see. One very visible feature, however, is the neuromast ridges that are plentiful on head and body. They are part of the lateral-line sensory system, used for monitoring mechanical vibrations in the water. The neuromast ridges are particularly numerous on the head and operculum. Along the sides, these neuromasts form short, parallel ridges. The cavefish brain has a large center for receiving vibrations and the nerves leading to this center are also large. This hypertrophied sensory system works best where "background noise" is limited. Cavefishes therefore prefer quiet, lentic habitats where turbulence is low. To further reduce disturbance (and conserve energy), these fishes move with slow, oar-like strokes of their long pectoral fins.

In the United States, adult cavefishes in the family Amblyopsidae range in size from two to about four inches total length, the largest being the northern cavefish. All cavefishes are carnivores and feed extensively on copepods, especially when young. Adults also eat isopods and amphipods, small crayfish, larval salamanders, and even fish of other species if they get into subterranean waters. When population density rises, at least some cavefishes will cannibalize young of their own species simply because they are readily available.

Reproduction of cavefishes has not been studied widely, but some observations have been made on the Ozark and northern cavefishes. Breeding occurs during the period of high water runoff, February through April, and the eggs hatch in mid-summer. Young are then recruited into the population when prey can be expected to be abundant. The northern and Ozark cavefishes, and probably all cave amblyopsids, incubate the young in the gill chamber. The vent, with the opening of the oviduct, is in the throat area just below the gill openings. The eggs are deposited into the gill chamber of the females and are incubated until they hatch. From twenty to seventy eggs are incubated at a time, depending on the species of cavefish. The young (fry) remain in the chamber until their yolk sacs are absorbed, which may take four or five months. Cavefish fry have an unusually high survival rate and most reach the free-swimming stage. Because the fry are fairly large when they leave the gill chamber and head into the open waters, they are seldom preyed upon. Cave crayfish sometimes capture and eat cavefish, but this is probably rare.

Unlike the cavefishes of the family Amblyopsidae, the so-called blindcats of the catfish family, Ictaluridae, are very poorly known. The reason for this difference is that the blindcat habitat is inaccessible compared to the cavefishes. While cavefishes and blindcats both inhabit waters of underground caverns, those where the blindcats are found have very few openings to the surface. In fact, all blindcats that have been seen have come to the surface in artesian well waters. Although very little is known about the biology of blindcats, it is safe to assume that their lifestyle is similar to other cave adapted fishes. This is based on the similarity of ecological factors operating in most subterranean aquatic ecosystems.

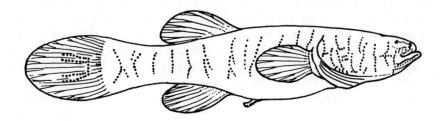

10–1
Northern cavefish with numerous neuromasts or sensory papillae on the head, side of body, and caudal fin. Illustration by R. D. Ono.

# The Blindcats
# Family Ictaluridae

## Toothless Blindcat and Widemouth Blindcat
### *Trogloglanis pattersoni and Satan eurystomus*

About forty species of the catfish family Ictaluridae are distributed throughout the freshwaters of eastern North America and Central America. These pugnacious, hardy fishes live in diverse habitats, including rivers, ponds, creeks, and lakes of a variety of sizes. Among the more bizarre habitats exploited by these fishes are the deep, lightless waters of caves where the blind catfishes, or blindcats, make their homes. Only three of the forty species of North American freshwater catfishes inhabit caves. Two of these blindcats, both of which are considered threatened species by the American Fisheries Society, occur in the United States. The third blindcat, *Prietella phreatophila,* commonly known as the Mexican blindcat, lives in deep aquifers in Coahuila, Mexico. In 1970, the U.S. government placed the Mexican blindcat on the federal endangered species list to protect the only known population in Mexico from being depleted through importation and trade in the United States.

The toothless blindcat, *Trogloglanis pattersoni,* and the widemouth blindcat, *Satan eurystomus,* live in the artesian waters of the Edwards Aquifer, a porous, honeycombed, limestone formation in southern Bexar County near San Antonio, Texas. Located underground at a depth of about five hundred feet, the Edwards Aquifer varies from five to forty miles wide along its 175 mile length, and is the sole source of drinking water for over one million residents around San Antonio. The San Antonio Pool area of the aquifer, which contains water under pressure, is penetrated by five 1000-feet deep artesian wells. Here the toothless blindcat and the widemouth blindcat live in water temperatures that average a warm 80° F. Similar artesian wells to the north and northwest in the same county are cooler, 72° F, and contain no populations of blindcats. We do not know if the cooler water keeps the blindcats away or if there is a physical barrier to that area. However, scientists have known for some time that fishes can detect subtle temperature fluctuations with sense organs located in their skin. This temperature sensitivity is so acute in certain fishes that they detect changes as small as 1° F if the temperature fluctuation is rapid. Scientists now believe that, due to their temperature sensitivity, many fishes tend to remain in preferred temperature ranges, limiting their consequent distributions.

The toothless and widemouth blindcats occur independently in two of the San Antonio Pool wells and coexist as predator and prey in the other three.

The toothless blindcat is the most highly specialized ictalurid catfish known. As its name implies, its unique jaw has no teeth and has a paper-thin construction. In addition, the toothless blindcat's digestive tract is convoluted, providing an increased surface area for the digestion and absorption of food. Scientists have obtained only scanty information on the toothless blindcat's diet. The fragile jaw and convoluted gut indicate that the toothless blindcat is a herbivore, probably feeding on the fungal growth and detritus found in the wells. The widemouth blindcat, on the other hand, appears to be a carnivore. Its strong, tooth-filled jaws give the widemouth blindcat's head a shape that ichthyologist Carl H. Eigenmann described as "similar to that of a tadpole." In addition to feeding on subterranean shrimp and amphipods, the widemouth blindcat occasionally makes a meal of its neighbor, the toothless blindcat.

The predator-prey relationship between these two blindcats correlates with the differences in their sensory development. Because sight is useless in the total darkness of their subterranean pools, both species have developed other senses to ensure their survival. The skin of the toothless blindcat contains taste buds that allow the fish to detect the presence of food. The skin of the widemouth blindcat does not contain taste buds and its nostrils are minute, indicating that its senses of taste and smell are not as well-developed as those of the toothless blindcat.

One sensory system is keenly developed in the widemouth blindcat. Fishes generally have a lateral line system that allows them to sense pressure changes caused by objects moving through the water near them. A group of fluid-filled canals embedded in the skin of the fish open to the surface in a row of small pits along the fish's sides to form the lateral line. The canals are lined with groups of special sensory cells called hair cells that project into the canals. When the fluid in the canals is displaced by a pressure wave impinging upon the pits, the movement of the fluid bends the hair cells causing associated nerve cells to fire. The direction of hair cell deflection conveys different information to the fish, allowing it to pinpoint the position of the moving object. The widemouth blindcat has superbly developed sensory canals around its mouth and along the sides of its head. The fish can sense the subtle pressure waves created by tiny shrimp and amphipods and the stronger pressure waves created by its unfortunate neighbor, the toothless blindcat.

Although the sensory systems of the blindcats are different, the unique subterranean habitat in which they dwell has allowed both species to develop some similar adaptations. The toothless and widemouth blindcats lack a swimbladder, the balloon-like organ that fish keep filled with gas to prevent them from sinking when they are not swimming. The Texas blindcats have developed instead a layer of fatty tissue that increases their buoyancy and facilitates swimming. This fatty tissue probably serves as a source of energy when food is scarce.

The toothless and widemouth blindcats are threatened by decreasing water levels in the Edwards Aquifer. The aquifer has been tapped by hundreds of Man-made wells supplying irrigation and drinking water to the area around San Antonio, Texas. Theoretical models indicate that an increase in the San Antonio population would lead to an increase in water usage that would lower the water level in the aquifer to below the rainfall recharge zone. In addition to the lowered water levels, the aquifer is threatened by contamination from chemical pollution. There is still time to correct these problems. State and federal agencies as well as private citizens must take action to effect changes in water use patterns. Some of these changes will probably be unpopular, but they are essential to the protection of the aquifer. In the end, what is good for the blindcats will be good for the human population of the area.

# The Cavefishes
# Family Amblyopsidae

## Ozark Cavefish
### *Amblyopsis rosae*

Probably the most intensively studied and the most specialized of the American cavefishes of the family Amblyopsidae is the Ozark cavefish, *Amblyopsis rosae,* which was found in caves and wells in seven counties in southwestern Missouri, two counties in northwestern Arkansas, and three counties in northeastern Oklahoma. The area inhabited by the Ozark cavefish is a limestone region with many caves and underground streams. Observations of this species since its discovery some ninety years ago indicate that it prefers small cave streams with chert or rubble bottom, but is occasionally found in pools over silt and sand bottom. This contrasts sharply with most other cavefishes which inhabit pools of underground streams or lakes.

At first glance it might appear that the only populations of Ozark cavefishes that might be threatened would be those in well known accessible caves. This is not the case. Because of the nature of the threats, the impact is far reaching. The major threat is habitat alteration, including groundwater pollution, lowering of the water table, and, in some areas, flooding by reservoirs. Other threats such as collecting for the home aquarium or as a curiosity and vandalism of cave habitats are more localized problems. Taken together, these threats represent a serious problem for the future of the Ozark cavefish.

The pollution or contamination of aquatic ecosystems in caves comes from a variety of sources. Sewage leaking from septic tanks and drainage fields and street runoff are common sources of pollution in cave systems in developed areas. In rural areas, contamination from pesticides and other agricultural chemicals pose serious problems for the Ozark cavefish. Once the pollutant enters the cave system, it can move through the underground channels far from its original source. Additional research is needed to determine how pollutants are affecting the decreasing Ozark cavefish population.

Results of a recent survey of the Ozark cavefish in sinkholes and wells in southwestern Missouri is cause for concern. Only two of the seven counties where the species formerly occurred had Ozark cavefishes. In these two counties, less than fifteen fish were sited in four caves. In an effort to locate additional undiscovered populations, caves in three other counties were examined. In all, about 75 caves in the ten southwestern Missouri counties were explored in search of the Ozark cavefish.

In northwestern Arkansas the situation appears somewhat better for the Ozark cavefish. Although there are fewer caves in this area, there is at least one very health population in a large cave system, Cave Springs Cave, in Benton County, Arkansas. Fortunately the cave entrance is well protected by a private landowner, and unauthorized entry is not permitted. Cave Springs Cave was near the path of a highway relocation project that would have posed a serious threat to the cave ecosystem. Once this potential threat surfaced, the Arkansas State Highway Department routed the highway around the area. At least one other cave, Logan Cave in Benton County, Arkansas, supports a population of the Ozark cavefish. The exact size of the Logan Cave population is not known, but it appears to be smaller than the one found in Cave Springs Cave.

The status of the Ozark cavefish in northeastern Oklahoma is not known because it was only recently found in the caves of this area. That it was not found earlier suggests that these populations are small. Cave systems in northeastern Oklahoma are exposed to the same threats as caves in other portions of the Ozark cavefish's range.

The Ozark cavefish has been considered rare or endangered in the states where it occurs. It was assigned threatened status by the American Fisheries Society in 1979. The Ozark cavefish is not currently on the U.S. list of endangered and threatened fishes, but its status is being reviewed by the U.S. Fish and Wildlife Service.

Conservation of the remaining populations of the Ozark cavefish will require a coordinated effort on the part of involved state and federal agencies. It is apparently not too late to protect this unique inhabitant of the Ozark region caves.

# Northern Cavefish
## *Amblyopsis spelaea*

(Color plate 10.)

The northern cavefish, the largest cavefish in the family Amblyopsidae, grows to four inches long and was the first species of cavefish to be described in scientific literature. The description, which appeared in 1842, was authored by James E. DeKay, a well known naturalist of that era. It was based on a single specimen collected in Mammoth Cave in west central Kentucky. As caves of that region were explored, populations of the northern cavefish were found 150 miles north of Mammoth Cave into south central Indiana.

Throughout its two state range, the northern cavefish has been observed in approximately twenty caves in five counties in Kentucky and about 25 caves in five counties in Indiana. This distribution pattern is somewhat misleading. Several of the citings have been in different caves within a few miles of each other. In southern Indiana most of the observations have been concentrated in the Lost River system in Orange County. This appears to be the largest concentration of northern cavefishes known.

Threats to the northern cavefish, like those of the Ozark cavefish, are centered around habitat alteration. While populations in areas like the Mammoth Cave system in a National Park are protected from direct threats of collecting and vandalism, contamination of the water outside the park remains a problem. Much of the recharge of underground streams in this area comes from sinkholes. The sinkholes that receive surface runoff from large areas are frequently used for unauthorized trash dumps for everything from junk cars and appliances to household garbage. Protection of the recharge zone, the sinkholes and their watershed would be an excellent start toward conserving cave ecosystems in this area.

Alteration of surface drainages through impoundment and channelization have posed serious threats to cave ecosystems in some areas. One such case involved a U.S. Soil Conservation Service watershed project on the Lost River in Indiana. As previously mentioned, this area supports one of the largest populations of the northern cavefish. The proposed watershed project would have increased siltation of waters flowing into sinkholes that recharge the cave system and would have decreased the overall volume of water entering the system. Fortunately, this project never came to fruition, decreasing by one the number of problems confronting the northern cavefish. Also, the benefits of the Lost River watershed project to the human population of the area were highly questionable.

Land and water conservation managers in karst areas must have a better understanding of how surface activities impact the cave ecosystem. This is important not just for the protection of the cave-adapted animal life, but also to the humans who use the same groundwater resources for drinking water.

# Alabama Cavefish
## *Speoplatyrhinus poulsoni*

The Alabama cavefish is undoubtably one of the rarest vertebrates in the world. It is known only from the lentic, subterranean waters of Key Cave that opens on the north bank of the Tennessee River west of Florence, Alabama. This is near the southeastern edge of the Highland Rim physiographic provence. The first specimen of this cavefish was collected on March 19, 1967, by biologists John and Martha Cooper while collecting cave crayfishes. Most of what we know about this fish comes from the nine specimens that were collected between 1967 and 1970. Additional information has been gleaned from observation of uncaptured specimens and general studies of the Key Cave ecosystem.

The Alabama cavefish's apparent rarity, restricted distribution, and the potential threats from groundwater pollution prompted the U.S. Fish and Wildlife Service to designate the Alabama cavefish a threatened species in 1977. At the same time, Key Cave was delineated as its critical habitat. Threats from groundwater pollution would most likely come from nearby agricultural fields. A recent analysis of water from the cave found very little sediment, indicating that pollution from agricultural activities is probably not a severe problem.

While this was encouraging news, additional samples taken through the year need to be analyzed before the area gets a clean bill of health. Other groundwater pollution problems could result from the development of an industrial park which was proposed for the Key Cave area in 1976. The current status of the plans for this development are not known.

After its discovery in Key Cave, hopes were high for locating other caves inhabited by the Alabama cavefish. Most biologists were optimistic about the possibilities of finding additional populations based on the distribution patterns of other cave-adapted animals. It would be very unlikely that a relict cavefish could survive in such a restricted area. So far, additional searches have turned up only the more widespread and common southern cavefish, *Typhlichthys subterraneus*. In fact, the southern cavefish has been collected from more than thirty caves in northern Alabama alone, with a half dozen near Key Cave. Biologists have not ruled out the possibility that the southern cavefish has outcompeted and displaced the Alabama cavefish. The southern cavefish is widespread, has a higher reproductive potential, and is aggressive. This supports this hypothesis. The caves of northwest Alabama and the adjacent portion of Tennessee will be searched further for this rare cavefish. In the meantime, protection of Key Cave and its groundwater supply is essential to the well being of the Alabama cavefish.

# XI.

# Cuatro Ciénegas Fishes

Just below the Texas border in northern Mexico lies the state of Coahuila, a largely desert and mountainous region in Mexico's Ridge and Basin Province. Near the center of Coahuila, about 110 miles northwest of Monterrey, lies a small, horseshoe-shaped basin 25 miles from east to west and roughly 20 miles from north to south, at an elevation of approximately 2000 feet. Enclosed on all but its southern end by steep mountains that rise 3000 to 9000 feet above the basin floor, the Bolson de Cuatro Ciénegas, or "basin of four marshes," is part of the Chihuahuan desert region.

Toward the end of the Cretaceous period the seas that covered the Mexican peninsula and inundated northern Coahuila began to recede, and the mountain ranges formed from upliftings of the former sea bed. As the basin took shape its internal drainage was periodically isolated from the surrounding Chihuahuan desert drainage system through various geological events. Sloping mounds of rubble accumulated at the base of the mountains, and the sediment-laden runoff from the mountains deposited elevated plains of sand and clay near the outlet of the basin. These sediments created natural barriers that separated the surface waters inside the basin from the river drainage outside, effectively isolating fishes inside the Cuatro Ciénegas basin.

Within the enclosed Cuatro Ciénegas basin, a network of subterranean waters created the present array of aquatic habitats that support a variety of endemic species. The spring outflows carved subterranean channels in the basin's soft limestone substrate. The channels occasionally caved in, creating open sinkholes that exposed the underlying water. The edges of the sinkholes continually crumbled into the water, often plugging the outflow and impounding its waters. As the sinkholes filled, a succession of aquatic vegetation took

143

root along the banks, gradually lining the bottom of the pits with flocculent detritus which provided food for fishes, snails, and other animals. Through this gradual process, the subterranean springs gave birth to the marshes that form an important aquatic habitat in the Cuatro Ciénegas basin.

Spring pools and lakes constitute major aquatic habitats in the basin, and likely represent the early stages in the continuous process of marsh formation. The spring pools, which are known to the locals as *posos*, develop in shallow depressions or sinkholes around headsprings. During periods of heavy rainfall the increased water flow often erodes the banks and overflows the pools, creating lakes, or *lagunas*. The Cuatro Ciénegas basin lakes range between 300 and 1500 feet in diameter. The lake bottoms consist of a flocculent ooze composed of organic detritus, shell fragments, and clay.

11–1
Posos de Becerra in Cuatro Ciénegas. Note the dredged irrigation canal leading from the posos. Photo by J. E. Johnson.

In some of the more recently formed lakes, the limestone substrate has not accumulated sufficiently to block the water outflow. In other lakes the water is constantly replaced, and the visibility rarely drops below 30 to 45 feet. Biologist Dwight Taylor, who visited the basin in 1965, wrote: "One who first dives into one of these large, clear lagunas with the numerous cichlid fishes, *Cichlasoma* sp., that are boldly colored and change color with startling speed, is immediately struck with the impression he is in an aquarium. The constant flow of water, lack of turbidity, and the virtual absence of plankton make these spring-pools conspicuously more clear than the lakes that are more nearly closed systems."

Some of the spring outflows, supplemented by mountain runoffs, surfaced from their subterranean channels to become desert streams that in turn created a diversity of habitats, ranging from deep, strongly flowing pools to riffles and fast chutes. Crystal clear, except for the periods following torrential rains when the water becomes turbid, these desert streams vary in their permanence. Some are stable throughout the year, fluctuating less than four inches in depth; while others undergo cycles of flooding followed by dry periods.

In these diverse aquatic habitats, an equally diverse fish fauna evolved. Fossil evidence suggests that some of the springs in the basin have existed for a few million years, and that surface waters capable of supporting fish populations probably existed in isolation for over tens of thousands of years. Isolated in the basin's various aquatic habitats, some of the fishes diversified morphologically and physiologically, becoming distinct from the ancestral species as they adapted to specific environmental conditions such as warm water temperature and high salinity. As a result, over half of the 20 species of native fishes in the Cuatro Ciénegas basin are endemic. Other fishes, already well-adapted to their particular habitats, changed very little over the millennia, retaining many of the morphological and physiological characteristics of their ancestral stock.

No one knew of these endemic and relict fishes until 1939, when biologist E. G. Marsh conducted the first scientific exploration of the basin and made the first collection of Cuatro Ciénegas fishes. Ichthyologist Carl L. Hubbs later examined Marsh's collection and noted the high degree of endemism among the specimens. Beginning in 1958, ichthyologist W. L. Minckley made a series of collecting trips to the basin, which he described as a "natural laboratory" where the specific adaptations to characteristics of the distinct habitats in the region could be identified. These scientific expeditions revealed additional endemic fish species as well as other unique vertebrate and invertebrate species. "One of the more interesting biological studies possible in the valley of Cuatro Ciénegas," wrote D. W. Taylor in 1966, "is the comparison of rates of evolution of different animals living in substantially the same habitat: the fishes, turtles, snails, Crustacea, and so on." He added, ". . . the mere naming and describing, let alone study of these groups has scarcely gotten underway."

The study of the Cuatro Ciénegas fauna may never progress beyond the discovery phase, for the basin's unusual environment is already threatened by encroaching human populations. The extensive construction of irrigation canals and the subsequent diversion of water from the lakes and marshes has produced a dramatic drop in water levels. This exposes the previously submerged soil along the banks, which is quickly colonized by sedges and cattails, creating new terrestrial habitats but destroying the habitats of many aquatic species.

145

The receding water level also concentrates the remaining fishes in a smaller volume of water. Competition for food and predation increases, altering the population structure and levels for most species. The canals also create confluences among aquatic habitats that have been geographically isolated for thousands of years. Species of fish that have evolved separately are suddenly brought together, and the reproductively compatible species risk extinction through mass hybridization.

The lake and marsh system known as Posos de la Becerra, ten miles southwest of the town of Cuatro Ciénegas, serves as a dramatic example of the severe impact that canalization has had on the basin's aquatic ecosystem. Minckley and a fellow biologist described Posos de la Becerra as "one of the largest and most complex aquatic habitats in the Cuatro Ciénegas basin" before a canal was constructed in 1964 to divert its waters for irrigation. When the canal was opened in December, the water level in the Posos fell eighteen inches in two days. By April 1965, the canal outflow had stabilized and the surface of the laguna had dropped more than three feet below its original level. The many connected marshes that received water from the lake and its springs also were depleted, and the total water surface of the posos and adjacent marshes plummeted from about four square miles to less than 0.1 square miles. Snails that constituted a principal source of food for some of the fishes in the laguna were greatly reduced and the remaining fishes were crowded into the depleted waters. By December 1965, few live snails remained in Posos de la Becerra and the survival of the fish was doubtful.

Canalization is not the only threat to the basin ecosystem. As towns and agricultural operations spread into Cuatro Ciénegas basin, the increased demand for water also depleted the desert streams. Agricultural runoff and sewage pollute the reduced stream waters. Reduced stream flow causes the currents to dwindle, and at the same time increases water temperature. The crystalline waters become turbid, and the deep pools, riffles and fast-flowing chutes that constitute the habitats of many native fishes disappear.

Only two large desert spring ecosystems with high rates of endemism remain on the North American continent: Ash Meadows in Nye County, Nevada, and the Cuatro Ciénegas basin of northern Mexico. Four of the fish species endemic to the Ash Meadows ecosystem are listed as endangered. The three Cuatro Ciénegas endemic fishes examined in this chapter are also endangered: the Cuatro Ciénegas Shiner *Notropis xanthicara*; the Cuatro Ciénegas Platyfish *Xiphophorus gordoni*; and the Sardinilla Cuatro Ciénegas *Lucania interioris*. Since 1964, the scientific community has attempted to persuade the Mexican government to establish the Cuatro Ciénegas basin as a national park. This effort has unfortunately not succeeded to date.

Clark Hubbs, son of ichthyologist Carl Hubbs and an ichthyologist himself, wrote the following about the Cuatro Ciénegas fishes: ". . . these populations may be as isolated as are the birds and reptiles studied by Darwin, Lack, and others in the Galapagos. As such they must be retained as 'living' examples of evolutionary processes . . . We must avoid the extinction of those natural resources whose true value only may become obvious after they are extinct."

Color Plate 1. Maryland darter—*Etheostoma sellare*

Color Plate 2. Orangefin madtom (left) and Roanoke
logperch (right)—*Noturus gilberti* and *Percina rex*

Color Plate 3. Shortjaw cisco—*Coregonus zenithicus*

Color Plate 4. Unarmored threespine stickleback—
*Gasterosteus aculeatus williamsoni*

Color Plate 5. Lahontan cutthroat trout (male top, female bottom)—*Salmo clarki henshawi* (courtesy of the Smithsonian Institution, Washington, D.C.)

Color Plate 6. Devils Hole pupfish—*Cyprinodon diabolis*

Color Plate 7. Humpback chub (foreground) and Colorado squawfish (top) —*Gila cypha* and *Ptychocheilus lucius*

Color Plate 8.  Bonytail chub (right) and Razorback sucker (left)—*Gila elegans* and *Xyrauchen texanus*

Color Plate 9. Greenback cutthroat trout—*Salmo clarki stomias*

Color Plate 10.  Northern cavefish—*Ambl yopsis spelaea*

156

Color Plate 11.  Slackwater darter—*Etheostoma boschungi*

Color Plate 12. Snail darter—*Percina tanasi*

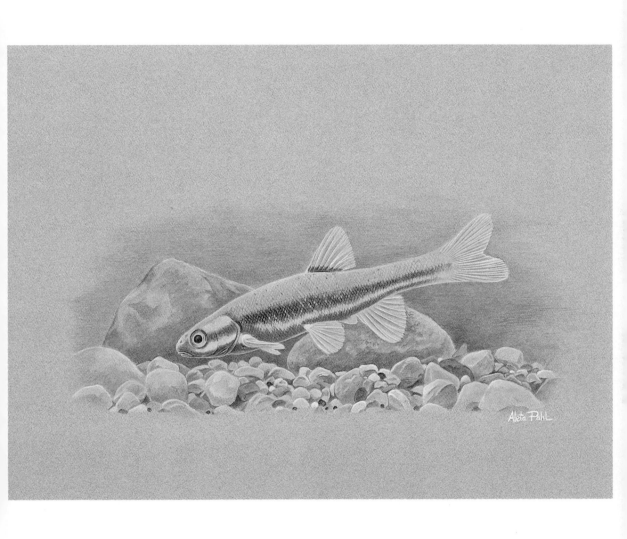

Color Plate 13.  Blackside dace—*Phoxinus cumberlandensis*

Color Plate 14.  Barrens topminnow—*Fundulus julisia*

Color Plate 15.  Shortnose sturgeon—*Acipenser
brevirostrum*

Color Plate 16.  Totoaba—*Cynoscion macdonaldi*

# Sardinilla Cuatro Ciénegas
## *Lucania interioris*

The chance was slim that anyone would discover this small, secretive member of the killifish family, Cyprinodontidae, known as the sardinilla Cuatro Ciénegas, *Lucania interioris*, for the sardinilla dives into the mud and remains buried up to its snout when chased. Nevertheless, Carl L. Hubbs managed to capture the sardinilla in the samples of fishes that he obtained during a 1939 collecting trip to the Cuatro Ciénegas basin.

The Cuatro Ciénegas sardinilla turned out to be related to an essentially marine North American killifish, *Lucania parva*, which is distributed along the Atlantic Coast from New England to south Texas. *Lucania parva* was introduced on the west coast in the early 1960s. Prior to Hubbs' discovery, only two species of *Lucania* were known: *Lucania goodei*, which generally occurs in the freshwater marsh and swamp habitats of Florida; and *Lucania parva*, which is found in a wide variety of habitats, including protected salt and brackish waters, low-salinity coastal marshes, and in some inland fresh waters.

*Lucania* probably entered the Cuatro Ciénegas basin during a period when the basin's internal drainage flowed into one of the coastal drainages, and remained within the basin's aquatic system following another period of isolation. Evidently possessing the ability to withstand a wide variety of environmental conditions, the isolated specimens adapted to the physical stresses of saline spring pools and marshes in the Cuatro Ciénegas basin, and eventually evolved into the distinct species, *Lucania interioris*. Despite attempts to find the species throughout northeastern Mexico, *Lucania interioris* has not been found outside the Cuatro Ciénegas basin.

The sardinilla Cuatro Ciénegas lives in a variety of habitats within the basin. Although the water is always clear but easily muddied due to the fine detritus and mud that covers the clay substrate, the salt content varies from slightly saline to highly alkaline, and the temperatures range from 62°–80° F. All of the marshes and spring pools in which sardinillas occur are almost devoid of shade or protective cover. To date, biologists have located the species in a system of limestone spring pools called Los Positos, in the Garabatal River in the northwestern region of the Cuatro Ciénegas basin, and in the river's associated marshes.

The sardinilla Cuatro Ciénegas does not exceed one inch in length. This small size is typical of isolated desert spring species. The small males have very bright colors. Adult male sardinillas have chalky blue dorsal fins and turquoise blue anal fins. The pelvic and pectoral fins range from weak to deep orange, and the pelvic fins are edged in black. Punctuating the bronze-gold background color of the body, a series of horizontal blue spots extend across seven rows of scales, and each row of spots is separated from the next by horizontal olive or orange lines. The head of the sardinilla male is no less spectacular. The orange-brown lower portion of the head blends into the olive top portion, a black bar extends across the lower eye, and behind each eye flash blue reflective patches. In sharp contrast to the gaudy males, the female sardinillas are yellowish brown all over.

While all three species of *Lucania* perform their courtship near the bottom of their respective habitats, only *Lucania interioris* also spawns there. *Lucania parva* and *Lucania goodei* spawn at or near the surface whether there is a suitable substrate to deposit the eggs in or not. The sardinilla Cuatro Ciénegas spawns on fibrous materials at or near the bottom. Ichthyologists who have studied this unique behavior suggest that the sardinilla's preference for bottom spawning may be a means of protecting the eggs and embryos from the basin's intense sunlight and the solar radiation at the surface of the water.

In the 1960s, the local government in the Cuatro Ciénegas basin constructed the La Angostùra irrigation canal to drain water from the Rio Garabatal. This initial threat to the sardinilla's habitat has since been compounded by the development of additional irrigation projects. One marsh pool, from which the species was first collected in 1961 and again in 1963, had dwindled by 1964 from its initial depth of eight inches to a mere two inches. Biologists returning to the pool in 1964 found the temperature of the depleted water elevated to a lethal 106° F. They also discovered that a variety of toxic compounds had been released from the bottom silt when the bottom was disturbed. Not one specimen of *Lucania interioris* remained in the pool.

Other habitats of the Cuatro Ciénegas sardinilla must be protected to prevent the extinction of this fish.

# Cuatro Ciénegas Platyfish
## *Xiphophorus gordoni*

Of all the endemic species of fish in the Cuatro Ciénegas basin, perhaps the least known is the Cuatro Ciénegas platyfish. Ironically, the ubiquitous platyfishes and swordtails of the genus *Xiphophorus* have been described since the 1930s. Their biology has been more closely examined and is better understood than the biology of most fishes. The Cuatro Ciénegas platyfish was not discovered, however, until 1961 when Carl L. Hubbs led a group of scientists on a collecting trip in the Cuatro Ciénegas basin.

The scientists discovered the one-inch-long Cuatro Ciénegas platyfish in Laguna Santa Tecla, a spring lake about twenty miles southeast of the town of Cuatro Ciénegas, at the southeastern end of the Cuatro Ciénegas basin. Subsequent explorations have revealed that the range of the Cuatro Ciénegas platyfish is apparently limited to a spring-fed ditch leading into Laguna Santa Tecla and a marsh area adjoining the lake outlet. The outlet is a channel varying in width from four to fifteen feet, and between one and two feet deep. The Cuatro Ciénegas platyfish inhabits an area with dense aquatic vegetation where the bottom is covered by loose silt and mud. The fish's olive coloration, suffused with yellow and marked by a horizontal black stripe along its sides, may allow the Cuatro Ciénegas platyfish to blend with the aquatic vegetation in which it dwells.

To date, no studies on the feeding, reproduction, biology, or life history of the Cuatro Ciénegas platyfish exist. Its restricted range puts the species at considerable risk as the increased demand for water from the basin results in the gradual drainage of the lagunas and marshes.

# Cuatro Ciénegas Shiner
## *Notropis xanthicara*

Ichthyologist W. L. Minckley and his collaborator Glady Lytle first described the Cuatro Ciénegas shiner, *Notropis xanthicara* in 1969, but no biologist has studied the life history of this new species. The species probably arose in the Pleistocene (about 2½ million years ago) when a population of a more common shiner, *Notropis rutilus*, was isolated in the aquatic ecosystem of the Cuatro Ciénegas basin. As individuals developed adaptations to their unique habitats, they became increasingly different from the ancestral species and eventually evolved into a new species.

The Cuatro Ciénegas shiners are distributed throughout the Cuatro Ciénegas basin, although the largest population is in the northeastern basin. The species inhabits the open waters of the large lakes and deeper marshes, and the desert streams in the upper reaches near the spring sources. Field observations reveal that the small fishes, which average between just over one inch to two inches in length, live primarily in the shear zone between currents and in quiet backwaters. Traveling in schools up to 25 individuals, the Cuatro Ciénegas shiners tend to remain near the bottom of their aquatic habitats at night. During the day, the schools rise to the surface where they feed on floating objects.

The silvery Cuatro Ciénegas shiner is distinguished from other shiner species by a black band, one scale-row wide, that extends the length of the body from behind the eye to the tail fin. During breeding, the males acquire a predominantly yellow color, particularly on the fins and head, from which the Cuatro Ciénegas shiner's scientific name *xanthicara,* or "yellow head," is derived. The brilliance of the male breeding colors is not limited to the head and fins alone. The yellow along the fish's back becomes overlaid with a brown cross-hatched pattern, while the sides below the distinguishing black stripe take on a pinkish-orange hue. The yellow pelvic fins become edged in iridescent blue and the intensely yellow tail fin develops jet black rays. Thus colored, the males acquire the appearance of animated jewels.

Habitat alteration is a constant threat to this endemic shiner of the Cuatro Ciénegas.

# XII.

# Interior Highlands Fishes

In the south central United States, two upland areas, the Ozark Plateaus and Ouachita Mountains, form what is commonly called the Interior Highlands. These highland areas are located in southern Missouri, northern and western Arkansas and eastern Oklahoma, and cover an area of about 75,000 square miles. Although separated from the Appalachian Highlands of the eastern United States by several hundred miles, these two highlands are similar in land form and the kinds of rocks found in each area. There are also biological similarities between the Interior and Appalachian Highlands, with some plants and animals being restricted to the upland habitats in each area. A few species are found only in the Interior Highlands with their closest relatives in the Appalachian Highlands.

*The Ozark Plateaus,* the northern portion of the Interior Highlands, are roughly bound on the north by the Missouri River, the east by the Mississippi River, and the south by the Arkansas River. They extend west to extreme southeastern Kansas and northeastern Oklahoma and gradually disappear beneath the plains. This area of approximately 40,000-square miles has a few areas with elevations over 2000 feet in northern Arkansas. Most of the Ozark Plateaus are underlain by limestone which contains large amounts of chert and dolomite that have been deeply dissected by the many streams of the region.

The deeply incised Ozark streams frequently occupy narrow valleys and are often bordered by sheer limestone bluffs more than one hundred feet high. The water, much of which flows from large springs, is clear, cool, and generally of high quality. The outstanding aquatic habitat provided by these high quality Ozark streams supports a diverse fish fauna of more than 65 species, of which

167

fourteen species are found nowhere else in the world. Two of the fourteen fishes found only in the Ozarks are considered threatened. They are the Niangua darter and the bluestripe darter.

# Niangua Darter
## *Etheostoma nianguae*

The Niangua darter, a threatened species, is a long slender darter with a pointed snout that reaches about four inches in length. It was originally discovered in the Niangua River near Marshfield, Webster County, Missouri in the summer of 1884. When formally described in 1888, this darter was assigned the specific epithet, *nianguae* after the river in which it was discovered. Subsequent to its discovery, it was found to inhabit several tributary streams of the Osage River in west central Missouri. The stream systems the Niangua darter inhabits today, from east to west, are the Maries River, Big Tavern Creek, Niangua River, the Pomme de Terre River, and the Sac River. Historically the Niangua darter occurred in these same stream systems, but was more widespread and much more abundant at most sites.

The Niangua darter is most closely related to the arrow darter, which occurs in southeastern Kentucky and southward across the state line into Tennessee. The darter that the arrow and Niangua darters evolved from was probably widespread and had a continuous distribution prior to the Pleistocene Ice Age. Its continuous distribution was interrupted by Pleistocene glaciers advancing into the north central United States southward to southern Ohio. This isolated populations in the Missouri Ozarks and mountains of southeast Kentucky and northeast Tennessee. After the glaciers retreated, environmental conditions prevented the isolated darter populations from repopulating the intervening area. They have remained isolated and evolved independently in response to different selective pressures giving rise to the arrow and Niangua darters. The arrow darter, unlike its close relative the Niangua darter, appears to be holding its own against Man's encroachment into its habitat.

Biologists recently studied the Niangua darter very thoroughly to discover the details of its habitat and life history and more precisely determine its conservation status. The results of the survey indicate that the darter inhabits approximately 125 miles of medium-sized Ozark creeks at elevations between 550 and 1175 feet. Usually these creeks are moderately clear upland streams with slight to medium current over a clean, silt free gravel or rocky bottom.

Depending on the season, the Niangua darters inhabit the pools, runs, and riffles of the streams. In the early spring Niangua darters can usually be found in shallow (one to two feet deep) pools and runs. As spawning season approaches the colorful males begin courtship behavior, chasing and attempting to mount females. Competing males often display their spiny dorsal fin in a threatening gesture and occasionally battle by quickly circling and biting each other. The males in their breeding dress of greenish yellow background color with dark saddles across the back, orange spots on the upper sides, alternating blue-green and orange blotches on the mid-sides, and orange-red belly move into shallow swift gravel riffles to spawn. This takes place in early April and lasts three to four weeks, the duration of the spawning period. The less colorful females remain in the pools adjacent to the swift riffles, move into the riffles briefly to spawn, and then return to the pool.

The actual spawning act is brief, but very intense. As the female moves into a riffle area she is joined by a male who follows her closely as she selects a spawning site. She then dives head first into the gravel, leaving only her head and tail exposed. The male positions himself directly over her and begins vibrating, pressing his tail into the substrate simultaneously releasing sperm to fertilize the eggs deposited by the female. This peculiar behavior leaves the fertilized eggs buried in the gravel, safe from most predators until they hatch. The parents do not protect the eggs or young. As the spawning season ends, the males leave the riffles and join the females in the deeper pools and runs. Upon retiring to the pools, Niangua darters rest on the bottom, as is typical of most darters.

As the larval Niangua darters emerge from their gravelly birthplace, they actively seek food items—microcrustaceans and aquatic insects. Growth is rapid during the first year. Most individuals reach a length of more than two inches, over half their adult size. Growth slows after the first year and most two year old Niangua darters are about three inches long. Most individuals do not live beyond two years of age, though a few reach four years. Throughout most of their life they feed primarily on the aquatic stages of mayflies and stoneflies which are abundant in clean Ozark streams.

Like the Niangua darter, the bluestripe darter, *Percina cymatotaenia*, is also restricted to the Ozarks in southcentral Missouri and is equally threatened. The bluestripe occurs in pools and backwaters over a sand bottom with aquatic plants and debris in clean medium-sized Ozark streams. In the late 1800s it was reported as "abundant," but today it is one of the rarest fishes in Missouri. The bluestripe darter no longer occurs in several streams where it was present around the turn of the century. It has also been eliminated from the headwater portion of some streams where it is presently found, indicating its range and habitat is still shrinking. The bluestripe darter is most closely related to a recently discovered unnamed species that occurs in the central uplands of Kentucky.

Although there are no large human population centers within the range of the Niangua and bluestripe darters, Man's activities are responsible for their decline. Threats to these darters also threaten the attractive and valuable, high quality stream fishery for which the Ozarks are known. The most significant threat to the Niangua and bluestripe darters is deterioration of the streams they inhabit. Siltation and enrichment from nutrient laden runoff has seriously polluted some areas. Channelization and removal of riparian vegetation along portions of stream channels has further deteriorated the habitat. Impound-ments of earlier years destroyed considerable habitat. No major dams are planned within the habitat of the Niangua darter.

When early settlers arrived they found most of the Ozarks covered with oak-hickory forest. As the forests were cleared and the land cultivated, siltation of streams increased. While the source of silt particles may change over time, they are ubiquitous and constantly enter stream systems. Silt in a stream environment can be lethal to gill breathing organisms. It clogs the gills of gill breathing organisms, preventing oxygen exchange, and eventually results in suffocation. Silt also settles in the small spaces between gravel, eliminating the prime habitat of many aquatic insects, and reduces food resources for fishes. A layer of silt covering the bottom can completely smother microscopic plants and greatly reduce the productivity of a stream.

Stream channelization projects, which typically straighten and widen the stream channel, are usually built to reduce flooding. There are not many channelization projects within the Niangua and bluestripe darters' range, but those few seriously threaten localized stream segments, usually less than one mile long. These projects are frequently associated with highway and bridge construction. In some areas local landowners will remove riparian vegetation and widen the stream to reduce flooding in agricultural areas. Stream channelization usually results in greater flooding downstream and also causes increased erosion and siltation.

Dams and their associated impoundments or reservoirs completely obliterate stream habitats within their pool. In the case of the Niangua darter, four large impoundments inundated habitat in several streams. Recent interest in the recreational potential of free flowing streams and stream fisheries should help prevent additional impoundments within the Niangua and bluestripe darters' range.

To maintain the Niangua darter and eventually bring about its recovery, existing habitat must be maintained and/or upgraded. Potential habitat within the Niangua darter's range could be renovated and the darter reintroduced. Public works projects involving channelization or impoundments within the range of the Niangua and bluestripe darters should be curtailed to prevent additional habitat loss.

*The Ouachita Mountains,* usually referred to as the Ouachitas, form the southern portion of the Interior Highlands and extend from central Arkansas west into southeastern Oklahoma. They are bound on the north by the Arkansas River, the east by the Mississippi River Alluvial Plain, the south by the Gulf Coastal Plain, and the west by the plains. The 225-mile long, 100-mile wide mountainous area is characterized by extensive folding with its ridges and valleys oriented roughly in an east–west direction. Streams of all sizes with good water quality are found throughout most of the area. Elevations along some of the higher ridges are over 2500 feet. Evidence supporting the connection between the Ouachitas and the Appalachians has been found in rock samples from deep wells drilled on the coastal plain of Alabama and Mississippi. Fishes of the Ouachitas are also similar to the Appalachians. This was pointed out by ichthyologists, Drs. David Starr Jordan and Charles H. Gilbert in 1886, who reported that "The general character of the streams resembles that of parts of East Tennessee, and the fish fauna is remarkably similar to that of the Tennessee River."

Streams of the Ouachitas support a very diverse fish fauna and several species are restricted to the area. Four species that occur in the Ouachitas are threatened by habitat alteration and pollution. The peppered shiner, *Notropis perpallidus,* and the leopard darter, *Percina pantherina,* are typical examples of threatened Ouachita fishes.

# Peppered Shiner
## *Notropis perpallidus*

Of the approximately 110 species of shiners, genus *Notropis*, the peppered shiner is among the smallest. The adults rarely exceed two inches in length. This diminutive shiner was reported to be "very abundant," when first collected in the Saline River, a tributary of the Ouachita River, near Benton, Saline County, Arkansas in 1884. As was typical of many collection of fishes in the late 1800s, the sample was taken just above the railroad bridge because trains were about the only means of transportation available. The stream was described as having moderately rapid flow with alternating gravel riffles, deep quiet pools, and very clear water.

When first collected in 1884, ichthyologists believed the peppered shiner was a new species. But because of its small size and frail appearance, it was ultimately referred to as the young of a larger species of *Notropis*. Here it remained for more than fifty years until Dr. Carl L. Hubbs from the University of Michigan, and his graduate student, John D. Black, formally described the shiner in 1940. After the description was published, the peppered shiner was found in several stream systems in the Ouachitas and the rolling hills of the Gulf Coastal Plain adjacent to the mountains in central Arkansas and southeastern Oklahoma.

Throughout its range the peppered shiner appears to be limited to clean, clear, free-flowing streams thirty to sixty feet wide. Within this general habitat it is further restricted to the quiet waters adjacent to channels with swift current, in water two to four feet deep over sand and gravel bottom. Here it is frequently found near aquatic plants, such as water willow, *Justicia americana*, and pondweeds of the genus *Potamogeton*, which probably serve as cover when escaping from predators.

The quiet backwater areas inhabited by the peppered shiner are ideal habitat for a variety of aquatic insects, the preferred food of this shiner. It feeds from the bottom upward throughout the entire water column, including the surface of the water. Although it consumes an array of aquatic insects, midge larvae and mayfly larvae are the peppered shiner's favorite prey. The peppered shiner appears to be an opportunistic feeder, finding prey by sight in the clear, quiet water habitat.

The conservation status of the peppered shiner has been reviewed at the state and national level several times during the past decade. Most conservationists assign the shiner a rare or threatened status. A recent study of the peppered shiner was undertaken to review its status and to learn more about the details of its life history, habitat, distribution, and threats. Results of that study indicate that the threatened status assigned by previous workers is appropriate. It also identified impoundments, stream alteration, clearcutting, and pollution as major threats to the long term survival of the peppered shiner.

While streams may recover from periodic siltation, the impact on streams of dams and impoundments is drastic and long lasting. Impoundments have taken their toll on the peppered shiner and its habitat, where six major dams were constructed during the past 25 years. These six, plus four older dams, bring the number of impoundments within the range of the peppered shiner to ten. The Saline River, the largest river without an impoundment that the peppered shiner inhabits, has been targeted for damming, even though no money has been allocated for construction. In addition to supporting a good population of the peppered shiner, the Saline River has an excellent stream fishery.

Any aquatic species whose very restricted habitat is bombarded by silt and other pollutants from the upstream watershed has a serious problem. The peppered shiner is no exception. Clearcutting, a timber harvesting technique that takes all trees in large areas, often hundreds of acres, is used in several watersheds of streams inhabited by the peppered shiner. Clearcutting obviously increases silt load and water temperature fluctuation within the stream system. Runoff from agricultural operations can add large quantities of nutrients to streams, causing excessive plant growth (especially algae) and deterioration of water quality. Insecticide runoff from freshly treated fields can be lethal to fishes and important food organisms such as aquatic insects. Chemical pollution from untreated or improperly treated industrial waste and chemical spills can kill miles of stream ecosystem. In 1978, a train wreck near Benton, Arkansas spilled a formaldehyde-type chemical into the Saline River, killing aquatic organisms for several miles. The key to conservation and recovery of the peppered shiner is habitat protection, especially the Saline River.

## Leopard Darter
### *Percina pantherina*

The leopard darter, like the Niangua darter and peppered shiner, was first collected in 1884 and shares with these fishes the unfortunate distinction of being a threatened species. After 1884, it was not collected again until 1927 and did not receive a specific name until 1955. Leopard is the common name and the specific name, *pantherina*, comes from the leopard or panther-like dark spots along its back and sides. The spots contrast sharply with the yellow-olive background, presenting a striking color pattern. Typical of the genus *Percina*, the leopard darter lacks bright colors, distinguishing it from almost all the gaudy darters of the genus *Etheostoma*. The leopard darter rarely exceeds 3½ inches in length. It lives three to four years, about average for darters of the genus *Percina*.

The geographic range and habitat of the leopard darter are limited to the upland portions of the Little River system and its major tributaries in extreme southeast Oklahoma and southwest Arkansas. Of the six upland streams that range from large creeks to small rivers, the leopard darter occurs in four—the Cossatot, Mountain Fork, Glover, and upper Little River. Within these larger upland streams the leopard darter is typically found in moderately swift riffles and chutes with gravel or cobble bottoms in clear water, one to four feet deep. This habitat supports a large population of aquatic insects, including blackfly and mayfly larvae, the most common food of the leopard darter. Occasionally the darter ventures into areas adjacent to the swifter waters where there are beds of aquatic vegetation. Unsuccessful efforts to locate populations of leopard darters in small creeks, reservoirs, and sluggish streams confirm its restricted habitat.

172

The leopard darter is not the only fish to recognize the productive habitat provided by the clear, swift, rocky bottomed mountain streams. At least eight other darters are known to share this habitat. There are almost as many potential predators in this habitat, including smallmouth bass, spotted bass, and longear sunfish. While these predators may, on occasion, prey on leopard darters, in a roundabout way they have helped ensure their survival. Streams inhabited by the leopard darter are popular and valuable recreational streams for fishing and for canoeing. Recognition of the value and importance of these streams as unique natural resources has helped keep them clean and free flowing.

The major threat to the leopard darter and its fellow inhabitants of the larger upland streams in the Ouachitas is habitat alteration, especially dams and their accompanying reservoirs. The Lukfata Lake (reservoir) project proposed by the U.S. Army Corps of Engineers for Glover Creek typifies the problem. This project, authorized as part of the Flood Control Act of 1958, involved a dam 176 feet high, 2000 feet long, that would flood about 6000 acres of land. The purposes, as stated in the Draft Environmental Statement, were flood control, water supply, and recreation, including fish and wildlife. After the Draft Environmental Statement was released in June 1975, the U.S. Fish and Wildlife Service initiated a study of the leopard darter to determine its status, distribution, and habitat. As data from the study became available, it appeared that the largest population of leopard darters was in Glover Creek. The study also left little doubt that the proposed Lukfata Dam would adversely affect or eliminate more than half the leopard darter habitat in the Glover Creek system.

On July 6, 1976, the U.S. Fish and Wildlife Service proposed to list the leopard darter as a threatened species and delineate its critical habitat under provisions of the Endangered Species Act. After this proposal appeared in the Federal Register, considerable controversy erupted concerning the leopard darter and the Lukfata Dam. Most of the agitation came from the Glover River Organization, a local pro-development group, who stirred up their congressman and the Army Corps. On the other side of the controversy were several local and state conservation organizations who supported the proposed threatened status for the leopard darter and wanted to maintain Glover Creek as a free-flowing stream. The U.S. Fish and Wildlife Service was caught, as is frequently the case, in the middle answering questions from both sides. The Army Corps charged that the authorized, proposed, and initiated projects in the Little River drainage would "reduce the potential habitat of the species by about 12 percent." On close examination it was found that the 12 percent figure was determined by considering every stream, large and small, as potential habitat. Even though the leopard darter had never been found in small streams or large sluggish streams, they were considered "potential habitat." They also considered as "potential habitat" several stream systems in the Little River drainage, where the leopard darter had never been known to exist.

After considerable debate and an examination of the Lukfata Project during the Water Projects Review conducted by the Carter Administration, the leopard darter was added to the federal list of threatened species on January 27, 1978. At this point it appeared that the project would not be constructed for a variety of reasons, only one of which was the leopard darter. Less than two months after the species was listed, March 17, 1978, the Glover River Organization filed suit against the U.S. Department of the Interior challenging the listing of the leopard darter. They claimed the Department of the Interior should have prepared an Environmental Impact Statement instead of the Environmental Assessment which had been prepared in conjunction with the listing. On hearing the case in the U.S. District Court for the Eastern District of Oklahoma, the judge ruled in favor of the Glover River Organization. The case was appealed to the Tenth Circuit Court of Appeals, which overturned the lower court decision, leaving the critical habitat and threatened listing of the leopard darter in tact. Once again it appears that the Lukfata Dam project will not be built, but it remains an authorized project. The leopard darter is one of four fishes which have been involved in legal challenges under the Endangered Species Act.

# XIII.

# Tennessee and Cumberland Fishes

When the first settlers arrived in the southeastern United States, they found it blessed with an abundance of rivers and creeks with high quality water. Because this resource was so abundant, it was generally taken for granted. Unlike the southwestern United States with its water rights and water allocation struggles, water in the southeast has generally been considered a free commodity. This abundance is in part responsible for the abuse and outright destruction of many biologically productive rivers and creeks. The Cumberland and Tennessee rivers are but two of the dozens of southeastern streams, magnificent in their pristine state, that have been altered to the point that in many places they can hardly be called rivers. Not surprisingly, two fishes and several freshwater mussels and snails that once inhabited the streams of the Tennessee and Cumberland river basins are now extinct. Many fishes, freshwater mussels, and snails that were common in these rivers are now among our endangered and threatened species.

*Tennessee River,* the largest tributary of the Ohio River, collects its waters from more than 40,000 square miles of seven states in the southeastern United States. More than half of its watershed is within the state of Tennessee with the remainder split between Alabama, Georgia, Kentucky, Mississippi, North Carolina and Virginia. It meanders some seven hundred miles and traverses landscapes ranging from mountain to plateau to plain along its course. Its headwaters are in the Appalachian Highlands of Virginia, North Carolina and Tennessee in an area of heavy rainfall. While most of the watershed receives fifty to sixty inches of rain per year, some isolated areas may get up to eighty inches per year. Average discharge is about 65,000 cubic feet per second, but during flood stage it may reach 500,000 cubic feet per second. At the other extreme, it is also subject to drought and in some of the driest years it receives less than forty inches of rainfall. Elevations in the watershed range from a high of more than 6,000 feet in the Smoky Mountains to about three hundred feet at the junction with the Ohio River in western Kentucky.

In 1820, C. S. Rafinesque, a French naturalist and professor of botany and natural history at Transylvania University, published his treatise on the fishes of the Ohio River and its tributaries. In this book, entitled *Icthyologia Ohiensis*, he briefly describes the Tennessee River, formerly called the Cherokee River, as a very large and fine navigable river almost as large as the Ohio. Rafinesque also noted the great width of the river and mentioned the lake-like area around Muscle Shoals in northwest Alabama which was full of small islands, rapids, and shoals. The striking beauty and abundance of plant and animal life found at Muscle Shoals also impressed another early naturalist, Timothy A. Conrad. In his book on *New Fresh Water Shells of the United States*, published in 1834, he described the area as follows:

> *The expansion of the Tennessee River, known by the name of Muscle Shoals, is of the character I have described; it is shallow, ornamented with a number of small islands, and its bed is full of the long grass which abounds in various species of* Naiades. *The lover of the grand and the beautiful in natural scenery, as well as the student in science, will here find abundant sources of interest. He will be delighted with a noble river, whose beautiful and numerous islands are clothed with gigantic trees; whose high and undulating shore on one hand is ornamented with thriving villages, and on the other spreads out an extensive alluvial, rich in all the gifts of Ceres, or rises abruptly from the river a mural escarpment of carboniferous limestone, which reflects its blue and somber aspect in the crystal waters at its base.*

The only aspect of this lovely view remaining at Muscle Shoals that resembles the scene described by Conrad in 1834 is the high limestone escarpment or bluff on the south side of the river. Even this unmovable landmark has been reduced by the murky backwaters of Pickwick Dam that cover the bottom of the bluff.

Muscle Shoals was perhaps the most extensive shoal area, but the scene there was duplicated on a smaller scale at many points along the river and its major tributaries. These scenes gradually disappeared as the human population along the river expanded. Along with more people came the increased demand for electrical power, flood control, and riverboat traffic. On May 18, 1933, the U.S. Congress approved the creation of the Tennessee Valley Authority to promote the economic and social well-being of the people in that region. This was the beginning of rapid development in the Tennessee Valley that brought profound and long lasting changes to the aquatic systems of the basin. First came the large dams on the main channel of the Tennessee River, followed by dams on the tributary streams. Today the Tennessee River system, with more than fifty major dams, is one of the most "developed" rivers in the world. Remains of the widespread and diverse fish fauna and other aquatic organisms of the system are tucked away in the few miles of unaltered rivers that have escaped development.

*Cumberland River* begins at the confluence of the Poor Fork and Clover Fork near the town of Harlan in southeastern Kentucky. From here it flows southwesterly through Kentucky into central Tennessee through the city of Nashville, where it turns, taking a northeasterly course back into Kentucky before spilling its waters into the Ohio River near Smithland, Kentucky. From its headwaters in the rugged Cumberland Mountain it meanders some seven hundred miles to its mouth on the alluvial valley of the lower Ohio River. The basin, which averages about fifty miles wide, drains about 18,000 square miles, approximately half the area drained by its neighbor to the south, the Tennessee River. Elevations in the Cumberland Basin are generally lower, ranging from about 4000 feet in the Cumberland Mountains to about 300 feet at its mouth. Most of the over fifty inches of rain falls during the winter and spring, which are periods of frequent flooding. The Cumberland River, like the Tennessee River, has been "developed" from its mouth to near its headwaters.

13–1
Tellico Dam on the Little Tennessee River, under construction. Photo by J. D. Williams.

# Slackwater Darter
## *Etheostoma boschungi*

(Color plate 11.)

On a Sunday evening in December, 1968, Ben Wall and I (JDW) were in the field zoology laboratory at the University of Alabama when a student, Dorothy Sentz, turned in a collection of fishes she had taken from a tributary to the Tennessee River in northwest Alabama. We were then graduate student lab assistants in the field zoology class and had been asked by Dr. Herbert T. Boschung to check the identification of fishes brought into the lab. As we sorted through a collection of fishes turned in by Dorothy Sentz, we came across one darter about two inches long that immediately caught our attention. The more we looked at this darter the more convinced we were that it was unlike any of the approximately 25 species of *Etheostoma* known to occur in Alabama. We worked into the early morning hours, carefully comparing this darter to other darters in the University of Alabama Ichthyological Collection, but came up with more questions than answers. Because we only had one specimen, was this darter an aberrant individual? Was it a hybrid? Was it a species that was common farther north, but that had never been reported as far south as Alabama? Or, was it in fact a new species?

During the next week we searched for answers to these and other questions and by week's end had decided to visit Cypress Creek near Florence, Alabama to examine the habitat and see if we could find additional individuals of this unusual darter. When we arrived at Cypress Creek, the stream looked as we had suspected it would, like hundreds of other streams in northern Alabama and southern Tennessee. As we ventured into the creek with our seine, we were somewhat apprehensive about what we would find. After only a few minutes of seining in swift water riffle areas without success, we moved to the slackwaters along the margin of the stream. Here, after a couple of runs with the seine through leaf litter and debris, we hit the jackpot. Once we had pinpointed the habitat we found a dozen individuals in a matter of a few hours. By the end of the day we had the answer to one question—these unusual darters did represent a new species. On returning to the university that evening, we made the decision to name the new species in honor of our professor, Dr. Herbert T. Boschung, who had contributed so much to the science of ichthyology in the southeastern United States.

As studies on the slackwater darter progressed, numerous questions had to be answered. Among the more interesting questions was where did it come from and what darter was it most closely related to? We were surprised to find that the slackwater darter was derived from a group of darters that occurred primarily west of the Mississippi River in the Ozarks, Ouachitas, and the Arkansas River system. One of these, the paleback darter, *Etheostoma pallididorsum*, is restricted to a few streams in the Ouachitas in southeastern Arkansas and is also a threatened species. Only one other species related to this group occurs east of the Mississippi River. The trispot darter, *Etheostoma trisella*, is restricted to the headwaters of the Coosa River system in Tennessee, Georgia, and Alabama, and is also threatened like its relatives.

Before publishing our new species description in 1974, more streams with similar habitat were sampled to locate additional populations of the slackwater darter. Two populations were found, one in the Flint River system of north-central Alabama and one in the Buffalo River system of south-central Tennessee. Subsequent to the description in 1974, two additional populations were found, one in Swan Creek, north-central Alabama, and one in Shoal Creek, south-central Tennessee. While the discovery of additional populations was encouraging, none were wide ranging or as large as the Cypress Creek population. How surprising that the slackwater darter escaped detection for so long, when one considers the hundreds of collections of fishes taken in this area through the years beginning as early as the late 1800s. The possibility of finding additional populations always exists, but because of the habitat requirements and unusual life history of the slackwater darter, this possibility seems unlikely.

The habitat of most darters is relatively constant throughout the year, and those that do move generally do so between areas of similar habitat within the same stream. Slackwater darters, however, have two very different types of habitat: one for the breeding season and the other during the nonbreeding season. The nonbreeding habitat for the slackwater darter is small to moderately large streams up to forty feet wide and six feet deep. They are most often found in slow current in the larger streams along the bank where the

13–2
Seining for slackwater darters in their spawning habitat. Photo by J. D. Williams.

179

bottom is a mixture of gravel, mud, and silt with an accumulation of twigs and decaying leaves. Slackwater darters can usually be found in this habitat from early April through December. During November and early December they begin to aggregate for their migration to the spawning habitat. At the same time, males begin to acquire their bright breeding colors and eggs carried by the female begin to enlarge. By early January the migration to their spawning waters is in full swing. Spawning habitat for the slackwater darter is most unusual for a fish and, with the exception of the slackwater's close relatives, it is a habitat that is not exploited by any other fish. However, this habitat is commonly used by some species of frogs, toads, and salamanders. This habitat is the clear seepage water, two to four inches deep, in open woods and grassy fields. These areas are usually twelve to eighteen inches above the adjacent stream that they drain into. The darters depend on the typical winter rains to raise the water level sufficiently to allow them to move from the stream into the fields.

Water level permitting, the slackwater darters begin to enter their shallow, grassy spawning habitat during the last week of January. By mid-February the males have attained their peak nuptial coloration and the females' 300–350 eggs are fully developed. Males at this point begin to stake out territories around clumps of grass and initiate courtship behavior. The eggs are deposited in the clumps of grass from the end of February through the end of March with a peak in spawning activity in mid-March. After the eggs hatch, the larval slackwater darters remain in the breeding habitat until April or May, when they leave to join their parents in the stream habitat. If they linger too long in the breeding habitat, they can be stranded and die as the water level drops and the area eventually dries out in early summer. If you walk through the breeding habitat during the summer or fall after it has dried out, it is very difficult to imagine that any fish could spawn in such an unlikely place as a pasture.

The limited distribution of the slackwater darter, combined with the proposed channelization of Cypress Creek by the U.S. Soil Conservation Service concerned southeastern ichthyologists. In 1972, even before the slackwater darter was described in the scientific literature, biologists at the first Alabama Endangered Species Symposium considered it vulnerable to extirpation. At the second Alabama Endangered Species Symposium in 1976, biologists reviewed the status of the slackwater darter and assigned it a threatened status. Within a year, September 1977, the U.S. Fish and Wildlife Service added the slackwater darter to the U.S. Endangered and Threatened Species List as a threatened species. The major threats to the slackwater darter were the Soil Conservation Service stream channelization projects on Cypress and Swan creeks and creeping urbanization from Huntsville, Alabama in the Flint River system. Since the species was added to the federal list in 1977, progress has been made in protecting its habitat in Cypress Creek. After a thorough study of its life history and distribution in the Cypress Creek watershed, the Soil Conservation Service reconsidered their design for the channelization project. Present Soil Conservation Service plans call for a project that will achieve the desired results without adversely affecting the slackwater darter habitat. Unfortunately, the slackwater darter was not discovered in Swan Creek until the channelization project was almost complete. The impact of that project on the darter has not been assessed. As for the problem of creeping urbanization, it continues to creep, gradually encroaching on the habitat of the slackwater darter.

# Snail Darter
## *Percina tanasi*

(Color plate 12.)

Tellico Dam on the lower end of the Little Tennessee River was one of many potential dam sites identified by the Tennessee Valley Authority in 1936. The Tellico project, like many other dam projects, was considered a means of reducing high unemployment and migration of young people out of the area. After a review of the Tellico project in the 1930s it appeared that the dam project would not be economically feasible to build. In 1942, the dam was reconsidered and plans were made to move forward with the project. This time it was interrupted by World War II. After the war, the Tennessee Valley Authority concentrated on larger dam projects and Tellico was not proposed again until 1963, at a cost of $41 million. While there was strong support for this project there was also considerable opposition from local citizens. The Tennessee State Planning Commission also questioned the need for the project. Opposition to the Tellico Dam Project continued during 1964 and in 1965 Supreme Court Justice William O. Douglas visited the area to express his support of the Eastern Band of the Cherokee Indian Nation's opposition to the project. In 1965 and 1966, congressional hearings examined the economic and environmental aspects of the project. These hearings were very stormy with proponents and opponents of the Tellico Dam project turning out in full force. The proponents won and in 1966, Congress approved Tellico Dam and authorized funds to start the project in 1967. With congressional approval and funding, initial work on the project began and the fate of the Little Tennessee River, referred to locally as the Little T, appeared sealed.

Passage of the National Environmental Policy Act in 1969 did not go unnoticed by the Tennessee Valley Authority nor by the opponents to Tellico. Soon after passage of the National Environmental Policy Act the opponents of Tellico Dam asked the Tennessee Valley Authority to prepare an Environmental Impact Statement for the project, but the Tennessee Valley Authority felt it was not necessary. In 1971, local farmers, landowners, and conservationists joined and filed a suit in Federal Court to halt the Tellico project because the Tennessee Valley Authority had not prepared an Environmental Impact Statement as required by the National Environmental Policy Act. The Tennessee Valley Authority countered by claiming that the National Environmental Policy Act was not applicable to the Tellico project because it was approved by Congress before the National Environmental Policy Act was passed. The courts did not see it that way and issued an injunction in 1971, stopping Tellico Dam until Tennessee Valley Authority submitted an Environmental Impact Statement for their project. The Tellico Dam project was idle for almost two years while Tennessee Valley Authority prepared their

13-3
Little Tennessee River provided habitat for the snail darter prior to impoundment by
Tellico Dam. Photo by J. D. Williams.

Environmental Impact Statement for submission to the Federal Court. During this period the opposition gained support from several camps, including Governor Winfield Dunn of Tennessee, who urged Tennessee Valley Authority to halt plans for Tellico Dam, pointing out the historical and cultural importance of the area and recreational value of the Little T in its natural free-flowing state. Tennessee Valley Authority rejected this request, maintaining that benefits from the Tellico Dam were more important. In 1973, the Federal Court ruled that the Tellico Dam Environmental Impact Statement was acceptable and dismissed the injunction. Once again work on Tellico Dam commenced and the fate of the Little T was sealed for the second time.

On December 28, 1973, President Richard Nixon signed the Endangered Species Act of 1973. This new act provided much broader coverage than the Endangered Species Conservation Act of 1969. One of the provisions of this law required federal agencies to examine their projects and activities to ensure that they would not jeopardize an endangered or threatened species, or destroy critical habitat. While Tennessee Valley Authority was aware of the impending new act, they were not aware of any potential endangered species conflicts in the Tellico Project area. The aquatic surveys of the Little T had revealed several rare fishes. Yet, all occurred in several other Tennessee River system streams as well.

This all changed on August 12, 1973, a hot summer day at the University of Tennessee. Dr. David Etnier and a graduate student, Bob Stiles, decided to cool off on a field trip to the Little T. They drove to a site on the lower part of the river called Coytee Springs. Decked out in face mask, snorkel, and flippers they waded into the clear, cool water flowing over a clean gravel bottom. They had collected fishes at this spot on several occasions and were not expecting any surprises. As they swam across the riffle, Etnier came across a small three-inch long fish with a brownish olive body and dark saddle-like markings across its back. At first glance this fish looked like a sculpin, genus *Cottus,* but after a closer look it was clearly a darter, genus *Percina.* After netting several specimens, they returned to the fish lab for a closer look. After several months of research it became clear they had discovered a new darter which fed largely on the small snails that were abundant in the gravelly shoals. They had discovered the snail darter.

In the fall of 1974, Dr. Etnier submitted a status report on the snail darter to the U. S. Fish and Wildlife Service. The report indicated that the darter was endangered and the major threat was the impoundment and siltation of its habitat behind Tellico Dam. On January 20, 1975, the Fish and Wildlife Service was petitioned to list the snail darter as an endangered species. After a review of all available data, a proposal to list the species was published in the Federal Register on June 17, 1975. Earlier in June the Tennessee Valley Authority, foreseeing a problem, transplanted snail darters into the Hiwassee River, a tributary of the Tennessee River south of the Little T. The Tennessee Valley Authority carried out the transplant without asking or telling the state of Tennessee or the U. S. Fish and Wildlife Service. In September, the Tennessee Valley Authority transplanted an additional 361 snail darters to the Hiwassee River to establish an additional breeding population. There was another transplant in February of 1976 that brought the total snail darter transplants to the Hiwassee River to more than seven hundred individuals.

After eight years the Hiwassee River population appears to be established, but only time will tell.

In October of 1975, the Fish and Wildlife Service placed the snail darter on the U. S. Endangered Species List and, on December 16, 1975, proposed critical habitat in an area that was to be flooded by Tellico Dam. Construction on the dam was proceeding at a rapid pace, with multiple shifts working day and night. The Tennessee Valley Authority was clearly working as fast as they could to complete the dam and force congressional action for its closure. Their actions were obviously in violation of the Endangered Species Act, yet they continued to build the dam. In February 1976, suit was brought against Tennessee Valley Authority for violation of the Endangered Species Act and requested the court to issue a permanent injunction on the completion of Tellico Dam. On April 1, 1976, the U. S. Fish and Wildlife Service took action on behalf of the snail darter by declaring the lower portion of the Little T as critical habitat. The trial was held on April 23 and was brief and concise. In May, Judge Robert Taylor issued a decision denying the request for a permanent injunction on completion of Tellico Dam. This decision was appealed to the U.S. Court of Appeals for the Sixth Circuit, but it appeared this action would come too late, as Tennessee Valley Authority announced that the gates of Tellico Dam would be closed on January 1, 1977. Once again the Little T appeared to be finished.

During the fall of 1976, the dozens of memos, letters, statements, etc. flowed between Tennessee Valley Authority, the U. S. Fish and Wildlife Service, the state of Tennessee, Congress, and conservation groups. As the January 1, 1977 closure date for Tellico approached, there was a feeling of desperation among proponents of the Little T and the snail darter. The news from Tennessee Valley Authority that construction was behind schedule and the closure date for Tellico Dam would be postponed was little consolation. On January 31, 1977, the Court of Appeals surprised everyone and reversed the District Court decision and issued a permanent injunction halting all activities relating to Tellico Dam that would harm the snail darter or its critical habitat. This, along with the inauguration of a conservation-minded President—Jimmy Carter— was cause for celebration throughout the conservation community. Once again a reprieve for the Little T.

Almost immediately after the court decision, Tennessee Valley Authority appealed the case to the Supreme Court, petitioned the U. S. Fish and Wildlife Service to delist the snail darter, and requested a permit to transplant all snail darters from the Little T. They claimed that the transplant population in the Hiwassee River was established and that the Tellico Dam was blocking the snail darter spawning migration. A further argument was that the darters in the Little T would disappear within two to four years if not transplanted. In July 1977, the U. S. Fish and Wildlife Service denied the Tennessee Valley Authority request to transplant the darters from the Little T and in December of 1977, formally denied Tennessee Valley Authority's petition to delist the snail darter. In the meantime darters were being picked up below the dam and moved above the dam to gravelly shoal areas upstream. At this point the outlook for the snail darter was looking a little better. In the spring of 1978, the snail darter received a big boost when newly appointed Tennessee Valley

Authority Director, David Freeman, suggested nonimpoundment alternatives to the Tellico Dam project. By this time the snail darter had made headlines throughout the country and grabbed the attention of Congress. It received even more attention when the Supreme Court, on June 15, 1978, upheld the Court of Appeals decision halting the dam. While the Supreme Court decision was great news for the Little T and snail darter, there was some "fine print" in the ruling. The Supreme Court recommended that the only relief for the Tennessee Valley Authority and their Tellico Project was through the U. S. Congress.

In the fall of 1978, after news articles and editorials debating the snail darter *vs.* Tellico Dam appeared in the news nationwide, Congress took action. They amended the Endangered Species Act, creating an exemption committee, also called "God Committee" or "Extinction Committee," to resolve life and death conflicts between endangered species and threatening projects. The amendments specifically named the snail darter–Tellico Dam project as a case to be decided by this committee. The committee thoroughly reviewed all aspects of the conflict and had to decide in favor of the darter *or* the dam. In January of 1979, after several months of research and careful consideration of alternatives, the committee was ready to decide. In a very tense and dramatic public meeting in the Department of the Interior, Washington, D. C., the vote on the question was called for—a unanimous decision in favor of the snail darter! Could this be? At last the Little T and snail darter had been saved!!

Saved for a few months! A very short amendment exempting the Tellico Project from all federal laws, including the Endangered Species Act, was attached to energy legislation and passed Congress without debate. Surprisingly, most of the Congress did not know the amendment had been added until the bill was clear and on its way to President Carter for his signature. The President reluctantly signed the bill into law and in so doing sentenced the Little T and its snail darters to death beneath the murky waters behind Tellico Dam.

In the final analysis, it appears that the President traded the Little T and its snail darters for crucial conservative votes for his Panama Canal legislation pending in Congress. In January of 1980, after more than fifteen years of battle, the gates of Tellico Dam were closed and the Little T went under for the last time, along with its snail darters. Other major natural resources that also went under include: an outstanding trout fishery, unequalled anywhere in the southeastern U. S.; more than 17,000 acres of high quality, productive agricultural lands; and many significant historical and archeological sites including the Cherokee Village of Tanasi, the namesake of the snail darter and the state of Tennessee. The final battle was over the snail darter. But the war was over natural resources whose value far exceeds the benefits of the Tellico Dam project—a classic BOONDOGGLE!!

So where is the snail darter today? Unlike the other natural resources that were drowned along with the Little T, this little darter is ironically doing fairly well. The Hiwassee River transplants survived and additional populations have been discovered across the Tennessee border in northwestern Georgia and northeastern Alabama. The future of the snail darter looks fairly secure. Long live the little darter that could.

# Blackside Dace
## *Phoxinus cumberlandensis*

(Color plate 13.)

This brightly colored dace, a threatened species, was first discovered in a stream tributary to the Cumberland River in Daniel Boone National Forest, Whitley County, Kentucky in 1975. Although a few specimens had been collected prior to 1975, the differences between the blackside dace and other related minnows went unnoticed. Further studies after 1975 confirmed the distinctive nature of this fish and, in 1978, Wayne and Lynn Starnes formally described the species, giving it the specific name, *cumberlandensis*, after the Cumberland River to which it is endemic. That such a distinctive fish went undetected for so long is somewhat surprising until one considers the restricted nature of its range or distribution. In a recent survey it was found to be largely restricted to the Cumberland Plateau area in the upper Cumberland River drainage of extreme southeastern Kentucky and adjacent portions of northern Tennessee. With a few exceptions, this area is entirely above Cumberland Falls on the Cumberland River in McCreary and Whitley counties, Kentucky.

The limited drainage area above Cumberland Falls where the blackside dace occurs may also be the area where the species evolved. The nearest relative of the blackside dace is the mountain redbelly dace, *Phoxinus oreas,* which occurs in streams of the upper Tennessee River, New River, and several Atlantic Coast drainages. The ancestral stock which gave rise to the blackside dace probably entered the area above the falls long before the Pleistocene Ice Age through a geologic process known as stream capture. This process involves the headward or upstream erosion or cutting of a stream in one drainage basin through its divide into another drainage basin where it "captures" a stream of that basin. This process, which is very slow, may involve the transfer of fishes into a new drainage basin where they were formerly absent. This appears to have been the case for the blackside dace when a stream in the upper Cumberland River drainage basin captured a stream from an adjacent drainage basin which contained the ancestral blackside dace stock. Cumberland Falls, an insurmountable barrier to fishes, also played a role in the evolution of the blackside dace, by preventing the upstream movement of another relative, the southern redbelly dace. The southern redbelly dace has only recently entered the upper Cumberland drainage above the falls, perhaps by stream capture. The blackside dace may be the only species of fish that has evolved in isolation above Cumberland Falls.

Habitat of the blackside dace is best characterized as small upland streams six to fifteen feet wide, where the riffle-area to pool-area ratio is about equal. Within these streams, blackside dace are found in pools with clear, cool water where the bottom is bedrock, rubble, or sand at depths up to one yard. Most of these streams are at elevations of 900 to 1600 feet and their banks are covered by dense stands of rhododendrons and hemlock. These small streams are sparsely populated with fishes with only three to five species commonly occurring with the blackside dace. The related southern redbelly dace is occasionally taken in the same pool as the blackside dace, but when the two are

186

found together, one species usually greatly outnumbers the other. This is due in part to the difference in habitat with the southern redbelly dace occupying slightly lower gradient streams, downstream from the blackside dace habitat. In areas where blackside dace habitat has been altered, the southern redbelly dace appears to have gained the upper hand and displaced the blackside dace.

Even though the small upland streams in the upper Cumberland produce a variety and abundance of aquatic invertebrates, these are a small fraction of the total diet of the blackside dace. The blackside dace seems to prefer plant matter such as algae, diatoms, root hairs of larger plants, and fragments of organic material throughout their three-year life span. They also ingest large quantities of sand, but the purpose or function, if any, behind this behavior is not known. The sand might be ingested along with other food, but could be eaten to help crush the plant material they feed on, or they may obtain nutrients from the bacteria which grow on the surface of the sand grains. The diet of the blackside dace is very similar to that of the bluntnose minnow, *Pimephales notatus,* and the related southern redbelly dace, *Phoxinus erythrogaster,* but these fishes are rarely found in the blackside dace habitat. When these two species are found in the same area as the blackside dace, they may, if food is limited, compete for this resource. Young white suckers, *Catostomus commersoni,* which occur along side the blackside dace, also feed on organic material, but invertebrates make up the major part of their diet. The other fishes which regularly occur in the blackside dace, habitat feed primarily on aquatic insects.

13–4
Drainage from coal strip mining often results in siltation and pollution of nearby streams. Photo by J. D. Williams.

187

As far removed as this area is from major human population centers and large dams, one might think the blackside dace habitat would be secure. Unfortunately this is not the case. This area is part of the extensive and valuable Appalachian Plateau coal field. While coal has been mined in this area since it was settled, mining had little impact on the blackside dace until the arrival of strip mining in the 1950s. Strip mining is a process where the soil and rock overlying a bed of coal is "stripped" away, exposing the coal bed. This technique increased coal output at reduced cost compared to underground mining. It also has created serious environmental problems in streams due to siltation and pollution from acid drainage from the mine. These problems not only threaten the blackside dace, they adversely affect stream ecosystems downstream from the dace habitat.

During a recent survey of the upper Cumberland River drainage, approximately 170 small upland stream sites were sampled to determine the extent and status of blackside dace populations. This survey found 26 populations of blackside dace. Seventeen are in some jeopardy from coal mining and accompanying problems; others are too small and isolated to make a substantial contribution to the future preservation of the species. Equally disturbing news from this survey was the speculation that more than fifty populations had been eliminated because of habitat alteration resulting from coal mining activities. The basis for this speculation was the evaluation of the habitat compared to the known habitat requirements of the blackside dace. Additional evidence came from conditions at five sites where populations of blackside dace are known to have been extirpated. Other streams examined during the survey had been possible habitat for the dace and may or may not have supported populations before they were altered by mining and other Man-induced changes. Among these changes are stream canopy removal and siltation which result from poor timber harvesting techniques and road construction. Note that the situation does not have to be "one *or* the other," coal mining *or* high quality streams. There are many actions that can reduce the effects of mining. While the actions would increase the cost of mining, they would greatly improve water quality and stream productivity. This one time cost to the mining operation would result in long term benefits to the area downstream.

At present, some of the larger and more stable populations of the blackside dace are within or adjacent to the Daniel Boone National Forest. This area is obviously very important in the conservation of this species. Steps should be taken to ensure the protection of stream habitat in this national forest. We hope conservation actions will be initiated on streams outside the Daniel Boone National Forest to help maintain other populations. These actions might include mine reclamation, land treatment to reduce siltation, renovation of small upland streams, and reintroduction of the blackside dace into its former habitat.

# XIV.

# Southeastern Spring Fishes

In addition to being endangered and threatened species, these three fishes also have a very limited and unique habitat—springs. A spring is defined as a natural discharge or flow of water from the soil or rock to the surface. Spring formations vary depending upon climatic conditions, geology of the area, and topography. Some springs are small, shallow areas a few inches deep, while others may become large ponds, and streams. While the potential exists for springs to form over much of the country, most large springs occur where the underlying rocks are limestone. As water percolates through the soil into cracks in the limestone it dissolves channels in the rock forming underground streams that often surface as large springs. Such limestone formations lie beneath almost all of Florida and large portions of Alabama, Kentucky, Tennessee, Arkansas, and Missouri. These areas have many large springs, underground streams, sinkholes, and caves. Silver Springs, near Ocala, Florida, is an example of a large spring with a flow of about twenty million gallons per hour, a surface area of two acres, and a depth of more than 35 feet. Most springs are smaller with a discharge measured in thousands or a few million gallons per day.

Springs which the barrens topminnow, spring pygmy sunfish, and watercress darter inhabit are considerably smaller than Silver Springs, but they still have several characteristics in common. The water temperature, which seasonally varies in surface streams, remains constant throughout the year. In most springs of the southeastern U. S. the water temperature is approximately the same as the average annual air temperature for the region. The water in these springs is typically very clear and does not become dingy after heavy rains and floods. The chemical content, dissolved gases and minerals, of springs also remains constant. The constant spring environment is ideal for ecological and biological studies and, in fact, has been used as an outdoor laboratory on numerous occasions.

Springs are usually populated with lush growths of aquatic plants that range from small filamentous algae and mosses to large rooted plants several feet long. These plants in turn support many aquatic insects and other invertebrates. Snails are often one of the most abundant animals present in the calcium-rich waters of springs. The shallow marshy areas around the edge of springs typically support healthy frog populations. With so many plants and invertebrates in such a constant environment, one would expect an abundance and variety of fishes. Large springs in Florida frequently do support a varied and abundant fish fauna—more than forty species of fishes have been reported from Silver Springs, Florida. However, other springs are practically fishless around their source because the water coming from the ground contains very little dissolved oxygen. Beyond Florida, most springs are inhabited by only a few (six to twelve) species of fishes, but they may be very abundant. Widespread and common fishes typically associated with upland southeastern springs include the central stoneroller, *Campostoma anomalum;* southern redbelly dace, *Phoxinus erythrogaster;* creek chub, *Semotilus atromaculatus;* blacknose dace, *Rhinichthys atratulus;* mosquitofish, *Gambusia affinis;* green sunfish, *Lepomis cyanellus;* and banded sculpin, *Cottus carolinae.* The whiteline topminnow, *Fundulus albolineatus,* which was known only from Big Spring in Huntsville, Alabama is extinct. Other southeastern fishes that are endemic to one or more springs include coldwater darter, *Etheostoma ditrema;* tuscumbia darter, *Etheostoma tuscumbia;* pygmy sculpin, *Cottus pygmaeus;* and the three species discussed below.

# Barrens Topminnow
## *Fundulus julisia*

(Color plate 14.)

Before a recent survey turned up additional populations of the threatened barrens topminnow, the last refuge for this small bluish-colored fish was a spring pool in the front yard of a home owned by Joseph and Bertha Banks, a self-employed carpenter and his wife, in Summitville, Coffee County, Tennessee. The Banks purchased the house in 1972 because of their fondness for the limestone bluff and cave that were next to it. Little did they realize that the 75 × 50-foot ornamental pond behind a small dam Mr. Banks built would contain a rare species of fish and bring notoriety to their home.

Banks constructed a concrete dam across the spring run outflow from the natural cave to create a small pond for rainbow trout. The stocked rainbow trout still disappeared downstream, but the pond provided a suitable home for the barrens topminnow. Schools of ten to twenty topminnows can be seen casually swimming about in the pond. Eventually the spring waters empty into West Fork Hickory Creek, which currently receives untreated effluents from a trailer court. In the protected pond, the topminnows probably feed on aquatic invertebrates and fallen terrestrial insects. Occasionally a topminnow will make it over the concrete dam and on downstream, but very few have survived the half mile journey to West Fork Hickory Creek. Even though a few stragglers have made it to West Fork Hickory Creek, that stream does not appear suitable to support a reproducing population. The topminnow requires the clear cold ground water that flows from the cave and cannot survive long without it. Also, the effluent from the trailer court may be toxic to the topminnow, especially during periods of drought.

First collected in the spring of 1937, during pre-impoundment surveys by the Tennessee Valley Authority, the barrens topminnow was unofficially recognized as a distinct species in 1938 by the late Dr. Carl L. Hubbs. The three 1937 collections of the barrens topminnow were deposited in the University of Michigan's Museum of Zoology and cataloged as the whiteline topminnow, *Fundulus albolineatus,* a species that is considered extinct by most ichthyologists. And there the matter sat, receiving little or no attention for several years. After these initial collections of the barrens topminnow in the 1930s, no further specimens were found until the mid-1960s.

For years the barrens topminnow and whiteline topminnow, because of their similarities, had been considered conspecifics; that is, belonging to the same species. The only known habitat of the whiteline topminnow was Big Spring and its outflow, Spring Creek, in Huntsville, Alabama. Springs are constant sources of clean, uncontaminated water and are used in many ways, not the least of which is as a water supply for homes and municipalities. Like many springs that were used as sources of water, Big Spring, whose spring outflow cut through Huntsville's city park, was drastically altered with cement-lined banks for a retaining wall around the spring's edge. A low dam was constructed across the spring run and carp, goldfish, and even ducks were placed in the impounded waters. The whiteline topminnow was last seen in 1889, before the massive habitat alterations. We believe that it is extinct.

Based on additional investigation of character traits from preserved specimens of the whiteline topminnow and the barrens topminnow, some ichthyologists felt that the two were, indeed, different from each other. Carl Hubbs, with his highly trained eye for detail and a feeling that the specimens were of a new species, helped put later ichthyologists on the right track. In July of 1982, James Williams and David Etnier, an ichthyologist at the University of Tennessee who discovered the snail darter, officially described the barrens topminnow as a new species and gave it the name, *Fundulus julisia.* The species epithet, *julisia,* comes from the Cherokee Indian language and means "watercress fish" which seems appropriate as lush matlike growths of watercress, *Nasturtium,* are often found where this fish occurs.

Living in waters from springs, spring runs, and tiny streams influenced by groundwater, the barrens topminnow used to inhabit Doak Springs and Lake Ovaca and several other local spring ponds. Like the Banks artificial pond, Little Duck River in Coffee County has luxuriant watercress mats, but despite much searching, no barrens topminnow have been found here since 1964. The absence of the barrens topminnow in several areas where it formerly occurred prompted the state of Tennessee and the U. S. Fish and Wildlife Service to support a status survey for the species. The survey called for the sampling of spring pools and streams with the characteristic barrens topminnow habitat to determine present abundance and distribution of the species. When the survey was completed in the winter of 1982, the survey team came in with great news! Over one hundred spring pools and streams in Conner, Coffee, and Warren County, Tennessee were checked. Eight had barrens topminnows. All eight localities are within a five mile radius of each other, and four of the eight had good populations that appear fairly secure. Total population estimates for the barrens topminnow now range from 4,000 to 6,000 individuals.

In August of 1980 Mr. Banks, the Nature Conservancy, and the Tennessee Wildlife Resources Agency drafted a management agreement to maintain landowner rights and monitor the barrens topminnow habitat. In this pact, the Tennessee Wildlife Resources Agency agreed to help keep the Banks spring pond algae-free and rectify other changes that might be detrimental to the well-being of the barrens topminnow population, but without interfering with the Banks' rights as owners. Because the pond was in the front yard of the Banks' house and the homeowners were quite concerned with protecting the rare fish, all parties involved felt that the Banks would be in better touch with the barrens topminnow than anyone else. So, Joseph and Bertha Banks remain crucial links in the survival of one of the best populations of barrens topminnows. With the knowledge that a threatened species of fish resides in their spring pond, they no longer talk of cementing its margin or draining it on a regular basis to remove excessive plant growth. Now they run water from the home-use well into the pond during periods of low spring flow to keep the fish alive and healthy.

The Banks have closely watched their resident population of topminnows from a homemade swing that dangles from a branch of an old tree at the edge of the pond. But even from the vantage point offered by this swing turned "observation deck," much is still unknown regarding the biology of this tiny minnow.

Biologists do know that when the water temperatures reach about 70°F the male engages in courtship behavior. The male barrens topminnow takes on a pale blue-green to yellow-green coloration with a smattering of orange to dark red spots on its head and body flanks. In addition, the male develops small sharp cone-shaped bumps called nuptial or breeding tubercles on its dorsal and anal fins. These tubercles are used by the male to physically stimulate the female during spawning. The actual spawning ritual begins when a sexually mature male chases a willing female until she retreats into dense vegetation which serves as spawning cover. The eggs she lays will adhere to the spawning substrate. Because of the extensive large floating mats of aquatic vegetation no one has actually observed the spawning act. Likewise, while the fecundity of the female barrens topminnow is still a mystery, a single spawning pair of topminnows have been found to produce over 25 eggs daily for several days. While the barrens topminnow has been successfully reared in aquaria, no formal efforts to propagate large numbers in captivity have materialized as yet.

At present the Tennessee Wildlife Resources Agency plans to continue support for monitoring existing barrens topminnows' habitats and search for new populations. Other plans call for the examination of spring pools and streams where the species formerly occurred with a view towards renovation of the habitat and eventual reintroduction of the topminnow. They are also considering management agreements with landowners, similar to the Banks agreement, to give added habitat protection to the recently discovered populations. All things considered, the future of the barrens topminnow appears bright. With continued conservation efforts this species could be on the road to recovery very soon.

# Spring Pygmy Sunfish
## *Elassoma* species

Of the millions of people who enjoy the pastime of fishing in North America, the odds are good that most freshwater anglers got their start by catching a sunfish, bluegill, crappie, or even a bass. There was always a good chance of hooking either a "sunny" or bluegill with a cricket, worm, or even a kernel of corn securely fastened to a hook. Most of the 33 species of the North American sunfish family, Centrarchidae, have provided untold hours of fishing enjoyment for countless Americans of all ages.

There is one group of sunfishes, however, that most people have never seen before, much less caught on hook and line. The pygmy sunfishes, genus *Elassoma,* are the smallest members of the sunfish family, rarely reaching two inches in length. They typically inhabit the dark-stained waters of sluggish streams, swamps, and ponds of the central and lower Mississippi Valley and the Coastal Plain from North Carolina to Texas. One exception to this is the spring pygmy sunfish which inhabits limestone springs in northern Alabama.

The spring pygmy sunfish seemed to have headed down the dead end road of extinction in 1941, the last year that it was seen swimming in Pryor Spring, a tributary to the Tennessee River. It was thought to be extinct until a University of Tennessee ichthyologist, Dr. David Etnier, found a single living individual in the Beaverdam-Moss Spring complex in 1973, 32 years later.

First discovered as a new species of sunfish in the waters of Cave Springs in 1937, by the Tennessee Valley Authority during its preimpoundment surveys, the spring pygmy sunfish still has not been officially described in the scientific journals. Instead this fish is recognized as an undescribed species of the genus *Elassoma*. Perhaps the most distinguishing characteristic of this species is the "window" found in both the dorsal and anal fins of the male. This "window" or clear spot in each fin is created by the transparent membrane covering the last four dorsal and last three anal fin rays respectively. The rest of the male's body is dark brown to blue-black in color. Six to eight irregularly spaced vertical bars of lustrous gold contrast boldly with the dark background. A variety of shades of brown with or without irregularly placed vertical bars makes up the body coloration of the female spring pygmy sunfish. Only ¾ to 1 inch in length as an adult, the tiny sunfish resides in dense, submerged aquatic vegetation in the shallow, 6 to 36 inches, spring waters.

The spring pygmy sunfish was originally found in three separate spring systems, all draining in the Tennessee River system in northern Alabama. Cave Springs, where it was originally discovered back in 1937, was covered over by a Tennessee Valley Authority reservoir called Pickwick Lake. This impoundment was the sole cause of extirpation of the sunfish in this former spring habitat. A second spring, called Pryor Spring, has had a history of disturbances. The original bank vegetation was replaced by an exotic aquatic plant native to South America, commonly known as Parrots Feather, *Myriophyllum brasiliense*. Found growing in dense stands along cool, spring-fed bodies of water, this tropical plant is widely distributed in the Tennessee Valley. In Pryor Spring, the Parrots Feather grew into a solid stand in the spring pool and its 1½ mile outflow. The tremendous bulk of this aquatic vegetation began to choke the spring's flow, backing up the water and flooding the neighboring forested areas. Not only were the forested areas becoming water-logged with the backed up spring water, but the shallow flooding was producing ideal breeding grounds for mosquitoes. The Parrots Feather was removed mechanically to maintain the flow through the spring run and to destroy potential mosquito breeding grounds, but, by the next breeding season, the aquatic plants had completely recolonized the spring system.

In May of 1945 the herbicide 2,4-dichlorophenoxyacetic acid or 2,4 D, was used to more efficiently control the parrots feather in Pryor Spring. More recently, the spring run has been channelized and even used as a dumpsite for a variety of unwanted junk. Whatever the reason or reasons for the present habitat conditions, no spring pygmy sunfish has been seen there since individuals were last collected during the spring of 1941 despite many attempts.

The only known habitat for the spring pygmy sunfish today is in the Beaverdam-Moss Spring complex in Limestone County, Alabama. The spring complex consists of Beaverdam and Moss Springs and other small unnamed springs which converge and flow into Beaverdam Creek. Ownership of the springs and the surrounding agricultural land is held by one landowner and an estate. Unaware of the presence of the spring pygmy sunfish, the owner dredged part of its habitat with a front-end loader in 1976, and cattle now water themselves at the spring. Shortly after the news of these habitat-altering events and other problems of siltation and pesticide runoff reached the U.S. Fish and Wildlife Service, the agency considered listing this tiny sunfish as an endangered species and proposed the Beaverdam-Moss Spring complex as its critical habitat. Although the spring pygmy sunfish was never listed as endangered or threatened, one of the landowners has indicated a willingness to help protect it by joining the state of Alabama and the U.S. Fish and Wildlife Service in a habitat management agreement. Currently, spring pygmy sunfishes inhabit most of Moss Spring and its spring run to Beaverdam Creek, the areas within Beaverdam Swamp, and "Lowe's Ditch," an artificial irrigation ditch formed by dynamite blasting about 25 years ago on the Lowe Estate. This ditch is fed with waters from Beaverdam Spring and a "blue hole" spring and was last used for irrigation ten to fifteen years ago. Subsequently, dynamite was also used to clear the ditch of beaver dams. Despite these literally "earth-shaking" incidents, the spring pygmy sunfishes are still fairly plentiful in Lowe's Ditch.

The Beaverdam-Moss Spring complex is relatively free from Man's presence because of its rather remote location. Metropolitan dangers from either industrial pollution or sewage effluents are of no immediate concern in this region, even though chronic bouts with siltation from rainfall erosion and potential battles with fertilizer and pesticide run-off from the adjacent cultivated fields can quickly change the complexion of the habitat. In this part of Alabama, cotton is a common crop and with this plant comes a host of pests such as the infamous boll weevil. Farmers in this area spray their cotton fields with toxic pesticides like toxaphene and methyl parathion with hopes of eliminating the cotton plant pests. Should heavy rains immediately follow the spraying, a serious toxic run-off could destroy much of the spring's fauna. Such a sudden catastrophe could close the chapter on the last remaining population of the spring pygmy sunfish.

Even more subtle, these toxic chemical run-offs may affect the spawning behavior or food supply of the spring pygmy sunfish. This fish may have a life span of only one year and probably breeds year round. About 35 percent to 40 percent of the 60 to 65 eggs in a spawn will survive. A missed opportunity to spawn because of less than ideal breeding conditions created by a run-off would result in a missed generation of offspring . . . and in this case, the reduction of the total population, or even complete eradication.

Fortunately, the threats to the spring pygmy sunfish are not major; but, because populations of this species have been reduced to the Beaverdam-Moss Spring complex, close monitoring and protection of this sunfish's last habitat must be of utmost concern to ensure its survival. The spring pygmy sunfish has been successfully spawned and its larvae raised to adulthood in the laboratory. It may be possible in the future to reintroduce a population. Although more than one hundred springs have been sampled to find additional populations of spring pygmy sunfish, none were found. The search will continue, and we hope spring habitats like Pryor Spring can be renovated to the point that a reintroduction would have a good chance of survival.

# Watercress Darter
## *Etheostoma nuchale*

In 1964, while dipnetting for salamanders in Glenn Springs at Bessemer, Jefferson County, Alabama, two scientists captured a small fish that neither of them recognized. A graduate student named W. M. Howell at the University of Alabama at Tuscaloosa later identified the specimen as a new species of darter previously unknown to science. Thus, the discovery of the watercress darter had been made.

A mere six years after its discovery, the watercress darter was officially given endangered species status. Initially, despite intense sampling by ichthyologists at other local springs and creeks in the Birmingham-Bessemer area, it appeared that Glenn Springs, a limestone spring, held the only population of watercress darters in the U.S. The endangered status was conferred to this little fish for several reasons, each of which could independently wreak irreparable damage upon the population.

In general, the watercress darter thrives in the deeper, slow-moving backwaters of springs that have thick growths of aquatic vegetation such as watercress, *Nasturtium,* from whence it derives its name. Here the darter perches on leaves and roots at mid-water depth; normally it does not live on the bottom as do most members of the darter family. The dense vegetation provides this 2½ inch fish with a varied diet of crustaceans, aquatic insect larvae, and snails. The deep, robust body of the watercress darter may, in fact, be an adaptation to help the fish move about in thick masses of aquatic vegetation. The species name, *nuchale,* means "pertaining to the nape" and refers to the slight bulging nature of the watercress darter's nape. The humped nape comes from the enlarged muscles connecting the darter's skull to its vertebral column.

Glenn Springs is a small spring twenty yards from a major highway with locally heavy traffic. The population of watercress darters, which ranges between four hundred to seven hundred individuals could be completely destroyed by an accident or construction along the highway. Water flow from the spring normally fluctuates depending on the recharge from local rains. During periods of drought, the water flow is cut almost in half. While these periods of drought are a major concern themselves, the situation is compounded by recent growth and expansion of shopping malls and apartment complexes in the Birmingham-Bessemer area. The asphalt parking lots that are constructed over the land quickly channel the available rainfall into drains and gutters instead of allowing the water to recharge local springs. Water levels of springs continue to drop. Some of the smaller springs in the area have completely dried up due to the lack of rainfall recharge.

These alarming observations prompted ichthyologists to attempt to transplant some watercress darters into an area called Prince Springs, just one mile away and which had similar ecological characteristics to Glenn Springs. Three separate samples were taken over nine years, but not one watercress darter was netted. A close relative, the redfin darter, *Etheostoma whipplei,* was consistently collected, suggesting that the watercress darter could have been outcompeted by its close kin.

Because of the precarious nature of this fish, the U.S. Fish and Wildlife Service's Office of Endangered Species formed a recovery team whose first mission was to determine the geographic distribution of the watercress darter. After much field work and seining every spring pool and small creek in the area, the team discovered two more populations, both near Glenn Springs: Thomas Spring, which was privately owned by Mr. Frank Thomas, and Roebuck Spring, a clear water spring thick with watercress located at the Alabama State Boys' Industrial School in Roebuck, Jefferson County, Alabama.

Soon after the watercress darter recovery team was formed, alarming news came from the Alabama Department of Public Health. The U.S. Fish and Wildlife Service had requested that water samples from Glenn Springs be run through a battery of tests. The results indicated that coliform bacteria were present and almost "too numerous to count!" The presence of a large number of coliform bacteria is a sure sign that the water is contaminated by some source such as surface water or fecal material from man or animals. If the water shows a coliform count of 4 in 100 milliliters of water, that particular sample of water is said to be contaminated. The Glenn Springs coliform count turned out to be 350 in 100 milliliters of water indicating that a severe deterioration in the watercress darter's habitat was taking place.

A coliform count of 350 would have been relatively good, if you were sampling the water quality in Roebuck Spring. This visibly clear spring chockful of luxuriant growths of aquatic vegetation covering most of the bottom has been condemned as a source of drinking water for ten years because of high coliform counts ranging from 440 to 3600. Historically, this spring was the drinking water supply for the students at the Industrial School. Although the exact cause of the high coliform counts is not known for certain, health department officials speculate that the coliform bacteria may have come from surrounding septic tank sewage seeping into the groundwater and surfacing at Roebuck Spring. The coliform counts were especially high after heavy rainfall. The bad water quality also adversely affected the population of watercress darters found in the spring. Not less than 50 percent of the population seemed to have "gas bubble" disease which gives the darter a pop-eyed condition. This disease can be caused by water that has been saturated with nitrogen or abnormally high levels of bacteria. Both high coliform counts and high levels of nitrogen were present in the Roebuck Spring water.

Although the visibility in Thomas Spring was quite good, the owner was not particularly happy with the dense growths of aquatic vegetation that carpeted the margin and bottom of the spring pool. The owner was well aware of the plight of the small fish that was grabbing local headlines and was sympathetic regarding the topic of the watercress darter. However, he strongly felt that the vegetation had to go by introducing grass carp, *Ctenopharyngodon idella,* to crop the dense growth. He was totally unaware of the potential impact of this action on the watercress darter. Subsequent collecting attempts in Thomas Spring pool yielded only a single female adult watercress darter. The introduction of the grass carp largely or completely eliminated the darter from the spring pool by efficiently grazing the vegetation where the darter lived with many species of aquatic insects and snails—choice morsels to the watercress darter.

Fortunately not all was lost at Thomas Spring. A small population of darters existed below the spring pool, beyond the range of the grass carp.

The fragile world of the watercress darter will need protection to guard the survival of the species. The recovery team outlined several recommendations that it felt were needed to ensure the darter's survival. First, the U.S. Fish and Wildlife Service should move forward with plans to lease the property on which Glenn Springs is located. A fence surrounding the springs to prevent trespassing should be erected. Thomas Spring has been purchased from Mr. Thomas and the grass carp has been removed so that the aquatic vegetation can repopulate the spring-pond. As soon as the vegetation bounces back, this habitat can once again support darters. Present plans call for the reintroduction of watercress darters into the spring pool from the small population just below the spring pool. Finally, Roebuck Spring, which is already state-owned, should be protected from outside development. In all three spring habitats, low level dams, one to two feet high, could be constructed to create the spring pool habitats preferred by the watercress darter.

We hope that the darters will freely spawn in these spring pool habitats. Unfortunately, little is known about the reproductive biology of this fish other than the fact that females with ripe eggs were found from March through July and that both sexes sport different breeding colors. The belly of the male watercress darter boasts a brilliant orange-red hue that sharply contrasts to the bright blue fins during courting. The male tries to coerce a female into mating by displaying its brightly colored robust body. Though beautifully marked in its own right, the female watercress darter's breeding colors are rather plain compared to the male: a wash of browns and blacks intermixed with the whites over most of the body.

Perhaps the population level will recover and increase to sizeable proportions, that will permit transplants into neighboring springs with similar ecological characteristics. These efforts will help ensure the survival of the watercress darter within its historic ranges.

# XV.

# Marine and Estuarine Fishes

The oceans and estuaries pose an especially perplexing challenge to biologists in assessing the numbers, ranges, and abundances of fishes. The National Marine Fisheries Service and coastal states keep information on the commerical species of fishes surrounding the continental U. S. Much of their data comes from tagging experiments implemented mainly to study the migratory habits of commercial and sport fishes moving up and down the coasts. Commercial fishermen's harvest records are also kept to follow the fluctuations in yield of the commercial fish stocks. Unfortunately, for those marine or estuarine fishes without commercial value, few if any records exist.

During the past decade coastal as well as inland states have hosted symposia on endangered species to establish base line data on the status of their fauna and flora. Ichthyologists and fisheries biologists present data at these meetings on the current status and threats to the fishes in their waters. By combining the information from the individual states into a coastal area, south Atlantic coast for example, the situation for a particular marine or estuarine species becomes clear. While this system is not as precise or foolproof as most biologists would like, it is the best assessment of endangered and threatened marine fishes we have. We are hopeful the system is working because very few endangered and threatened marine fishes have been identified to date.

One of the reasons so few marine fishes are endangered or threatened is that most species are widespread along the coast. In fact most marine fishes are distributed along several hundred miles of coastline. The exceptions to this generality are some of the reef fishes in southern Florida. The Key blenny is known only from Looe Key, several miles offshore from Big Pine Key in the lower Florida Keys. This rare species, known only from six individuals found between rows of coral in about fifteen feet of water, may exist on other keys. In fact, it could have been found on several of the Florida Keys prior to Man's intrusion into the area. Before the Key blenny is labeled as endangered or threatened, additional research on distribution and life history should be carried out.

Most of the marine fishes considered endangered or threatened are anadromous, or they are found in estuarine areas where streams flow into the ocean. Two of the three species highlighted in this section are anadromous, and the third spawns in the brackish waters at the mouth of a river. The factors that have led to the demise of anadromous fishes have most frequently been problems associated with the freshwater portion of their habitat. Future efforts to conserve nearshore estuarine and marine fishes should begin in freshwater.

15–1
Altamaha River near Jessup, Wayne County, Georgia is utilized by shortnose sturgeon on the spawning runs from nearby coastal waters. Photo by J. D. Williams.

# Shortnose Sturgeon
## *Acipenser brevirostrum*

(Color plate 15.)

*On the white sand of the bottom*
*Lay the monster Mishe-Nahma,*
*Lay the sturgeon, King of Fishes;*
*Through his gills he breathed the water,*
*With his fins he fanned and winnowed,*
*With his tail he swept the sandfloor,*
*There he lay in all his armour. . . .*
*"Take my bait," cried Hiawatha. . . .*
*"Take my bait, O King of Fishes!"*

The Song of Hiawatha *by*
*Henry Wadsworth Longfellow*

If the "king" in Hiawatha's waterway was *Acipenser brevirostrum*, the short-nose sturgeon, then the population size of that species probably had nothing to do with its royal label. Although the shortnose sturgeon made the endangered species list in 1967 and came under the protective measures of the Endangered Species Act of 1973, which made it unlawful to catch, kill, or otherwise retain it, recent evidence seems to indicate that this "king of fishes" probably never was abundant. The National Marine Fisheries Service is considering changing the shortnose's status from endangered (in danger of extinction through all or part of its range) to threatened—likely to become endangered. Fishery biologists cite the fish's apparent historic rarity and more important, claim that the numbers of shortnose may be more than what was once thought as justification for a status change. A Georgian fisheries researcher, who set out to study the movements of the shortnose in the Altamaha River, was surprised at the number of sturgeon that repeatedly turned up in nets—a phenomenon reminiscent of pre-turn-of-the-century fishing days.

Then, and for generations before, the five rows of lateral bony scutes, or spiny plates extending along the back and sides of the sturgeon were the bane of the shad fishermen who spent many nights repairing nets victimized by the sharp-edged scutes of a tangled sturgeon. Although they were sold in the fish markets, sturgeon were very inexpensive and not highly prized: An entire fish could be purchased for 25 cents, sturgeon steaks for a few cents a pound.

But in 1855 the birth of commercially prepared caviar in Sandusky, Ohio, using the related lake sturgeon, changed the American food industry's near neglect of sturgeon. Green, or unripe, eggs were removed from the sturgeon, gently rubbed over a fine-meshed screen to separate them from their enveloping membrane and washed in vinegar or white wine. After washing, the eggs fell through the screen to a trough and on into tubs where salt was added. The addition of salt drew water from the eggs and formed a copious brine. The briny eggs dried on fine sieves and then were placed into casks or cans.

By 1860, smoked sturgeon also caught the eye of the food industry and a sudden intense demand for sturgeon developed. Several other sturgeon-based products became commercially important. Isinglass, a gelatin made from the inner lining of the sturgeon air bladder, was used as a clarifying agent in wine-making, a cement for pottery, a textile stiffener, a waterproofer, and an additive in jams and jellies. This gelatin initially sold for one dollar per pound, or per about ten sturgeon bladder linings. Another sturgeon product, liver oil, was used as an anti-rheumatism ointment by the elderly people of Quebec. The Russians produced a commercial product from the spinal cord called "vyaziga." Finally, sturgeon skins were tanned for leather.

Although the sturgeon market created an east coast industry based on Atlantic sturgeon, it may also have adversely affected the shortnose population, which extends from New Brunswick, Canada to Florida. Like all members of the sturgeon family, Acipenseridae, the shortnose sturgeon is a primitive fish whose skeleton and skull are composed of cartilage, not bone. Their caudal fin is also sharklike. The sturgeons are not related to sharks, however. The shortnose long has been confused with the larger, more common Atlantic sturgeon. The slender body of the shortnose is colored with dark browns and blacks on its head, back, and sides. Below the lateral scutes, these dull colors give way to lighter browns and olive green that progressively lighten ventrally until reaching the white underside. White barbels dangle from the underside of the head, just in front of its mouth. As its namesake implies, the shortnose has a shorter and blunter snout. This fish, incorrectly labeled "mammose" or young Atlantic, was scooped up by the commercial fish industry.

15-2
Fisheries biologist, Dr. Ronnie Gilbert, about to release radio tagged shortnose sturgeon (note cylindrical transmitter attached just behind sturgeon's head). Photo from R. Gilbert, U.S. Fish and Wildlife Service.

Sturgeon authorities are fairly certain that the intensification of the sturgeon-based industries affected that fish's population size. Swedish immigrants moved from Delaware and began fishing the Winyah Bay in South Carolina each spring following the Civil War, as the sturgeon catch in Delaware Bay declined. By 1880, there were two sturgeon camps on Winyah Bay at Georgetown, South Carolina where fish were slaughtered and dressed in preparation for steamer trips to Charlestown and rail journeys to New York and other northern metropolitan centers where sturgeon meat and caviar were sold at a very good price. Nowadays the sturgeon meat and caviar sold in the United States is most likely imported European sturgeon or Mississippi River paddlefish, rather than east coast sturgeon.

There is doubt regarding the shortnose sturgeon's actual status, but it appears safe to consider it threatened. The confusion between the shortnose and young Atlantics, for example, has kept fish experts guessing at the actual numbers, past and present, of shortnose sturgeon. The seesaw nature of the early records maintained by the U. S. Bureau of Fisheries—with some records distinguishing between the Atlantic and shortnose and others lumping them together in one category—clouds a true picture of these numbers.

But an ambiguous record of population size is not the only reason for keeping tabs on the shortnose: Officials recognize several environmental phenomena that threaten the fish. One such threat is the pollution of rivers. The shortnose sturgeon spends much of its life in coastal waters around the mouth of a river. Pollutants entering any point along the watershed of that river have a good chance of reaching the shortnose sturgeon's habitat. Although most species of the sturgeon family are anadromous, the shortnose ventures into brackish water, but there is little evidence that they actually enter the sea itself. Scientists reason that this is why shortnose sturgeon are more susceptible to fungal infections in the Hudson River system. Approximately 75 percent of the observed shortnose in the Hudson River system had fin rot. Researchers speculate that the river, which was contaminated with polychlorinated biphenyls and other Man-made effluents directly linked to health problems, probably caused the fin rot. The shortnose does not appear to leave the river system like its cousin, the Atlantic sturgeon (which is not afflicted with this disease). So, perhaps the additional time the shortnose spends in the river adversely affects them.

Shortnose sturgeon also are found in large river channels. These channels are occasionally dredged for navigational purposes which poses drastic habitat alterations to the sturgeon. In addition to dredging, damming rivers for hydroelectric power blocks upstream spawning runs. The use of large quantities of water in steam electric power plants cause entrainment of the eggs and larvae on screens as large pumps suck water from the river. This is a serious problem for the shortnose sturgeon which deposits eggs only once every five or six years. Sturgeons are also slow growing and late maturing. Males reach sexual maturity at age eight to ten; females even later at fifteen to seventeen years.

The sturgeon should not be regarded as a maladapted fish in these turbid waters. They have remained virtually unchanged over millions and millions of years. Visual cues probably play a small role in their mode of living as witnessed by the two small eyes. Instead, sturgeon seem to rely heavily on chemical cues they sense with four barbels or feelers which are well-equipped with taste buds. Once these feelers have located food, the shortnose uses its ventrally positioned, protrusible mouth to suck in algae and various sorts of crustaceans, aquatic worms, small aquatic insects, fingernail clams and gastropods.

How long the shortnose sturgeon remains suitably adapted to its environment will most certainly depend on our awareness of environmental problems effecting the species. The polluting, dredging, and damming of the habitat of the shortnose sturgeon constantly threaten this relict species. Aquatic biologists and fishery management staff must continue to monitor the "white sand of the bottom for the monster, Mishe-Nahma."

# Acadian Whitefish
## *Coregonus canadensis*

The only North American endangered fish to be featured on a postage stamp, the Acadian whitefish, formerly known as the Atlantic whitefish, is one of only a half dozen species of freshwater fishes restricted to Canada.

The Acadian whitefish has an elongated, terete body about fifteen to twenty inches long. It belongs to the genus, *Coregonus* (meaning "angle-eye"), which includes the whitefishes and ciscoes, both noted for their commercial importance as food fishes. The Acadian whitefish is an anadromous species endemic to the southern part of Nova Scotia where it is infrequently found in coastal waters and a few streams and lakes. The construction of a hydroelectric dam in 1929 on the Tusket River and the installation of an inadequate and unattended fish ladder contributed to the demise of the whitefish in this river system. Because the design of the fish ladder did not properly attract the whitefish, large numbers were destroyed by the whirring blades of the turbines when they attempted to move down the sluices.

The ineffective fish ladder exposed the Acadian whitefish to poachers who ruthlessly exploited the migrating population moving from Yarmouth Harbor upstream between mid-September and early November. The Nova Scotia Fishery Regulations were amended in 1970 to prohibit the taking of the Acadian whitefish from all waters in the province at any time of the year and by any method, but poaching on the remaining populations still continued. Whatever individuals remain after the pressures from either the turbine blades or poacher's nets, return to the sea from mid-February to late March, feeding on amphipods, small periwinkles, and marine worms in the harbor.

The historic range of the Acadian whitefish included the Millipsgate Lake, but there have not been any reports of this endangered fish in the lake for some time. Even in undeveloped Nova Scotia, the effects of acid rain are being felt in the Tusket River system. Acid rain in Canada has already wiped out the natural population of one native subspecies of trout, the aurora brook trout. In fact, the remaining individuals of the Acadian whitefish may already be extirpated from this river by the acid rain with a pH of 4.7. Because there is some doubt whether the population of the Acadian whitefish still exists in Millipsgate Lake, acid rain may have been the final blow for the survival of this endangered Canadian species unless additional populations are found.

*       *       *

During a survey in September of 1982, Dr. Don McAllister of the National Museum of Canada found a small population of Acadian whitefish in Millipsgate Lake and three other small lakes in the same drainage system. Two individuals were also found in the Annis River estuary. None were found in the Tusket River where they were formerly abundant. Acid rain threatens these remaining populations. We can only guess how many Acadian whitefish will continue to survive in Nova Scotia waters . . . and for how long.

# Totoaba
## *Cynoscion macdonaldi*

(Color plate 16.)

Most fishes have a glossy white organ inside the body cavity called the swimbladder that provides a variety of vital services for coping with the aquatic environment. This long, gas-filled, balloon-like structure mainly serves as a hydrostatic organ, or float, enabling a fish to remain at a given level in the water column by adjusting its body density to that of the surrounding water. The gas volume within the swimbladder will change automatically to match a new hydrostatic pressure as the fish changes its level in the water column. In addition to this function, the swimbladder is connected with hearing in some fishes. Other fishes have a specialized set of sound-producing muscles that envelop the swimbladder. By rapidly contracting these muscles, the fish is able to vibrate the walls of the swimbladder. The swimbladder by its very construction acts like a resonator and intensifies the sound produced by the vibrations.

Humans have found yet another function for this anatomical apparatus. With proper preparation, the swimbladder becomes a delicacy, sold as a condiment for use in soup stock and even by itself as a side dish or garnish. The dried swimbladder, known as "Seen Kow" by the Chinese, brings a hefty price in the marketplace. A soup called "Seen Kow Ching Tong" or clear soup of fish bladders was one of the most popular recipes for this delicacy.

The desire for this Chinese delicacy both in the Orient and California's Chinese communities led to the birth of a new fishing industry in the Gulf of California during the 1920s and started the demise of a North American marine fish, the totoaba. The largest member of the family Sciaenidae which includes the croaker, corvina and the weakfish or seatrout, the totoaba can reach six feet in length and attain weights exceeding two hundred pounds. With dark blue coloring on its back and dusky silver sides, the totoaba is also referred to as the "white sea bass," "Mexican bass," and "totuava." The totoaba is endemic to the Mexican waters of the Gulf of California and consequently falls under the jurisdiction of the Mexican government.

For the Mexican villagers living in the dry, desert-like coastal areas adjacent to the Gulf of California, food came from the waters of the Gulf and not from tilling the arid land. It is easy to see how the totoaba, with its firm, succulent flesh and large size, became a favorite food item for these people. In the former seaport of Guaymas on the mainland shore of the Gulf, the resident Chinese population also discovered that the totoaba's swimbladder, when properly prepared, tasted very similar to the swimbladders of fishes used in the Orient. More importantly, if the totoaba swimbladder could be dried and dressed in the same manner as those across the Pacific Ocean, then there might be a commercial market overseas as well.

As a marketing experiment the Mexicans shipped dried totoaba swimbladder to China. To their delight it was well received. The Chinese were willing to pay high prices for the swimbladder; the financial incentive induced many Mexicans to head out to sea searching for the totoaba from their narrow dugout canoes. The method of catching these large fishes was rather simple and primitive. Fishing tackle consisted of a handline and a single large hook baited with a small dead fish. A successful day of fishing in the Gulf would find the dugout canoe piled with dozens of totoaba each of which could tip the scales at nearly one hundred pounds! Large totoaba yielded swimbladders that weighed over three pounds.

Hearing about the unusually large profits that were being made by the totoaba fishermen of Guaymas, a small band of former German seamen who had originally come to Mexico in search of gold began to fish for the totoaba's organ of "gold" in a serious manner. These new fishermen outfished the Mexican villagers and extended the range of fishing after the Guaymas waters were depleted. In fact, the German fishermen sailed so far north that they reached the mouth of the Colorado River. Here the numbers of totoaba were unbelievable! Little did they know that they had stumbled onto the spawning grounds of the totoaba.

Because this rich fishing ground was in such a remote region, a camp, later named San Felipe, was set up. When the Germans sailed back to Guaymas loaded down with stacks of dried swimbladders, the villagers were so overwhelmed that they all wanted to go to the mouth of the Colorado River. San Felipe grew within a few short seasons from a small camp started by five entrepreneurial Germans to a sizable temporary town composed of hundreds of Mexicans and Indians searching for the totoaba's swimbladder. The beginnings of a commercial fishing industry were in the making.

Shortly after the Great Depression the totoaba fishing industry boomed—swimbladders commanded over five dollars per pound. However, totoaba meat sales did not even come close to the market for its swimbladder. Sadly, the gutted bodies of totoaba were either strewn on the beach to rot or cast back out to sea.

Upon returning from the sea, the fisherman would line up his catch of totoaba on the beach, behead the fish and remove the swimbladders, or "buches," as the fishermen called them. The swimbladders were carefully scraped clean of all adhering tissues and then slit along one side of the oval structure. The fisherman could now open up the swimbladder into a large flat sheet. The swimbladder was meticulously cleaned again and placed on a rack to dry in the intense sun for two or, at most, three days. Periodically the swimbladder sheets would be turned, showing a gradual transition from the dense glossy white appearance to the translucent, tea-colored glassiness—the sign that they were hard, dry, and ready to be marketed. The season for processing and shipping buches out began in October and lasted until April. After that, San Felipe became practically deserted until the next October.

Through the early 1920s, the sole concern of fishermen was to harvest the totoaba only for its buche. But totoaba meat was becoming increasingly popular as a food item in the United States during the late 1920s, creating still another means of profitably exploiting this sciaenid fish. Following in the footsteps of San Felipe, two more fishing villages sprang up to share in the newfound market for this Mexican natural resource. The villages of Golfo de Santa Clara and Puerto Penasco, both found in the State of Sonora, along with San Felipe eventually accounted for 95 percent of the total annual catch of totoaba. From 1929 onward, the growing demand in the United States for totoaba meat created a burgeoning market that was aggressively met by the commercial totoaba fishing industry. More efficient, sophisticated fishing gear and boat facilities were developed to meet the demand. Furthermore, the fishing industry redesigned their refrigeration and transportation systems to handle the larger yields of totoaba that were being caught.

The annual totoaba yield continued to rise astronomically, reaching a peak in 1942 of over 2300 tons. Experienced totoaba fishermen had known for a long time that the most critical aspect of the industry was the annual spring spawning migration from the deeper waters in the northern Gulf of California to the mouth of the Colorado River which put many of these fishes in a relatively confined area. Here the nets closed in among hundreds of totoaba concerned only with spawning.

Without question, the totoaba ranked as the most important commercial fish to come out of the Gulf of California and represented the second most valuable fishery in Mexico; the shrimp industry being the most valuable. Fishermen in the Gulf would fish for either shrimp or totoaba, whichever was more abundant at the time. During the spring migrations of the totoaba, the shrimp trawlers would concentrate on this fish and bypass the shrimp. Despite the fishermen's intensified efforts to catch more totoaba, the annual yields slipped year after year to an all-time low in 1958. Overfishing was definitely dwindling the numbers of totoaba available to replenish its stocks. The tremendous numbers of shrimp that were being taken by the shrimpers may have affected the totoaba by exploiting a valuable element of its diet. Also, large numbers of juvenile totoaba were trapped in the shrimp nets and perished. The years between 1959 and 1966 saw a slight increase in the annual yields of totoaba; perhaps because of a 45-day moratorium during the spring spawning migrations and the Mexican government's creation of a sanctuary at the mouth of the Colorado River. This action allowed some recovery of the population from 1966 to 1975. A steady decline put the yield of totoaba at a new all-time low. It seemed that the totoaba faced habitat threats in addition to overfishing.

One of the major threats to the totoaba in addition to commercial fishing is the general deterioration of its spawning grounds. The Morelos Dam has diverted a substantial amount of water flow into the Mexicali Valley for irrigation. This dam has, in effect, reduced the flow of water into the mouth of the Colorado River, consequently drying up the marshes where the totoaba spawns. Hoover Dam and other large dams on the Colorado River have also contributed to this problem. The reduction of fresh water into the mouth of the Colorado River also means that the brackish water in which the totoaba spawns is replaced by more saline water from the Gulf of California. Unlike the rest of the estuaries in the northern Gulf of California, the Colorado River estuary receives large quantities of freshwater from the Colorado River. Because the totoaba only spawns in this particular estuary, perhaps the brackish water is essential to its reproductive success.

Biologists have found that all rivers and streams have their own unique scent or odor. For migrating fish species that return to their home rivers to spawn, olfactory cues give the fish species a chemical "roadmap" to follow. In some species, only a few molecules of the river odor are needed to guide the particular species successfully to its home stream. Amazingly, some fishes like the salmon can home in on this chemical signal from hundreds of miles away. As the freshwater inflow decreases, the spawning grounds become more saline and the river odor may be altered, thus reducing the number of totoaba that participate in the spring migration.

In 1969, there was also talk of installing a nuclear power and desalination plant at El Golfo de Santa Clara near the mouth of the Colorado River. Not only would the thermal and saline pollution produced by the plant disrupt the habitat, but the impact of agricultural development, industrialization, and urbanization would be devastating to the nursery and breeding grounds of the totoaba. This project never came to fruition.

The totoaba was officially declared to be an endangered species on May 21, 1979. How the totoaba will fare in the future is anybody's guess. Some biologists feel there is a chance that the totoaba will be extinct by the year 2000. Others see a bright spot on the horizon—the Mexican government established a total closed fishing season for this species in 1975. The National Marine Fisheries Service, in conjunction with the Bureau of Customs and officials from the U.S. Food and Drug Administration, in 1978 banned all totoaba imports to the United States. Without awesome fishing pressure the totoaba just might rebound to its former abundance. It will be interesting to watch. Still, the spawning grounds at the mouth of the Colorado River may have to be improved before this species truly recovers.

# XVI.

# Extinction and Extinct Fishes

Extinction is the disappearance of an animal or plant from its entire range. Essentially, it no longer exists. Nothing is quite so final as extinction. Once a species becomes extinct, it is irretrievably lost. Its potential for solving the problems of Mankind will never be revealed. While extinction is a natural biological process continually faced by all living species, recently there has been an alarming increase in the rate of extinction of animal and plant species. Many plant and animal species are disappearing long before their time according to the earth's natural scheme.

Man has accelerated the rate of extinction of wildlife with a variety of self-centered activities. Commercial hunting for exotic food and clothing and animal trade demands have contributed to the decline of some wildlife species. But by far the majority of human-interference extinctions result from habitat destruction. Certainly the most serious threats, today and in the past, are the environmental changes that result from human exploitation of natural resources. Previous extinctions have usually occurred because of Man's ignorance or lack of understanding of the consequences of habitat altering activities. This is no longer a valid excuse.

Habitat alteration for fishes comes in a variety of physical and chemical forms. Impoundment of rivers is a major threat, especially for those species restricted to the main channel of large rivers. In creeks and small rivers channelization has wrecked havoc on a number of fish habitats. Groundwater pumping and diversion of streams, especially in aquatic desert ecosystems, can quickly bring a fish species to the brink of extinction. Through runoff and seepage, pesticides and fertilizers make their way into aquatic ecosystems to create an unhealthy and eutrophic state. Water pollution from untreated industrial and municipal waste posed serious problems for fishes and other aquatic organisms in segments of streams and portions of lakes. While many of our waterways are being cleaned up, this problem still threatens some streams. Perhaps the most widespred pollutant of streams today is silt. Although silt is not toxic itself, it is still lethal. The adverse effects of silt on aquatic systems have long been recognized by biologists, but little has been done to correct increasing siltation of streams.

The biological alteration of aquatic habitats through the introduction of non-native organisms is a continuing threat. Introducing non-native fishes into habitats of native, often endemic fishes with restricted distribution has frequently devastated local populations. In some cases native fish species have never had the pressure of a major predator or competitor in their habitat. Such introductions can lead to rapid declines in the native fishes, especially in areas where the habitat is limited. Often the introduction of closely related non-native fishes results in massive hybridization of an endemic species, ultimately bringing about its extinction. Hybridization is particularly serious for endemic trouts in the western United States.

During the past century, at least fourteen species and seven subspecies of fishes have become extinct in North America; most of them finished for good because of habitat destruction as a result of human intervention. The fishes that have become extinct are not confined to a certain geographic area or a specific type of habitat. They are widely scattered across North America, yet most are in the southwestern United States. Extinctions have occurred in at least seven families of fishes. To date, six killifishes, five minnows, four trouts, three suckers, and a perch, sculpin and lamprey have been eliminated. While there is no doubt that habitat alteration was the leading cause of the extinctions that we list, in many instances several habitat altering events together led to the extermination of some fishes. In these cases it is difficult to identify with precision the specific factor that caused the extinction. Unfortunately the end result is the same.

The sad tales of four fishes that have become extinct in the last hundred years illustrate this problem. Extinction is forever! Endangered means there is still time to save them.

210

# Harelip Sucker
## *Lagochila lacera*

In the late 1800s the harelip sucker was widely distributed in clear streams of the east central portion of the United States. This species was given the common name of harelip because of its peculiar mouth and lips. The scientific name, *Lagochila,* means having a harelip. First collected in 1859, it was mistaken for another species of sucker and was not collected again until 1876, when Dr. D. S. Jordan and A. W. Brayton took two specimens in Chickamauga Creek near Ringold, Georgia. On this same collecting expedition they also found this unusual species in the Elk River at Estell Springs in Tennessee. After Jordan and Brayton described the harelip sucker they began to receive specimens that ichthyologists had collected in Ohio, Kentucky, Virginia, and Indiana. In 1886, the first and only individuals found west of the Mississippi River were found in the White River near Eureka Springs, Arkansas. Based on distribution patterns of other fishes, the harelip sucker probably occurred in several other states such as Missouri, West Virginia, and the western part of Pennsylvania.

Although the distribution of the harelip sucker was extensive—in fact it was the most wide ranging of recently extinct fishes—its habitat was somewhat restricted. It was usually found in pool areas of large clear streams, fifty to one hundred feet wide and three to twelve feet deep, with a gravel or rocky bottom. Although less than thirty specimens are preserved in museums, it was reported to be abundant. When it was discovered by Jordan and Brayton in 1876, they reported that "fishermen tell us that this is the commonest and most valued species of sucker found in the region." The last specimens collected were taken in the summer of 1893 from the Maumee River in northwestern Ohio.

The early demise of the harelip sucker precluded any biological or life history studies. However, some information can be gleaned from the specimens preserved in museums. The unusual modification of the lips and mouth suggest the harelip sucker was very specialized in its feeding habits. Examination of stomach contents reveals that the harelip sucker fed very heavily on small mollucks, snails, and limpets. Anatomical studies indicate that it was a sight feeder, probably seizing its prey individually rather than indescriminately picking up potential food items. Large adults were 1 to 1½ feet long and weighed several pounds. Like most suckers, the harelip sucker spawned in the spring and early summer. In Columbus, Ohio local fishermen called it "May sucker" because of the large spawning runs during the month of May.

The decline and ultimate extinction of the once common widespread harelip sucker is not unlike the passenger pigeon, a common widespread bird that became extinct in the early 1900s. Although the date of extinction for the harelip sucker is not known, we assume it was in the early 1900s. The decline of the harelip sucker probably began with the clearing of the land for farming when poor agricultural practices increased the amount of silt washing into streams. Increased silt and turbidity smothered the snails and reduced visibility for the sight feeding harelip sucker. In addition to silt, pollution from untreated industrial and municipal waste in rapidly developing areas further deteriorated the water quality and probably contributed to the harelip sucker's extinction.

The harelip sucker's disappearance was first noticed in the early 1940s. During the past forty years considerable effort has been spent to locate a population of the harelip sucker tucked away in some remote stream. All attempts have failed. In recent years, most ichthyologists that have reviewed the case of *Lagochila* have in mind one last stream where they are sure it is still hanging on. Most of us, however, no longer continue the search and accept the sad conclusion that this unique, once common, large sucker is gone. One also wonders how many other fishes adapted to clear rivers and creeks were lost before they were discovered.

# Tecopa Pupfish
## *Cyprinodon nevadensis calidae*

The Tecopa pupfish, typical of many southwestern fishes, was isolated in a small desert spring system nestled along the former shoreline of a Pleistocene lake. This distinctive pupfish was described by Dr. Robert R. Miller in 1948 and was pronounced extinct about thirty years later. Like many plant and animal extinctions, the demise of the Tecopa pupfish could easily have been prevented.

Tecopa Hot Springs, the only known habitat of the Tecopa pupfish, is located just north of the desert community of Tecopa in Inyo County, California about 35 miles east of the southern entrance to Death Valley. The springs are located on the east side of the Amargosa River Valley more than 75 feet above the valley floor. The two springs, about ten yards apart, have a combined flow of approximately 225 gallons per minute. Their outflow meanders about one mile before flowing into the Amargosa River which, at this point, is barely more than a trickle for most of the year. Tecopa pupfish were not found in the head spring where the water temperature was 108°–110° F, but were abundant several hundred yards downstream where the water had cooled to 96°–102° F.

There were signs of trouble in the Tecopa pupfish habitat as early as 1940. Bath houses were erected around the two springs to take advantage of the hot mineral water. Over the years the hot mineral water baths became very popular and attracted a fairly large seasonal and resident population. As people came so did trailer parks and houses which required alteration of the landscape. It was only a matter of time until the springs were altered. In 1965, the outflow of the two springs were joined and the remaining channel straightened. When the outflow from the springs were joined, the rate of flow and the temperature in downstream areas increased to levels unsuitable for the pupfish's survival and reproduction.

At some point two non-native fishes, mosquitofish, *Gambusia affinis,* and bluegill, *Lepomis macrochirus,* were introduced into the outflow of Tecopa Hot Springs. The role of these exotic fishes in the extinction of the Tecopa pupfish is not known. However, based on past experience, the presence of non-native fishes, especially in restricted environments, invariably reduces population

212

levels of native fishes. In view of this evidence, it is reasonable to suspect that the presence of non-native fishes decreased population levels of the Tecopa pupfish.

On January 19, 1982, when the U.S. Fish and Wildlife Service removed the Tecopa pupfish from the U.S. list of endangered species, a sad milestone was reached. It was the first time any plant or animal had been removed from the list due to its extinction. This action was taken after surveys in 1977–1979 failed to locate a single Tecopa pupfish. More than forty aquatic habitats in the Tecopa Hot Springs area were sampled in an effort to find a population. Occasionally, pupfish are reported from springs in the Tecopa area, but on checking they turn out to be the Amargosa River pupfish, *Cyprinodon nevadensis amargosae*.

On reviewing the Tecopa pupfish case, one can not help but wonder how many more species and subspecies of fish, wildlife, and plants will be lost before the extinction lesson is learned.

16–1
Extinct Tecopa pupfish. Photo by E. Theriot, U.S. Fish and Wildlife Service.

# Whiteline Topminnow
## *Fundulus albolineatus*

On May 27, 1889, Philip H. Kirsch of the U.S. Bureau of Fisheries stopped in Huntsville, Alabama to sample fish populations in the local streams. One of the areas sampled that day was Big Spring and its outflow, Spring Creek, in downtown Huntsville. Among the fishes taken in Spring Creek were 25 specimens of a unique topminnow. These specimens were deposited in the United States National Museum in Washington, D.C. In 1891, Dr. Charles Gilbert described the topminnow as a new species, *Fundulus albolineatus*. Its specific name *albolineatus* means white lines and refers to the prominent white stripes or lines along the sides of this three inch long topminnow. The common name, whiteline topminnow, is also taken from these distinctive markings.

When Kirsch first collected the whiteline tipminnow in 1889, and Gilbert described it in 1891, no one could have imagined that the one collection of 25 specimens would be the first and only collection of this species. The habitat of Spring Creek was described by Kirsch as follows: "Spring Creek, Huntsville, May 27, 1889. Temperature 65° F. This small stream about eighteen feet wide is formed by a single spring in the town of Huntsville. It is about one quarter mile long and flows into Pin-hook Creek. Its bottom is similar to that of the former creek (Pin-hook Creek, bottom of blue limestone). It is full of fishes, darters being very numerous." While this description would fit most spring creeks in northern Alabama and southern Tennessee, hundreds of collections from springs and streams flowing from springs in this area have failed to locate a single whiteline topminnow. Although discovery of the whiteline topminnow in some isolated spring creek remains a possibility, the probability is greater that the species is extinct.

The extinction of the whiteline topminnow went unnoticed by the rest of the world. Ichthyologists during the 1940s and 1950s noticed that no recent collections of the species had been taken. By the 1960s it was presumed to be extinct. When ichthyologists did return to Big Spring and Spring Creek to search for the whiteline topminnow, they found the habitat considerably altered. The spring pool had a concrete wall around it which eliminated all shallow water marginal habitat, a very important habitat for topminnows. Water flowing from the spring had been impounded to form a small duck pond in the city park. Carp and goldfish had also been introduced into the duck pond. Spring and Pin-hook creeks below the duck pond had been channelized for several miles. Further inquiry regarding the status of the spring revealed that it had been "pumped dry" on several occasions to repair the wall and remove debris. While there is no way of knowing what caused the extinction of the whiteline topminnow, any one of the habitat altering events mentioned could have delivered the final blow.

# Blue Pike
## *Stizostedion vitreum glaucum*

As early as the late 1800s, fishery biologists and commercial fishermen around the Great Lakes knew that there were two color forms of the walleye in Lakes Erie and Ontario. But these early biologists did not know the significance of the difference between the blue form and the yellow or "normal walleye." It was not until the 1920s that the differences in the two forms were analyzed. In 1926, the blue form was described as a distinct species, the blue pike, *Stizostedion glaucum,* but later, in 1936, it was relegated to subspecies status, *Stizostedion vitreum glaucum.* In addition to its blue color, the blue pike differed from the walleye, *Stizostedion vitreum vitreum,* in having a larger eye and bluish white fins. The blue pike was also smaller than the walleye and spawned later.

When the blue pike was described, it was found in central and eastern Lake Erie, the Niagara River, and western and southern Lake Ontario. Although reported from other lakes and streams in the vicinity of the Great Lakes, these reports were never confirmed. Within Lakes Erie and Ontario the blue pike inhabited the deep, clear, open waters. There were fewer in shallower turbid waters. There is some evidence that blue pike did move into shallower near-shore waters during the fall and winter. This habitat preference contrasts sharply with the walleye which typically inhabits somewhat turbid waters in shallow inshore lake areas and streams.

Blue pike were smaller and had a slower growth rate than its relative, the walleye. Adult blue pike were nine to sixteen inches long and weighed from half a pound to 1½ pounds. In spite of its small size the blue pike was a very popular sport and commercial fish. In the late 1930s and early 1940s, fishery biologists reported that fishing for blue pike in Lake Erie near Cleveland, Ohio was so intensive it looked more like a "food fishery" than a "sport fishery." As recently as the early 1950s the sport fishery, largely for blue pike, supported a fleet of more than twenty charter boats operating out of Erie, Pennsylvania. The blue pike was equally important in the sport fishery of Lake Ontario.

The commercial fishery for the blue pike was also large and intense. Based on Great Lakes fishery records between 1885 (beginning of records) and 1962 (last reported catch), about one billion pounds of marketable blue pike were landed. Blue pike contributed about 27 percent of the total production for Lake Erie between 1915 and 1959. In some years the blue pike exceeded 50 percent of the total Lake Erie production. Blue pike landings in Lake Ontario were much smaller, averaging about one-tenth the production of Lake Erie. The loss of the blue pike in the fishery of Lake Ontario was serious because it was the last of the valuable deepwater fishes to disappear, preceded by the Atlantic salmon, *Salmo salar,* lake trout, *Salvelinus namaycush,* and lake white-fish, *Coregonus clupeaformis.*

The collapse of the blue pike fishery and this fish's demise began in the late 1950s. The decrease in abundance was noted as early as 1958 and 1959, but fishery biologists were not alarmed because the decline appeared to be part of the extreme fluctuation in abundance that had been witnessed several times during the previous twenty years. By the time fishery managers realized that the blue pike was endangered, it was almost extinct. Commercial fishing regulations that prohibited taking blue pike went into effect several years after the last blue pike was taken. The blue pike was listed as endangered by the U.S. Fish and Wildlife Service in 1967.

The last blue pike was seen in fishery landings in 1965. The rapid decline and ultimate disappearance of such an abundant species is still hard to believe. What happened to the blue pike? What caused its extinction? Why did it disappear so rapidly? These are questions that will never be answered with certainty, but we do have some possible answers. Extinction of the blue pike was most likely caused by a combination of pollution, oxygen depletion, exploitation by commercial and sport fishermen, and the introduction of non-native fishes.

The turn of the century saw changes in the aquatic ecosystems of Lakes Erie and Ontario, but these alterations were nothing compared to what was coming between 1900 and 1970. The changes during these seventy years earned Lake Erie the distinction of being one of the largest polluted bodies of water in the world. The pollution originated from the surrounding population and industrial center which did not have or did not enforce water quality standards to maintain a healthy aquatic environment. For example, during the 1950s more than 225 tons of phosphates entered Lake Erie each year. This "fertilizer" caused microscopic plant populations to explode to twenty times their normal level. As these plants died and sank to the bottom they began to decompose, a process which removes oxygen from the water. Aquatic insects and other benthic fauna, important in the blue pike's diet, died from the low oxygen levels. These changes in the habitat, coupled with the removal of blue pike by overfishing, favored the increase in the walleye population. Some biologists believe the final blow to the blue pike came from competition and hybridization with the walleye.

Unlike many of our threatened, endangered, and extinct fishes, the dollar and cents value of the blue pike could be determined. Unfortunately the blue pike, a renewable natural resource, disappeared before its value was realized.

# XVII.

# Biogeography of Endangered and Threatened Fishes

Plant and animal species are not equally distributed over the surface of the earth. Each species has a definite geographical range which is determined by physical features such as the climate, geology, and abundance of water. The boundary of the range of a species is also limited by the distribution of other species in its environment. Every type of plant and animal sharing a particular environment is linked together into an interdependent network that has evolved over years of adaptation and natural selection.

In pinpointing the geographical locations of the numbers of endangered and threatened fishes, it is clear that these fishes are distributed in specific regions of North America. Within North America, 78 percent of the endangered and threatened fishes on our list inhabit U.S. waters while 10 percent are found in Mexico, and 1 percent in Canada; 8 percent are shared between the U.S. and Mexico, and 3 percent shared between the U.S. and Canada. Of the endangered and threatened fishes inhabiting the U.S., almost 80 percent of them are confined to two major geographical regions—the southwest and the southeast. Interestingly enough, many of the fishes from the southwestern region live in bodies of water that are the remnants of receding Pleistocene glaciers that retreated from the northern third of the U.S. approximately 10,000 to 12,000 years ago. The southeastern region has abundant rainfall and is blessed with a profusion of perennial streams. Today, the continuing degradation of stream resources in both regions could easily increase the total number of fishes to be placed on the endangered and threatened species list from each area.

Surprisingly, for the time being, the northeast, the central states, and the Great Lakes regions combined contribute only 8 percent to the total number of endangered and threatened fishes. However, with acid rain continually reducing or eliminating habitats in the northeast, more fishes may shortly join the ranks. The marine and estuarine environment as well as the state of Hawaii contribute about 4 percent of the total number.

Of the fishes currently endangered or threatened in the U.S., over 60 percent inhabit streams. In these streams, nine out of every ten fishes is a warmwater stream species, while the remaining one is a coldwater stream fish, a member of the salmon family in this case. One quarter of the remaining fishes find solitude in spring pools. About 4 percent are restricted to the subterranean waters of caves in the east central U.S., central Texas, and one species in Mexico. The Great Lakes, Lake Waccamaw in North Carolina, and lakes in the western U.S. are home for approximately 6 percent of the endangered and threatened fishes.

Excluding North America, the world's threatened and endangered fishes according to the Red Data Book of the International Union for the Conservation of Nature (IUCN), number only 77 species. Using a modification of the biogeographic region concept first conceived in 1876 by naturalist Alfred Russel Wallace, these species of fishes are found to be spread amongst six of the eight regions: the Palearctic Region (all of Europe, USSR, Japan, and China), Ethiopian Region (most of Africa and Madagascar), Oriental Region (the Philippine and Indonesian Islands, the western border of Afghanistan and Pakistan), Neotropical Region (South and Central America, the Caribbean Islands), Australasian Region (Australia, New Zealand, Tasmania, New Guinea), and the Ocean and Oceanic Islands Region. The Ethiopean Region currently holds the most endangered and threatened fishes of any biogeographic region outside of North America (Nearctic Region). The Ethiopean Region's endangered or threatened fishes, when combined with the number of fishes from the Oriental Region, represents one-fifth of the entire number of troubled fish species found in these six biogeographic regions. So far there are no reports of endangered and threatened fish species from the Antarctic Region.

North American endangered and threatened fishes currently comprise roughly 70 percent of all of the world's endangered and threatened fishes. This does not automatically mean that North America possesses the most polluted bodies of water or has interfered with and altered habitats of fishes to a greater extent than any other region on earth, although there is probably a fair amount of truth to this statement. More to the point, one wonders about other nation's efforts to keep up-to-date status information on their native fish populations. The statistic that less than 6 percent of the entire endangered and threatened fishes in the world are found in the Neotropical Region of South and Central America is, in all likelihood, far off base.

Biologists have no idea how many new species are lurking in the streams and lakes hidden deep within the recesses of the lush tropical rain forests in South America. Many South American governments are allowing the large-scale destruction of their rain forests to clear the jungles for expansion in the name of "progress." Not only will this razing of tropical rain forests have adverse effects on our weather patterns, but a tremendous number of fishes' habitats will be wiped out. Because biologists do not even know how many species of fishes live in this region, how can they reasonably determine the number of endangered and threatened fishes living in this ecosystem?

The next edition of the Red Data Book may reveal a much more accurate picture of the international situation as the public grows increasingly aware that environmental pollution with habitat destruction of plants and animals is not just a regional or national problem to be used as a political tool, but rather a problem that holds global consequences for everyone on earth.

# XVIII.

# Acid Rain

In much of the northeastern United States and across eastern Canada, a modern day horror known as acid rain is insidiously spreading like a cancer. Lakes, streams, and rivers are being reduced to silent, lifeless bodies of water as life at all levels of the food web are killed off. Acid rain has already been cited as a major reason for the decline and current threatened status of Quebec's copper redhorse. We suspect that acid rain is also removing mineral nutrients from the soil—reducing the productivity of forests as well as hopelessly corroding plumbing systems and the buildings themselves in particularly affected areas. Finally, acid rain has been implicated in causing respiratory diseases in humans and contamination of public drinking water.

Sulfur dioxide, hydrogen sulfide, and nitrogen oxide emissions are by-products from the burning of fossil fuels used in smelters, power plants, and factories. To a lesser extent, automobile exhaust fumes escaping into the atmosphere combine with moisture from the atmosphere to form droplets of sulfuric and nitric acids. These highly corrosive liquids then fall back to the ground as rain, snow, fog, hail, or any other form of precipitation. The sulfur and nitrogen oxides that do not make it into the atmosphere, but remain near the ground after being spewed out, can combine with the ground moisture to form the same acids. Natural processes such as forest fires, decomposition of organic matter, and volcanic eruptions also produce the corrosive compounds, but the millions of tons of sulfur and nitrogen oxides emitted from fossil fuel combustion represents the main problem by far.

The standard chemical scale for measuring acidity or alkalinity in a solution is the pH scale which ranges from 0 to 14. With a pH of 7 being neutral, the lower the pH value, the more acidic is the solution and the higher the pH

221

value, the more alkaline. Acidity in a solution such as rain is synonymous with the presence of hydrogen ions. The more hydrogen ions present in a solution, the more acidic the solution becomes. The pH is defined as the negative logarithm of the hydrogen ion concentration present in the solution. Because the scale is logarithmic, a change of only one point on the pH scale indicates a ten-fold change in acidity. If the pH of rain drops from 5.6, its average natural level, to 4.6, for example, then the rain has become ten times more acidic. A drop in pH to 3.6 from 5.6 would mean that the rainfall has become one hundred times more acidic. Acid rain is defined as precipitation having a pH under 5.6. Some extreme cases of acid rain reported in the recent past had the acidic equivalent of vinegar—a pH of only 2.4!

Acid rain has received the most attention and research in Europe where the post-industrial phenomenon is thought to have killed all fishes in hundreds of Scandinavian lakes and is considered to be a contributing factor in the ongoing disintegration of the Parthenon in Athens and the Coliseum in Rome. Probably the most important initial research into acid rain resulted from the work during the 1950s by Hans Egner, a Swedish soil scientist, who had hopes of gathering data on the fertilization of crops by atmospheric nutrients. Egner's studies served as a catalyst for two Swedish scientists and a British colleague who provided the basis for understanding acid rain genesis and how it could disperse hundreds or even thousands of miles away from its source. These pioneering studies completed by the early 1960s went unnoticed by the public and the scientific community.

Through the efforts of a young colleague of the Swedish scientists by the name of Svante Odén, the environmental problem was finally publicized in a leading Swedish newspaper in 1967. Odén's article warned that the phenomenon called acid rain knew no political boundaries and therefore was not just a local problem, but one which had large-scale, international consequences. Because the airborne compounds could disperse over great distances, a solution to the problem might require the cooperation of several jurisdictions. This article brought a great deal of attention to the acid rain issue because southern Scandinavia is so vulnerable to acid rain generated in western Europe and England.

Human nature is such that unless a problem affects one directly, no problem is recognized to exist. Unfortunately, this was the case in North America. All of North America remained fairly apathetic toward the problem of acid rain during the late 1960s. It was not that acid rain did not exist in North America. As more and more lakes, streams, and ponds in the northeastern U.S. and eastern Canada took on the strange "empty" blue appearance characteristic of acid rain-stricken waters, and fishermen complained about fishing entire days without nary a bite, North Americans gradually realized that acid precipitation was a universal phenomenon, not restricted to Europeans. Almost a decade lapsed after Odén's article for Americans to realize the severity of acid rain.

The northeastern U.S. and southeastern Canada have taken major beatings at the hands of acid rain over the years. Because of the circulatory wind patterns, the prevailing westerly winds of the upper atmosphere tend to transport pollutants east from their industrial sources in the Great Lakes region. Particularly during the summer months, the emissions collect and hang above the Great Lakes, trapped within high pressure systems which then rotate clockwise. The high mountains in the northeast cause these pollutant-laden air masses to rise and cool, forming the dreaded acid precipitation. Today over 10 percent of the lakes and ponds in the Adirondack Mountains have succumbed to acid rain pollution. At least 10 percent of the 226 largest lakes in New England have lost similar battles.

Because the air flows across North America from west to east, the eastern portions of the continent are particularly hard hit by this Man-made nightmare. The problem is not a regional one confined only to the northeast. Acid rain has been found from the Mississippi River to the Atlantic coasts and in California, Florida, and the Rocky Mountains as well.

The rapid spread and increase in acid precipitation in North America was partially related to the Environmental Protection Agency's (EPA) efforts to curb local air pollution problems. In a move to eliminate much of the emissions from industrial plants, the EPA hastily ordered plants to build taller smokestacks. Because of this naïve regulation, pollutants were released higher into the atmosphere where they formed droplets of acid rain which were carried much farther afield. Since this regulation went into effect in 1970, more than four hundred tall stacks have dotted the U.S. landscape, over one-third of them reach five hundred feet or more! The copper and nickel smelter, International Nickel Company, located in Sudbury, Ontario has a smokestack rising over 1200 feet into the sky. This Canadian smokestack could be the single largest source of acid pollutants in the world. The annual sulfur emissions belched out by this behemoth is said to equal the amount of emissions thought to have been released by all the volcanoes in the world!

Interestingly enough, there is a way to see how human activities have altered the pH of precipitation over the years. Studying cores of ice in Greenland, which have nicely preserved the annual layers of precipitation for thousands of years, reveals that the pH of precipitation prior to the Industrial Revolution was thirty to forty times less acidic than the rain now falling in the northeastern U.S.

There are very good reasons why the northeastern U.S., southeastern Canada, and Scandinavia seem to be more prone to damage by acid rain than other areas. Certainly their geographic locations are directly in line with the paths typically taken by pollutant-laden winds and all three regions have high precipitation rates. But certain freshwater ecosystems just seem to be more sensitive than others to the assaults of acid precipitation. It just so happens that these regions have siliceous types of bedrock (such as quartz or granite) which are highly resistant to weathering. Because these rocks are so resistant to dissolution through weathering, the surface waters contain very low concentrations of ions that could provide neutralizing power. The sensitivity of the freshwater ecosystem depends on the buffering or neutralizing capacity of its surface waters against the onslaught of acid rain. Without the buffering capacity which could be provided by a region rich in alkaline limestone, for instance, to resist the threat of acid rain, the siliceous bedrocks of the three regions cannot resist the advances of acid rain. Therefore, the pH of the surface water will drop quite rapidly. Furthermore, acid rain during the winter months becomes acid snow. During the spring melting, the lakes and ponds receiving this runoff are hit by "acid shock." This added booster of acidic waters may occur during the spring spawning of various species of fishes, making the phenomenon especially dangerous.

With an increased number of areas in North America and Europe currently considered sensitive to the ravages of acid rain, several environmentalists fear that the environment will deteriorate much more before the situation improves. Canadians project that 48,000 lakes will be lost by the year 2000. It seems highly unlikely that the burning of fossil fuels will significantly decline in the near future, unless a new form of clean and efficient form of energy is discovered. In fact, the usage of fossil fuels will probably accelerate.

Conservationists are also more and more concerned that industrialists will delay making expensive improvements necessary to reduce their plant's emission levels. "Scrubbers" or flue gas desulfurization units that collect harmful substances before they are expelled into the atmosphere can reduce as much as 90 percent of these toxic emissions. Industrialists claim that the installation of scrubbers is an expensive proposition that could break the economic backbone of the industries, especially in recessionary times. The industrialists further express opposition to decreasing emissions by arguing that the research on acid rain is still preliminary, particularly regarding who is ultimately responsible for damages to the environment.

Canadians are asking that very question: Who is responsible for acid rain and its effects? Canada claims that as much as 70 percent of its acid rain damage is the direct result of pollutants originating in the U.S., especially in the Ohio Valley where coal-fired utilities spew forth millions of tons of sulfur dioxide. The Canadians stand to lose a lot to acid rain as their three largest industries intimately depend on the well-being of the environment. Their largest industry, forest products, brings in revenues of $24 billion dollars a year and employs 10 percent of the entire Canadian work force. The pristine condition of the forests and lakes are crucial to tourism, Canada's second most lucrative industry. Commercial fishing, the third largest industry, could face irreparable damage from acid rain.

As a possible solution to the crisis, Canadians have proposed a massive cutback in industrial emissions of both countries to be put into immediate effect. The Canadians have admitted that their country is partially to blame for the acidification of hundreds of lakes and ponds in the northeastern U.S., but they feel that the damages are unbalanced. Many more sessions around the conference table will be required to solve this sticky issue involving a political boundary and the lethal airborne compounds that do not acknowledge such a boundary. Many more similar problems will no doubt surface in the years to come as the presence of acid rain becomes increasingly prevalent.

In the meantime, as controversies and heated debates continue to flare up between industrialists and conservationists, and funding for acid rain research is juggled around with seemingly little commitment by governments, life continues to ebb from the lakes, streams, and ponds.

# XIX.

# Outlook

How many more species of fishes in our lifetimes will follow in the footsteps of the blue pike, Tecopa pupfish, whiteline topminnow, or any of the other extinct fishes to become memories, preserved only in the pages of a book or in alcohol-filled bottles on dusty shelves in a museum? Each species of fish that becomes extinct as a result of our reckless, shortsighted overutilization of natural resources concludes another chapter in the history of life.

The twentieth century has witnessed the birth of some truly remarkable advances in technology, medicine, and science. Since the turn of the century we have seen the advent of the airplane, automobile, television, space travel, and the recent advances of computers and biotechnology. During this period, North America has switched from an agrarian society to a manufacturing society. During both of these phases in the U.S., Man's primary focus has been to exploit natural resources for economic gain.

After many years of this manufacturing phase of society, the computer industry is rapidly transforming the U.S. into still another phase, that being the information-based society. According to researchers involved in forecasting change in society, only 13 percent of the U.S. work force is employed in manufacturing while 60 percent either processes or produces information. The shift to deindustrialize the country will become global, eventually affecting Japan, Germany, and the other industrialized nations of the world as well. By the year 2000, the work force of the Third World will be manufacturing much of the world's goods because the goods can be produced for less.

While the agrarian society can be blamed for much of the initial damage to aquatic habitats as agricultural operations silted streams and diverted surface waters to irrigate fields, the transformation of the Industrial Revolution brought even greater pressures upon our water resources. Factories were built on rivers and other bodies of water to use them as sources of energy, water supply, transportation, and other purposes. Along with the manufacturing centers came the hordes of people needed to run them. Many farmers put down their shovels and became laborers in the cities. The creeks, rivers, and lakes were needed for both industrial and domestic uses. The aquatic habitats were ravaged by channelization, dammings, toxic chemical dumpings, and just excessive use by too many people for too many purposes. The drive to progress, to improve Man's quality of life, brought with it a lack of concern for the quality of life of many species of fishes. Habitat after habitat succumbed under the tremendous pressures of urbanization and industrialization.

While the dozens of fishes we have highlighted in this book need protection from Man's continuing encroachment, we do not wish to paint a doomsday picture for the future. On the contrary, we feel that the outlook is promising. The public's awareness and sentiment towards the plight of endangered and threatened fishes is rapidly growing as media coverage and educational materials spread the word. Groups such as the Audubon Society, American Rivers Conservation Council, Environmental Policy Center, Desert Fishes Council, National Wildlife Federation, and the Sierra Club draw the public's attention to the plight of endangered fishes. The Nature Conservancy's policy of acquiring land is the only hope for some of the endangered fishes. All of these private conservation organizations contribute invaluable time and effort in helping to conserve the aquatic environment and its inhabitants.

Management and recovery efforts will be greatly enhanced as more knowledge of the life history and habitat requirements of these endangered and threatened fishes is discovered. State and federal agencies have worked together with great determination and purpose to create and implement recovery plans for several endangered and threatened fishes. These plans have as their goal the protection, monitoring, and maintenance of an individual species of fish that is in danger. A number of success stories in which the endangered fishes have made comebacks are the direct results of a mutual cooperation among state, federal, and academic factions.

Hatchery programs for restocking fishes have been successful for some endangered and threatened fishes in recent years. For those species of fishes that have had their habitats altered and their ranges cropped, hatcheries may provide a stock for repopulating areas formerly inhabited.

The shift towards an information-based society from a manufacturing society could mean that the intense use of our water resources may slacken or certainly level off in the future as manufacturing moves out of the U.S., thus giving some aquatic ecosystems a chance to recuperate to some extent. We hope similar environmental problems that the U.S. faced during its growth phase as a manufacturing society will not be repeated in the Third World countries that will shoulder much of the manufacturing responsibilities. Perhaps they will learn from our mistakes. These countries are becoming universally aware that protection of any habitat is, ultimately, protecting Man's own environment.

There is a growing global appreciation for the values of wildlife and the protection of the environment. In the Soviet Union, environmental topics including the protection of rare and endangered species are being introduced into the universities and secondary schools. The Society for the Protection of

Nature in addition to hunting and fishing organizations function to preserve the environment in the USSR. Article 18 of the Constitution of the Union of Soviet Socialist Republics could be considered to be the Soviet analogue to the Endangered Species Act of 1973 in the U.S. Where the Endangered Species Act of 1973 not only provides rigid protection for endangered and threatened species, it also provides a means whereby the ecosystems upon which endangered and threatened species depend may be conserved. The Soviet legal article states, "In the interests of present and future generations, the necessary steps are taken in the USSR to protect and make scientific, rational use of the land and its mineral and water resources, and the plant and animal kingdoms, to preserve the purity of air and water, ensure reproduction of natural wealth, and improve the human environment."

How rapid is the universal awareness for conservation measures? According to the World Environment Center in New York, 144 countries had established environmental agencies as of mid-1982, compared to only 26 countries at the time of the 1972 United Nations Conference on the Human Environment. It is especially encouraging to see that in non-industrialized nations, the number of environmental agencies increased about ten times from 1972 to 1982. The outlook for Planet Earth is encouraging. The nations of the world are finally beginning to heed Henry David Thoreau's insightful statement:

*"In wildness is the preservation of the world."*

# XX.

# APPENDICES

# List of Endangered, Threatened, and Extinct Fishes of North America

Although biologists were aware of and noted the decline of some fishes as early as the late 1800s and early 1900s, serious concern was not aroused until the 1950s and detailed accounts and lists were not compiled until the 1960s. In 1964, Dr. Robert Rush Miller of the University of Michigan, Museum of Zoology published the first list of endangered fishes. He reported 38 fishes as endangered and indicated 21 species were "urgently threatened." All 38 fishes were from the arid lands of the western United States except one species, the Maryland darter.

During the 1960s the American Fisheries Society and the American Society of Ichthyologists and Herpetologists formed a joint Committee on Fish Conservation. The list compiled by this committee was published in 1972 and included fishes threatened at the state and national level. The most recent effort to compile a comprehensive list of endangered and threatened fishes of North America was published by the American Fisheries Society in 1979. There were 251 species and subspecies included in three categories—endangered, threatened, and special concern. This last category was for fishes whose status could change quickly or those species which required additional data before their conservation status could be established.

A worldwide conservation organization, the International Union for the Conservation of Nature (IUCN), published the first Red Data Book for fishes in 1969, which contained status reports for 79 rare and endangered fishes. In 1971, the IUCN released status reports for an additional 91 fishes and, in 1979, they published a completely revised Red Data Book for fishes, which contains almost two hundred status reports for threatened fishes worldwide. Data for the IUCN Red Data Book for fishes was compiled by Dr. Robert

Rush Miller. In the early 1960s, while the IUCN and professional societies were gathering data on endangered and threatened fishes, the U.S. Department of the Interior and several state fish and game agencies were also preparing federal and state lists of rare and endangered species. The results of the federal effort, entitled "Rare and Endangered Fish and Wildlife of the United States" was released in 1966. The publication, usually referred to as the "U. S. Redbook," contained data sheets for 38 rare or endangered fishes plus 45 fishes which were listed as status undetermined, four as peripheral to the U. S., and six as extinct. The second edition of the "U. S. Redbook," published in 1973, listed 55 U. S. fishes as rare and/or endangered.

In the late 1960s and 1970s, development of state endangered species lists was very important in the identification of endangered and threatened fishes. At present, approximately two-thirds of the states have publications on their endangered fishes.

# ENDANGERED, THREATENED, AND EXTINCT FISHES OF THE UNITED STATES

The following list of endangered, threatened, and extinct fishes was compiled by the authors from many sources. The species included and the conservation status assigned (E = endangered, T = threatened, and X = extinct) represent the views of the authors and may or may not be in agreement with the IUCN, U.S. Fish and Wildlife Service, or other sources. Two undescribed species (an entity which is generally recognized by ichthyologists, but has not been formally named) are included because they are distinctive and are generally known. There are other undescribed fishes that are endangered and threatened, but are not well known and have been omitted from our list. The threats have been categorized as follows:

1 = Habitat alteration. This category includes a variety of problems faced by aquatic ecosystems such as pollution, siltation, channelization, impoundments (dams), diversions, and flow reduction.
2 = Overutilization for commercial purposes.
3 = Disease.
4 = Introduction of exotic or non-native fishes. The most obvious problems resulting from the introduction of non-native fishes include predation, competition for food and space, and hybridization in cases where the exotic species is closely related to the endangered or threatened species.
5 = Restricted natural range. Some species with a limited range or restricted distribution could be eliminated by a single catastrophic event.

| Status | Common Name | Scientific Name | Distribution | Threats |
|---|---|---|---|---|

## Lampreys, Family Petromyzontidae

| Status | Common Name | Scientific Name | Distribution | Threats |
|---|---|---|---|---|
| X | Miller Lake Lamprey | *Lampetra minima* | Oregon | |

## Sturgeons, Family Acipenseridae

| Status | Common Name | Scientific Name | Distribution | Threats |
|---|---|---|---|---|
| *E | **Shortnose Sturgeon** | *Acipenser brevirostrum* | U.S. Atlantic Coast, Canada | 1 |
| T | Lake Sturgeon | *Acipenser fulvescens* | Southern Canada; Great Lakes, St. Lawrence River drainage; Mississippi River system; Mobile Basin, Alabama | 1 |
| T | Gulf Sturgeon | *A. oxyrhynchus desotoi* | Alabama, Florida, Mississippi, Louisiana | 1 |
| T | Pallid Sturgeon | *Scaphirhynchus albus* | Mississippi, Missouri, and Yellowstone rivers | 1 |

## Trouts, Family Salmonidae

| Status | Common Name | Scientific Name | Distribution | Threats |
|---|---|---|---|---|
| X | Longjaw Cisco | *Coregonus alpenae* | Great Lakes: Lakes Erie, Huron, Michigan | |
| E | **Acadian Whitefish** | *Coregonus canadensis* | Nova Scotia | 1,2 |
| X | Deepwater Cisco | *Coregonus johannae* | Great Lakes: Lakes Huron, Michigan | |
| X | Blackfin Cisco | *Coregonus nigripinnis* | Great Lakes: Lakes Huron, Michigan, Ontario, Superior | |
| T | Kiyi | *Coregonus kiyi* | Great Lakes: Lakes Huron, Michigan, Ontario, Superior | 1,2,4 |
| E | **Shortnose Cisco** | *Coregonus reighardi* | Great Lakes: Lakes Ontario, Huron, Michigan | 1,2,4 |
| E | **Shortjaw Cisco** | *Coregonus zenithicus* | Great Lakes: Lakes Huron, Michigan, Superior | 1,2,4 |
| *T | Little Kern Golden Trout | *Salmo aguabonita whitei* | California | 1,4 |

233

| Status | Common Name | Scientific Name | Distribution | Threats |
|--------|-------------|-----------------|--------------|---------|
| *T | Apache Trout | *Salmo apache* | Arizona | 1,4 |
| *T | Lahontan Cutthroat Trout | *Salmo clarki henshawi* | California, Nevada, Utah, Washington | 1,4 |
| T | Colorado River Cutthroat Trout | *Salmo clarki pleuriticus* | Colorado, Utah, Wyoming | 1,4 |
| *T | Paiute Cutthroat Trout | *Salmo clarki seleneris* | California | 1 |
| *T | Greenback Cutthroat Trout | *Salmo clarki stomias* | Colorado | 1,4 |
| T | Utah Cutthroat Trout | *Salmo clarki utah* | Utah, Wyoming, Nevada | 1,4 |
| *E | **Gila Trout** | ***Salmo gilae*** | New Mexico, Arizona | 1 |
| X | Silver Trout | *Salvelinus agassizi* | New Hampshire | |

## Minnows, Family Cyprinidae

| Status | Common Name | Scientific Name | Distribution | Threats |
|--------|-------------|-----------------|--------------|---------|
| T | Mexican Stoneroller | *Campostoma ornatum* | Arizona, Texas, Mexico | 1,3 |
| T | Devils River Minnow | *Dionda diaboli* | Texas | 1 |
| E | **Saltillo Roundnose Minnow** | ***Dionda episcopa punctifer*** | Mexico | 1,5 |
| E | **Flatjaw Minnow** | ***Dionda mandibularis*** | Mexico | 1,4 |
| T | Desert Dace | *Eremichthys acros* | Nevada | 1,5 |
| E | **Fish Creek Spring Tui Chub** | ***Gila bicolor euchila*** | Nevada | 1,4,5 |
| T | Sheldon Tui Chub | *Gila bicolor eurysoma* | Nevada, Oregon | 1,5 |
| T | Independence Valley Tui Chub | *Gila bicolor isolata* | Nevada | 1,4,5 |
| *E | **Mohave Tui Chub** | ***Gila bicolor mohavensis*** | California | 1,4 |
| T | Newark Valley Tui Chub | *Gila bicolor newarkensis* | Nevada | 1,5 |
| E | **Owens Tui Chub** | ***Gila bicolor snyderi*** | California | 1,4,5 |
| T | Cowhead Lake Tui Chub | *Gila bicolor vaccaceps* | California | 1 |

| Status | Common Name | Scientific Name | Distribution | Threats |
|---|---|---|---|---|
| E | **Borax Lake Chub** | *Gila boraxobius* | Oregon | 1,5 |
| X | Thicktail Chub | *Gila crassicauda* | California | |
| *E | **Humpback Chub** | *Gila cypha* | Arizona, Colorado, Utah, Wyoming | 1,4 |
| T | Sonora Chub | *Gila ditaenia* | Arizona, Mexico | 1 |
| *E | **Bonytail** | *Gila elegans* | Arizona, California, Colorado, Nevada, Utah, Wyoming | 1,4 |
| T | Gila Chub | *Gila intermedia* | Arizona, New Mexico | 1,5 |
| E | **Chihuahua Chub** | *Gila nigrescens* | New Mexico, Mexico | 1,4 |
| E | **Yaqui Chub** | *Gila purpurea* | Arizona, Mexico | 1,4 |
| T | Gila Roundtail Chub | *Gila robusta grahami* | Arizona, New Mexico | 1,4 |
| *E | **Pahranagat Roundtail Chub** | *Gila robusta jordani* | Nevada | 1,4 |
| E | **Virgin River Roundtail Chub** | *Gila robusta seminuda* | Arizona, Nevada, Utah | 1 |
| *T | Slender Chub | *Hybopsis cahni* | Tenessee, Virginia | 1 |
| T | Oregon Chub | *Hybopsis crameri* | Oregon | 1 |
| *T | Spotfin Chub | *Hybopsis monacha* | Alabama, Georgia, North Carolina, Tennessee, Virginia | 1 |
| X | Pahranagat Spinedace | *Lepidomeda altivelis* | Nevada | |
| T | White River Spinedace | *Lepidomeda albivallis* | Nevada | 1,4 |
| T | Virgin Spinedace | *Lepidomeda mollispinis mollispinis* | Arizona, Nevada, Utah | 1 |
| E | **Big Spring Spinedace** | *Lepidomeda mollispinis praetensis* | Nevada | 1,4,5 |
| T | Little Colorado Spinedace | *Lepidomeda vittata* | Arizona | 1 |
| T | Spikedace | *Meda fulgida* | Arizona, New Mexico | 1,4 |
| *E | **Moapa Dace** | *Moapa coriacea* | Nevada | 1,3,4,5 |

| Status | Common Name | Scientific Name | Distribution | Threats |
|--------|-------------|-----------------|--------------|---------|
| T | Chihuahua Shiner | *Notropis chihuahua* | Texas, Mexico | 1 |
| T | Beautiful Shiner | *Notropis formosus* | Arizona, New Mexico, Mexico | 1 |
| T | Cape Fear Shiner | *Notropis mekistocholas* | North Carolina | 1 |
| X | Phantom Shiner | *Notropis orca* | New Mexico, Texas, Mexico | |
| E | **Conchos Shiner** | ***Notropis panarcys*** | Mexico | 1,5 |
| T | Peppered Shiner | *Notropis perpallidus* | Arkansas, Oklahoma | 1 |
| T | Proserpine Shiner | *Notropis proserpinus* | Texas, Mexico | 1 |
| E | **Pecos Shiner** | ***Notropis simus pecosensis*** | New Mexico | 1 |
| X | Bluntnose Shiner | *Notropis simus simus* | New Mexico, Texas | |
| E | **Cuatro Ciénegas Shiner** | ***Notropis xanthicara*** | Mexico | 1 |
| E | **Cahaba Shiner** | ***Notropis* sp.** | Alabama | 1 |
| T | Blackside Dace | *Phoxinus cumberlandensis* | Kentucky, Tennessee | 1 |
| *E | **Woundfin** | ***Plagopterus argentissimus*** | Arizona, Nevada, Utah | 1 |
| X | Clear Lake Splittail | *Pogonichthys ciscoides* | California | |
| *E | **Colorado Squawfish** | ***Ptychocheilus lucius*** | Arizona, Colorado, Utah, California, New Mexico, Nevada, Wyoming, Mexico | 1,3,4 |
| E | **Independence Valley Speckled Dace** | ***Rhinichthys osculus lethoporus*** | Nevada | 1,4,5 |
| T | Moapa Speckled Dace | *Rhinichthys osculus moapae* | Nevada | 1,4 |
| E | **Ash Meadows Speckled Dace** | ***Rhinichthys osculus nevadensis*** | Nevada | 1,4 |
| E | **Clover Valley Speckled Dace** | ***Rhinichthys osculus oligoporus*** | Nevada | 1,4,5 |
| E | **Grass Valley Speckled Dace** | ***Rhinichthys osculus reliquus*** | Nevada | 1 |

| Status | Common Name | Scientific Name | Distribution | Threats |
|--------|-------------|-----------------|--------------|---------|
| *E | **Kendall Warm Springs Dace** | *Rhinichthys osculus thermalis* | Wyoming | 5 |
| T | White River Speckled Dace | *Rhinichthys osculus velifer* | Nevada | 1,5 |
| T | Loach Minnow | *Tiaroga cobitis* | Arizona, New Mexico, Mexico | 1,4 |

## Suckers, Family Catostomidae

| Status | Common Name | Scientific Name | Distribution | Threats |
|--------|-------------|-----------------|--------------|---------|
| T | White River Desert Sucker | *Catostomus clarki intermedius* | Nevada | 1 |
| T | Lost River Sucker | *Catostomus luxatus* | California, Oregon | 1,4 |
| E | **Modoc Sucker** | *Catostomus microps* | California | 1,4 |
| T | Warner Sucker | *Catostomus warnerensis* | Oregon | 1,4 |
| T | Shortnose Sucker | *Chasmistes brevirostris* | California, Oregon | 1,4 |
| *E | **Cui-ui** | *Chasmistes cujus* | Nevada | 1 |
| X | First June Sucker | *Chasmistes liorus liorus* | Utah | |
| T | June Sucker | *Chasmistes liorus mictus* | Utah | 1,4 |
| X | Snake River Sucker | *Chasmistes muriei* | Wyoming | |
| X | Harelip Sucker | *Lagochila lacera* | Alabama, Arkansas, Georgia, Indiana, Kentucky, Ohio, Tennessee, Virginia | |
| T | Copper Redhorse | *Moxostoma hubbsi* | Canada | 1 |
| T | Razorback Sucker | *Xyrauchen texanus* | Arizona, California, Colorado, Nevada, Utah, Wyoming | 1,4 |

## Freshwater Catfishes, Family Ictaluridae

| Status | Common Name | Scientific Name | Distribution | Threats |
|--------|-------------|-----------------|--------------|---------|
| T | Yaqui Catfish | *Ictalurus pricei* | Arizona, Mexico | 1 |
| T | Smoky Madtom | *Noturus baileyi* | Tennessee | 1 |

| Status | Common Name | Scientific Name | Distribution | Threats |
|--------|-------------|-----------------|--------------|---------|
| *T | Yellowfin Madtom | *Noturus flavipinnis* | Georgia, Tennessee, Virginia | 1 |
| T | Carolina Madtom | *Noturus furiosus* | North Carolina | 1 |
| T | Orangefin Madtom | *Noturus gilberti* | North Carolina, Virginia | 1 |
| T | Ouachita Madtom | *Noturus lachneri* | Arkansas | 1 |
| T | Frecklebelly Madtom | *Noturus munitus* | Alabama, Georgia, Louisiana, Mississippi, Tennessee | 1 |
| T | Neosho Madtom | *Noturus placidus* | Kansas, Missouri, Oklahoma | 1 |
| T | Pygmy Madtom | *Noturus stanauli* | Tennessee | 1 |
| *E | **Scioto Madtom** | ***Noturus trautmani*** | Ohio | 1,5 |
| *E | **Mexican Blindcat** | ***Prietella phreatophila*** | Mexico | 1,5 |
| T | Widemouth Blindcat | *Satan eurystomus* | Texas | 1,5 |
| T | Toothless Blindcat | *Trogloglanis pattersoni* | Texas | 1,5 |

## Cavefishes, Family Amblyopsidae

| Status | Common Name | Scientific Name | Distribution | Threats |
|--------|-------------|-----------------|--------------|---------|
| T | Ozark Cavefish | *Amblyopsis rosae* | Arkansas, Missouri, Oklahoma | 1 |
| T | Northern Cavefish | *Amblyopsis spelaea* | Indiana, Kentucky | 1 |
| *T | Alabama Cavefish | *Speoplatyrhinus poulsoni* | Alabama | 1,5 |

## Killifishes, Family Cyprinodontidae

| Status | Common Name | Scientific Name | Distribution | Threats |
|--------|-------------|-----------------|--------------|---------|
| T | White River Springfish | *Crenichthys baileyi* | Nevada | 1,4,5 |
| E | **Railroad Valley Springfish** | ***Crenichthys nevadae*** | Nevada | 1,4 |
| E | **Media Luna Killie** | ***Cualac tessellatus*** | Mexico | 1,4 |
| E | **Perrito de Potosí** | ***Cyprinodon alvarezi*** | Mexico | 1,4,5 |
| *T | Leon Springs Pupfish | *Cyprinodon bovinus* | Texas | 1,4,5 |

| Status | Common Name | Scientific Name | Distribution | Threats |
|---|---|---|---|---|
| *E | **Devils Hole Pupfish** | *Cyprinodon diabolis* | Nevada | 1,5 |
| *E | **Comanche Springs Pupfish** | *Cyprinodon elegans* | Texas | 1 |
| T | Conchos Pupfish | *Cyrpinodon eximius* | Texas, Mexico | 1,5 |
| T | Desert Pupfish | *Cyprinodon macularius* | Arizona, California, Mexico | 1,4 |
| X | Tecopa Pupfish | *Cyprinodon nevadensis calidae* | California | |
| E | **Ash Meadows Amargosa Pupfish** | *Cyprinodon nevadensis mionectes* | Nevada | 1,4 |
| *E | **Warm Springs Pupfish** | *Cyprinodon nevadensis pectoralis* | Nevada | 1,4,5 |
| X | Shoshone Pupfish | *Cyprinodon nevadensis shoshone* | California | |
| *E | **Owens Pupfish** | *Cyprinodon radiosus* | California | 1,4 |
| X | Raycraft Ranch Killifish | *Empetrichthys latos concavus* | Nevada | |
| *E | **Pahrump Killifish** | ***Empetrichthys latos latos*** | Nevada | 1,4,5 |
| X | Pahrump Ranch Killifish | *Empetrichthys latos pahrump* | Nevada | |
| X | Ash Meadows Killifish | *Empetrichthys merriami* | Nevada | |
| X | Whiteline Topminnow | *Fundulus albolineatus* | Alabama | |
| T | Barrens Topminnow | *Fundulus julisia* | Tennessee | 1 |
| T | Waccamaw Killifish | *Fundulus waccamensis* | North Carolina | 1 |
| E | **Sardinilla Cuatro Ciénegas** | ***Lucania interioris*** | Mexico | 1 |
| E | **Perrito Enano de Potosí** | ***Megupsilon aporus*** | Mexico | 1,5 |

239

| Status | Common Name | Scientific Name | Distribution | Threats |
|---|---|---|---|---|

## Livebearers, Family Poeciliidae

| Status | Common Name | Scientific Name | Distribution | Threats |
|---|---|---|---|---|
| E | Guayacón de San Gregorio | *Gambusia alvarezi* | Mexico | 1 |
| *E | Amistad Gambusia | *Gambusia amistadensis* | Texas | 1,5 |
| *E | Big Bend Gambusia | *Gambusia gaigei* | Texas | 1,4,5 |
| *E | San Marcos Gambusia | *Gambusia georgei* | Texas | 1,4,5 |
| *E | Clear Creek Gambusia | *Gambusia heterochir* | Texas | 4 |
| *E | Pecos Gambusia | *Gambusia nobilis* | Texas, New Mexico | 1,4 |
| *E | Gila Topminnow | *Poeciliopsis occidentalis* | Arizona, New Mexico | 1,4 |
| E | Monterrey Platyfish | *Xiphophorus couchianus* | Mexico | 1,5 |
| E | Cuatro Ciénegas Platyfish | *Xiphophorus gordoni* | Mexico | 1,5 |

## Silversides, Family Atherinidae

| Status | Common Name | Scientific Name | Distribution | Threats |
|---|---|---|---|---|
| T | Waccamaw Silverside | *Menidia extensa* | North Carolina | 1 |

## Sticklebacks, Family Gasterosteidae

| Status | Common Name | Scientific Name | Distribution | Threats |
|---|---|---|---|---|
| *E | Unarmored Threespine Stickleback | *Gasterosteus aculeatus williamsoni* | California | 1,4 |

## Sunfishes, Family Centrarchidae

| Status | Common Name | Scientific Name | Distribution | Threats |
|---|---|---|---|---|
| T | Spring Pygmy Sunfish | *Elassoma* species | Alabama | 1,5 |
| T | Guadalupe Bass | *Micropterus treculi* | Texas | 1,4 |

| Status | Common Name | Scientific Name | Distribution | Threats |
|---|---|---|---|---|
| | | Perches, Family Percidae | | |
| T | Eastern Sand Darter | *Ammocrypta pellucida* | Illinois, Indiana, Kentucky, Michigan, New York, Ohio, Pennsylvania, West Virginia | 1 |
| T | Sharphead Darter | *Etheostoma acuticeps* | North Carolina, Tennessee, Virginia | 1 |
| T | Coppercheek Darter | *Ethesotaoma aquali* | Tennessee | 1 |
| *T | Slackwater Darter | *Etheostoma boschungi* | Alabama, Tennessee | 1 |
| T | Coldwater Darter | *Etheostoma ditrema* | Alabama, Georgia, Tennessee | 1 |
| *E | **Fountain Darter** | ***Etheostoma fonticola*** | Texas | 1,5 |
| T | Niangua Darter | *Etheostoma nianguae* | Missouri | 1 |
| *E | **Watercress Darter** | ***Etheostoma nuchale*** | Alabama | 1,5 |
| *E | **Okaloosa Darter** | ***Etheostoma okaloosae*** | Florida | 1,4 |
| T | Paleback Darter | *Etheostoma pallididorsum* | Arkansas | 1 |
| T | Waccamaw Darter | *Etheostoma perlongum* | North Carolina | 1 |
| *T | Bayou Darter | *Etheostoma rubrum* | Mississippi | 1 |
| *E | **Maryland Darter** | ***Etheostoma sellare*** | Maryland | 1 |
| T | Trispot Darter | *Etheostoma trisella* | Alabama, Georgia, Tennessee | 1 |
| T | Tuscumbia Darter | *Etheostoma tuscumbia* | Alabama, Tennessee | 1 |
| T | Amber Darter | *Percina antesella* | Georgia, Tennessee | 1 |
| T | Goldline Darter | *Percina aurolineata* | Alabama, Georgia | 1 |
| T | Bluestripe Darter | *Percina cymatotaenia* | Missouri | 1 |

| Status | Common Name | Scientific Name | Distribution | Threats |
|--------|-------------|-----------------|--------------|---------|
| T | Freckled Darter | *Percina lenticula* | Alabama, Georgia, Louisianna, Mississippi | 1 |
| *T | Leopard Darter | *Percina pantherina* | Arkansas, Oklahoma | 1 |
| T | Roanoke Logperch | *Percina rex* | Virginia | 1 |
| *E | **Snail Darter** | ***Percina tanasi*** | Tennessee | 1 |
| X | Blue Pike | *Stizostedion vitreum glaucum* | Great Lakes: Lakes Erie, Ontario | |

## Drums, Family Sciaenidae

| Status | Common Name | Scientific Name | Distribution | Threats |
|--------|-------------|-----------------|--------------|---------|
| *E | **Totoaba** | ***Cynoscion macdonaldi*** | Mexico, Gulf of California | 2 |

## Cichlids, Family Cichlidae

| Status | Common Name | Scientific Name | Distribution | Threats |
|--------|-------------|-----------------|--------------|---------|
| E | **Mojarra Caracolera** | ***Cichlasoma bartoni*** | Mexico | 1,4 |
| E | **Mojarra** | ***Cichlasoma labridens*** | Mexico | 1,4 |

## Gobies, Family Gobiidae

| Status | Common Name | Scientific Name | Distribution | Threats |
|--------|-------------|-----------------|--------------|---------|
| T | Tidewater Goby | *Eucyclogobius newberryi* | California | 1 |
| T | O'opu Alamo'o | *Lentipes concolor* | Hawaii | 1 |

## Sculpins, Family Cottidae

| Status | Common Name | Scientific Name | Distribution | Threats |
|--------|-------------|-----------------|--------------|---------|
| T | Rough Sculpin | *Cottus asperrimus* | California | 1 |
| X | Utah Lake Sculpin | *Cottus echinatus* | Utah | |
| T | Shoshone Sculpin | *Cottus greenei* | Idaho | 1 |

*On U.S. Department of the Interior List of Endangered and Threatened Species

# Map of Endangered and Threatened Fishes of North America

Approximate distribution of the endangered and threatened fishes discussed in the text. The numbers on the map correspond to the species and areas listed below. Fishes are arranged in the order they appear in the text.

1. Copper redhorse
2. Maryland darter
3. Roanoke fishes
4. Lake Waccamaw fishes
5. Okaloosa darter
6. Lake sturgeon
7. Shortnose cisco
8. Shortjaw cisco
9. Borax Lake chub
10. Warner sucker
11. Modoc sucker
12. Unarmored threespine stickleback
13. Lahontan cutthroat trout
14. Cui-ui
15. Desert dace
16. Ash Meadows fishes
17. Pahrump killifish
18. Humpback chub
19. Bonytail chub, Colorado squawfish, razorback sucker
20. Woundfin
21. Moapa dace
22. Apache trout
23. Greenback cutthroat trout
24. Gila trout
25. Comanche Springs pupfish
26. Clear Creek gambusia
27. San Marcos River fishes
28. Texas blindcats
29. Ozark cavefish
30. Northern cavefish
31. Alabama cavefish
32. Cuatro Ciénegas fishes
33. Niangua darter
34. Peppered shiner
35. Leopard darter
36. Slackwater darter
37. Snail darter
38. Blackside dace
39. Barrens topminnow
40. Spring pygmy sunfish
41. Watercress darter
42. Shortnose sturgeon
43. Acadian whitefish
44. Totoaba

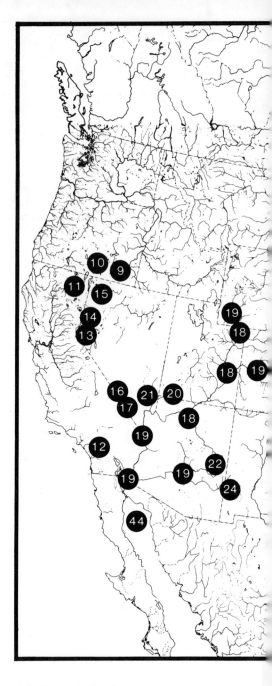

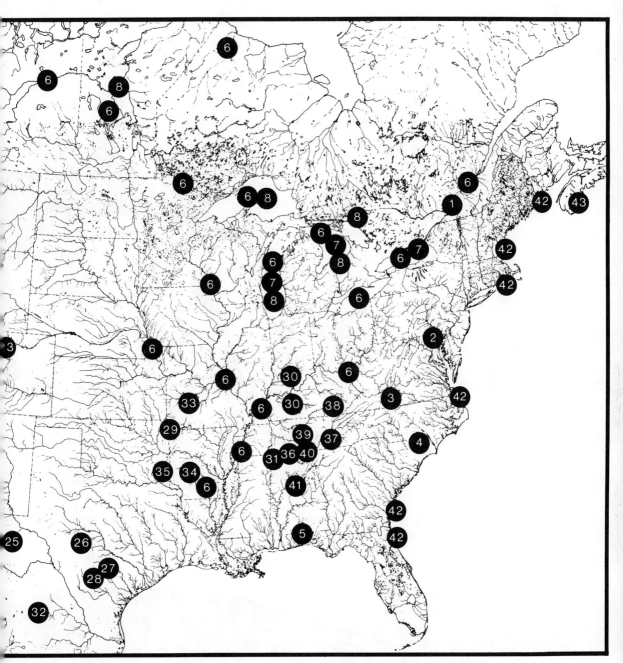

Map From North Carolina State Museum of Natural History

# Parts of a Fish

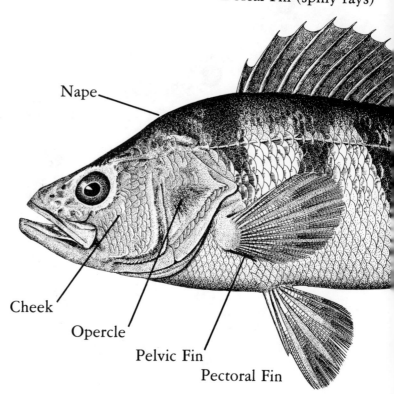

Dorsal Fin (spiny rays)

Nape

Perch

Cheek

Opercle

Pelvic Fin

Pectoral Fin

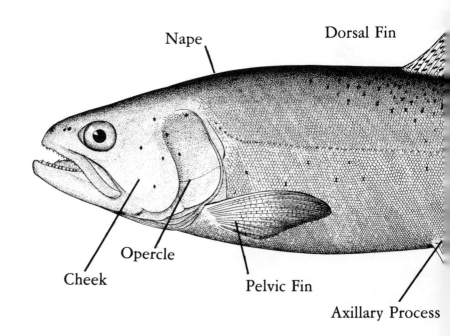

Nape

Dorsal Fin

Opercle

Cheek

Pelvic Fin

Trout

Axillary Process

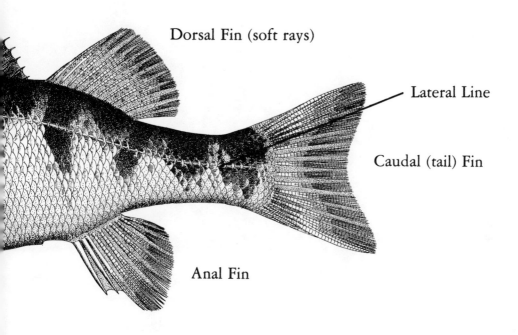

Dorsal Fin (soft rays)

Lateral Line

Caudal (tail) Fin

Anal Fin

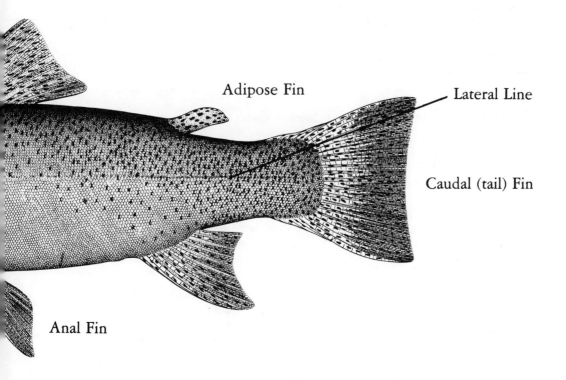

Adipose Fin

Lateral Line

Caudal (tail) Fin

Anal Fin

# Glossary

adaptive radiation = evolutionary diversification of species derived from a common ancestor, each adapted to a particular ecological role.

algal = primitive, chiefly aquatic, single or multicellular plants lacking true roots, stems, and leaves, but containing chlorophyll. Includes the seaweeds and kelps.

alkaline = having the chemical qualities of a base; a pH value of more than 7.

alluvial = sediment deposited or laid down by flowing water; a river bed, flood plain, delta, or fans at the foot of a mountain slope.

anadromous = migrating up rivers from the sea to spawn in fresh water.

aquifer = an underground water-bearing rock, rock formation, or group of formations.

artesian well = ground water which is under enough internal hydrostatic pressure to flow from a well without being actively pumped.

canalization = the process of building a system of canals usually from existing rivers and creeks.

channelization = process of straightening, widening, and removal of obstructions from a stream channel in an effort to reduce flooding. Usually this results in greater flooding downstream and increased erosion and siltation.

chemoreception = utilization of the sense of smell or taste in searching for food, finding mates, and avoiding predators.

conspecifics = individuals belonging to the same species.

critical habitat = portion of environment which is considered to be essential for the continued existence of an endangered or threatened species. This concept from the Federal Endangered Species Act provides a means by which endangered species can be protected from adverse impacts resulting from Federal action, but it does not create a refuge or nature preserve. It also does not limit private, local, or state projects unless Federal permits or funds are involved.

cyprinid = belonging to the freshwater fish family, Cyprinidae; the minnows.

denature = to change natural qualities of a substance.

electrofishing = use of electrical current to capture fishes.

endangered = any species or subspecies of fish or wildlife or plant, and any distinct population segment of any species of vertebrate fish or wildlife which interbreeds when mature that is in danger of extinction throughout all or a significant portion of its range within the foreseeable future.

endemic = native or confined to a certain region, often having a comparatively restricted distribution.

endorheic = an area with only interior drainage; no outlet, closed basin.

eutrophication = a process in which the increase of mineral and organic nutrients in a body of water usually caused by sewage and runoff from agricultural operations results in an excessive amount of plant growth leading to a decrease in the dissolved oxygen content of the water.

extirpate = to wipe out, eradicate, exterminate.

flocculant = substance that promotes the aggregation of particles into small lumps.

genome = the entire genetic complement of the individual.

gill rakers = comblike structures arising from each individual gill arch within the buccal chamber of a fish which act as a filter-feeding device; entrapping and straining out prey such as plankton from the water column. Used as a taxonomic character in identifying some species of fishes.

gravid = pregnant; laden with eggs or young.

Great Basin = drainage basin comprising most of Nevada and Utah with portions in California, Oregon, Idaho, and Wyoming. In actuality, it is a combination of about 90 valleys separated by more than 160 mountain ranges.

hybridization = crossing of individuals belonging to two genetically unlike natural populations or different species.

impoundment = accumulation or collection of water in a reservoir as a result of damming.

introgression = incorporation of genes of one species into the gene pool of another species.

lentic = lakelike, still waters.

mechanoreception = the ability to sense particle displacement or pressure wave disturbances in the environment. This sensory information is used by the organism to search for mates, hunt for prey, or to avoid predators.

pH = the negative logarithm of the hydrogen ion concentration present in a solution. The pH scale which ranges from 0 to 14 measures the acidity or alkalinity of a solution. A pH of 7 is neutral.

piscivores = carnivorous predators that feed on fishes.

pluvial = formed by abundant rainfall during cooler intervals of the Pleistocene Epoch; the last pluvial period occurred between 8,000–12,000 years ago.

potadromous = living in lakes, but making spawning runs into creeks and rivers.

Recovery Plan = formal plan of action prepared by a team of biologists combining the efforts of state and federal agencies as well as interested individuals who have responsibility for protecting a particular species and its habitat.

redd = oval depression in gravelly substrate constructed by spawning adult trout which serves as a nest for trout eggs.

relict species = a species that is a persistent remnant or survivor of an otherwise extinct group. A species left in a locality after earlier climatic or environmental changes.

riparian = existing along the banks of a river, lake, or other body of water.

rotenone = a toxic compound derived from the root of a tropical plant.

saline = salty. Mineral substances (salts) left by evaporating water or dissolved in water.

salmonid = fish belonging to the trout, salmon, or whitefish family, the Salmonidae.

seine = a net with weights on one edge and floats on the other; pulled vertically through the water to capture fishes.

species = groups of interbreeding natural populations that are reproductively isolated from other such groups.

strain = any of various lines of ancestry; kind; sort; of same species having distinctive characteristics.

stream capture = diversion of a portion of one stream by the headward or upstream erosion of a stream in another drainage.

stripmining = the mining of minerals and ores close to the surface by removing or stripping off the topsoil and other material to expose the minerals.

subspecies = populations within a species that are distinguishable by morphological, physiological, or behavioral characteristics and are usually geographically defined.

taxa = formal unit of classification of a group of organisms based on common characteristics in varying degrees of distinction.

terete = cylindrical, tapering at each end.

thermocline = layer of water in which a sudden change in temperature takes place, usually between the upper warm water layer and the lower cold water layer in large bodies of water.

threatened = any species or subspecies of fish or wildlife or plant, and any distinct population segment of any species of vertebrate fish or wildlife which interbreeds when mature that is likely to become an endangered species throughout all or a significant portion of its range within the foreseeable future.

trophic = pertaining to the use of a kind of food by an organism.

viviparous = bears living young.

# References

For further information we recommend the following publications and organizations. For specific information about the endangered and threatened fishes in your region contact your state fish and game department or the U. S. Fish and Wildlife Service.

## Threatened and Endangered Fishes

*At the Crossroads 1980.* A report on California's Endangered and Rare Fish and Wildlife. State of California Resources Agency, Fish and Game Commission and Department of Fish and Game. 1980  147 pp.

*Endangered and Threatened Plants and Animals of Alabama.* Edited by Herbert T. Boschung. Bulletin of the Alabama Museum of Natural History, University of Alabama. Bulletin Number 2. 1976. 93 pp.

*Endangered and Threatened Plants and Animals of North Carolina.* Edited by John E. Cooper, Sarah S. Robinson, and John B. Funderburg. North Carolina State Museum of Natural History, Raleigh. 1977. 444 pp.

*Endangered and Threatened Plants and Animals of Virginia.* Edited by Donald W. Linzey. Center for Environmental Studies, Virginia Polytechnic Institute and State University, Blacksburg. 1979. 665 pp.

*Endangered and Threatened Species of Illinois. Status and Distribution.* Illinois Department of Conservation. 1981. 189 pp.

*Endangered and Threatened Wildlife of Kentucky, North Carolina, South Carolina, and Tennessee.* Edited by Warren Parker and Laura Dixon. The North Carolina Agricultural Extension Service. 1980. 116 pp.

*Endangered and Threatened Wildlife of the Chesapeake Bay Region—Delaware, Maryland, and Virginia.* Christopher P. White. Tidewater Publishers, Centreville, Maryland. 1982. 148 pp.

"Fishes of North America—Endangered, Threatened, or of Special Concern: 1979." James E. Deacon, Gail Kobetich, James D. Williams, and Salvador

Contreras. American Fisheries Society, *Fisheries.* Volume 4, Number 2. 1979. pp 29–44.

*Fishes. Rare and Endangered Biota of Florida.* Edited by Carter R. Gilbert. University Presses of Florida. Volume 4. 1978. 58 pp.

*Rare and Endangered Species of Missouri.* Missouri Department of Conservation and U. S. Department of Agriculture's Soil Conservation Service. 1974. 75 pp.

*Red Data Book, Pisces.* Edited by Robert Rush Miller. International Union for Conservation of Nature and Natural Resources, IUCN, Morges, Switzerland. Volume 4. 1977.

*Tennessee's Rare Wildlife.* Edited by Daniel C. Eagar and Robert M. Hatcher. Tennessee Wildlife Resources Agency, Nashville. Volume 1. 1980. 337 pp.

"The Endangered Species Act and Southwest Fishes." James E. Johnson and John N. Rinne. American Fisheries Society, *Fisheries.* Volume 7, Number 4. 1982. pp 2–8.

*The Natural History of Native Fishes in the Death Valley System.* D. L. Soltz and R. J. Naiman. Natural History Museum of Los Angeles County, Science Series. Number 30. 1978. 76 pp.

# Selected Regional and State Books on Fishes

## Canada

*Freshwater Fishes of Northwestern Canada and Alaska.* J. D. McPhail and C. C. Lindsey. Fisheries Research Board of Canada Bulletin. Number 173. 1970. 381 pp.

*Freshwater Fishes of Eastern Canada.* W. B. Scott. University of Toronto Press. 1967. 137 pp.

*Freshwater Fishes of Canada.* W. B. Scott and E. J. Crossman. Fisheries Research Board of Canada Bulletin. Number 184. 1973. 966 pp.

## United States

### Alabama

*Freshwater Fishes of Alabama.* W. F. Smith–Vaniz. Auburn University Agricultural Experimental Station. 1968. 211 pp.

## Arizona

*Fishes of Arizona.* W. L. Minckley. Arizona Game and Fish Department, Phoenix. 1973. 293 pp.

## California

*Inland Fishes of California.* P. B. Moyle. University of California Press, Berkeley. 1976. 405 pp.

## Connecticut

*Freshwater Fishes of Connecticut.* W. R. Whitworth, P. L. Berrien, and W. T. Keller. State Geological and Natural History Survey of Connecticut. Bulletin Number 101. 1968. 134 pp.

## Hawaii

*Handbook of Hawaiian Fishes.* W. A. Gosline and V. E. Brock. University Press of Hawaii, Honolulu. 1960. 372 pp.

## Illinois

*The Fishes of Illinois.* P. W. Smith. University of Illinois Press, Urbana. 1979. 314 pp.

## Kansas

*Handbook of Fishes of Kansas.* F. B. Cross. Museum of Natural History Miscellaneous Publications. Number 45. 1967. 357 pp.

*Fishes in Kansas.* F. B. Cross and J. T. Collins. University of Kansas Museum of Natural History Miscellaneous Publications, Public Education Series. Number 3. 1975. 189 pp.

## Kentucky

*The Fishes of Kentucky.* W. M. Clay. Kentucky Department of Fish and Wildlife Resources, Frankfort. 1975. 416 pp.

## Louisiana

*Freshwater Fishes of Louisiana.* N. H. Douglas. Claitor's Publication Division, Baton Rouge. 1974. 443 pp.

## Michigan

*Fishes of the Great Lakes Region.* C. L. Hubbs and K. F. Lagler. University of Michigan Press, Ann Arbor. 1964. 213 pp.

## Mississippi

*Freshwater Fishes in Mississippi.* F. A. Cook. Mississippi Game and Fish Commission, Jackson. 1959. 239 pp.

## Missouri

*The Fishes of Missouri.* W. L. Pflieger. Missouri Department of Conservation, Columbia. 1975. 343 pp.

## Minnesota

*Northern Fishes, With Special Reference to the Upper Mississippi Valley.* S. Eddy and J. C. Underhill. University of Minnesota Press, Minneapolis. 1974. 414 pp.

## Montana

*Fishes of Montana.* C.J.D. Brown. Montana State University, Bozeman. 1971. 207 pp.

## Nevada

*Fishes and Fisheries of Nevada.* I. La Rivers. Nevada State Fish and Game Commission, Carson City. 1962. 782 pp.

## New Mexico

*Guide to the Fishes of New Mexico.* W. J. Koster. University of New Mexico Press, Albuquerque 1957. 116 pp.

## Ohio

*The Fishes of Ohio.* M. B. Trautman. Ohio State University Press, Columbus. 1981. 782 pp.

## Oklahoma

*The Fishes of Oklahoma.* R. J. Miller and H. W. Robison. Oklahoma State University Press, Stillwater. 1973. 246 pp.

## Utah

*Fishes of Utah.* W. F. Sigler and R. R. Miller. Utah Game and Fish Department, Salt Lake City. 1963. 203 pp.

## Wyoming

*Wyoming Fishes.* G. T. Baxter and J. R. Simon. Wyoming Game and Fish Department Cheyenne. Bulletin Number 4. 1970. 168 pp.

# Other endangered and threatened species references

*Endangered Species Technical Bulletin.* Endangered Species Program, U. S. Fish and Wildlife Service, Office of Endangered Species, Washington, D. C. 20240 (July 1976 to present.)

*The Endangered Species Handbook.* Greta Nilsson. Animal Welfare Institute. 1983. 245 pp.

*Extinction, The Causes and Consequences of The Disappearance of Species.* Paul and Anne Ehrlich. Random House, New York. 1981. 305 pp.

*Special Issue: Endangered Species.* National Wildlife Federation. April–May, 1974. Washington, DC

*These Are The Endangered.* Charles Cadieux. Stone Wall Press, Washington D.C. 1981. 256 pp.

# Conservation Organizations

By joining conservation organizations you not only help the conservation movement with your membership dollars, but learn more about the threats wildlife faces, the legislation pending in state and federal legislatures, and what individuals in your area are doing to protect endangered species. Many of these organizations publish newsletters, magazines, or the notes from their proceedings. The name of the publication follows the mailing address.

American Fisheries Society
5410 Grosvenor Lane
Bethesda, MD 20014
(Professional association, *Fisheries*)

American Rivers Conservation Council
323 Pennsylvania Ave., SE
Washington, DC 20003
(*American Rivers*)

American Society of Ichthyologists
and Herpetologists
Florida State Museum
University of Florida
Gainesville, FL 32611
(Professional association,*Copeia*)

The Desert Fishes Council
407 West Line St.

Bishop, CA 93514
(*Annual Proceedings*)

International Atlantic Salmon Foundation
P.O. Box 429
St. Andrews, New Brunswick
Canada EOG 2XO
(*IASF Newsletter*)

The Southeastern Fishes Council
Florida State Museum
University of Florida
Gainesville, FL 32611
(*Annual Proceedings*)

Trout Unlimited
501 Church St., NE
Vienna, VA 22180

## General Conservation Organizations

Center for Environmental Education
1925 K St. NW #206
Washington, DC 20006
(*The Whale Report; Environmental Education Report*)

Defenders of Wildlife
1244 19th St. NW
Washington, DC 20036
(*Defenders*)

Environmental Defense Fund
472 Park Ave., So.
New York, NY 10016
(*EDF Letter; The Associate*)

Friends of the Earth
124 Spear St.
San Francisco, CA 94105
(books on conservation)

League of Conservation Voters
317 Pennsylvania Ave. SE
Washington, DC 20003
(voting records for individual congressmen on conservation bills)

National Audubon Society
950 Third Ave.
New York, NY 10022
(*Audubon; American Birds*)

National Parks and Conservation Association
1701 18th St. NW
Washington, DC 20009
(*National Parks & Conservation*)

National Speleological Society, Inc.
Cave Ave.
Huntsville, AL 35810
(*NSS News; Bulletin*)

National Wildlife Federation
1412 16th St. NW
Washington, DC 20036
(*International Wildlife; National Wildlife; Ranger Rick's Nature Magazine*)

National Resources Defense Council, Inc.
122 E. 42nd St.
New York, NY 10168
(*The Amicus Journal*)

The Nature Conservancy, Inc.
1800 N. Kent St.
Suite 800
Arlington, VA 22209
(*The Nature Conservancy News*)

New York Zoological Society
The Zoological Park
Bronx, NY 10460
(*Animal Kingdom; Annual Report*)

Sierra Club
530 Bush St.
San Francisco, CA 94108
(*Sierra* magazine and other bulletins)

World Wildlife Fund – U.S.
1601 Connecticut Ave. NW
Washington, DC 20009
(*Focus*)